Ar
Kno........ᵤ

Contemporary Philosophical Monographs
Peter Ludlow, editor

Anti-Individualism and Knowledge

Jessica Brown

A Bradford Book
The MIT Press
Cambridge, Massachusetts
London, England

This book was set in Palatino by SNP Best-set Typesetter Ltd., Hong Kong, and was printed and bound in the United States of America.

Library of Congress Cataloging-in-Publication Data

Brown, Jessica.
  Anti-individualism and knowledge / Jessica Brown.
      p.   cm.—(Contemporary philosophical monographs ; 4)
  "A Bradford book."
  Includes bibliographical references (p.   ) and index.
  ISBN 0-262-02558-2 (hc. : alk. paper)—ISBN 0-262-52421-X
  (pbk. : alk. paper)
    1. Knowledge, Theory of. 2. Individualism. I. Title. II. Series.
BD161.B765 2004
121'.3—dc21
                                                              2003054115

10 9 8 7 6 5 4 3 2 1

Contents

Preface

This book examines the epistemological consequences of a view that dominates contemporary philosophy of mind—anti-individualism. According to this view, a subject's thought contents are partly individuated by her environment. By contrast, individualists deny this and argue that a subject's thought contents are wholly individuated by her "internal" states, such as her brain states. Many have taken anti-individualism to have radical consequences for our knowledge of our minds, our ability to reason, and our knowledge of the world. In this book, I investigate whether anti-individualism does have such radical consequences. The discussion weaves together central topics in the philosophy of mind, such as rationality, psychological explanation and the nature of thought, with general issues in epistemology such as skepticism and the nature of knowledge and warrant.

If, as anti-individualism suggests, what a subject thinks depends partly on her environment, it may seem that a subject can know what she thinks only by investigating the nature of her environment. But this seems deeply counterintuitive. A subject may use empirical evidence in forming a belief, but, once the belief is formed, it seems she can know that she has this belief without further reliance on empirical evidence. Certainly, a subject can know what she thinks without investigating those features of the environment that anti-individualists have argued partly individuate her thoughts, such as the chemical composition of substances and the linguistic conventions of her community. It would be a serious objection to anti-individualism if it had the result that a subject can have only empirical knowledge of her thoughts. I examine the challenge raised to a priori knowledge of one's thoughts both by standard versions of anti-individualism and by those versions that allow that a subject may suffer an illusion of thought. The main compatibilist response to this challenge emphasizes the reliability of a subject's beliefs about her thoughts. I offer a different response, which focuses on the epistemic notion of a relevant alternative. The discussion of whether anti-individualism undermines a priori knowledge of thoughts involves an examination of the nature of knowledge—does knowledge require discriminative abilities or merely the ability to reliably form true beliefs? If the latter, what sort of reliability does knowledge require?

It may seem to follow from the anti-individualist claim (that what thoughts a subject has depends partly on the environment) that a subject may need empirical information to know whether two thoughts or thought constituents have the same or different content. Sameness and difference of content are crucial to the logical relations between thoughts. Thus, anti-individualism seems to have the consequence that a subject may need empirical information to know the logical relations between her thoughts and that, without such empirical information, she may make mistakes about their relations. But, if so, then anti-individualism undermines the concept of a rational subject as one who would not believe simple contradictions or make simple invalid inferences. I defend anti-individualism against this objection by rejecting this conception of rationality. However, I use the results of the discussion to raise a new problem for the attempt to combine anti-individualism and Fregean sense. I argue that the assumptions of transparency and rationality behind the Fregean argument for sense are in tension with anti-individualism. This argument applies even to the notion of object-dependent sense developed by modern defenders of Fregean anti-individualism, such as Evans, McDowell, and Peacocke.

Even if anti-individualists can overcome the objection that their view is incompatible with a subject's having a priori knowledge of her own thoughts, a further issue arises. If it were the case both that what a subject thinks depends on her environment and that she can have a priori knowledge of her thoughts, then this might seem to provide her with a novel and a priori route to knowledge of the world. Since anti-individualism is supported by philosophical arguments, it may seem that a subject could use those arguments to gain a priori knowledge that her having a certain thought entails that she is in a certain kind of environment. Combining this knowledge with her a priori knowledge of her thoughts she could come to have a priori knowledge that she is in a certain kind of environment.

Some have taken this line of reasoning to show that anti-individualism can provide a novel response to skeptics who argue that we can never have knowledge of the existence and nature of the external world. Others have taken it to be an objection to anti-individualism since they think it absurd that one could gain knowledge of the nature of the world just by reflection on one's thoughts and philosophy. Either way, it would be an interesting and substantive result if it were a consequence of anti-individualism that one could gain a priori knowledge of the world. Davies and Wright have attempted to block the idea that anti-individualism has this consequence by arguing that warrant and hence knowledge do not always transmit across a valid inference. They suggest that a subject who knows the premises of a valid argument and knows that the argument is valid cannot always gain warrant for, and knowledge of, the conclusion by thinking through that argument. I argue against this limitation on the transmission of warrant and knowledge by considering the nature of warrant. Instead, I suggest a different reason for supposing that anti-individualism does not provide a novel a priori way of discovering facts about one's environment, namely, that anti-individualism undermines the type of knowledge required to use a priori knowledge of one's thoughts to gain a priori knowledge of the world.

I conclude that anti-individualism does not have the kind of radical epistemic consequences many take it to have. Certainly, anti-individualism provides a new source of mistakes about the logical properties of thoughts; and this raises a problem for the attempt to combine anti-individualism even with the notion of object-dependent sense. However, anti-individualism's potential threat to a priori knowledge of one's own thoughts can be largely defused by appeal to the epistemological notion of a relevant alternative. In addition, on a proper understanding of rationality, anti-individualism does not undermine the notion that we are rational subjects. Last, anti-individualism does not provide a new a priori route to knowledge of the world. Many would agree that anti-individualism lacks the radical epistemic consequences commonly suggested. However, I support this conclusion by a range of new arguments that link central issues in the philosophy of mind with the epistemological literature on knowledge, warrant, justification, and reliability.

Most of the material in the book has not been previously published. However, the discussion in chapter 4 overlaps substantially with my earlier article, "Reliabilism, Knowledge, and Mental Content," *Proceedings of the Aristotelian Society*, 2000. Chapter 8 draws on, but reaches a different conclusion from, my previously published papers on the reductio: "The Incompatibility of Anti-Individualism and Privileged Access," *Analysis* 1995, "Boghossian and Privileged Access," *Analysis* 1999, and "Anti-Individualism and Agnosticism," *Analysis* 2001. My paper "The Reductio Argument and the Transmission of Warrant" (in *New Essays on Semantic Externalism and Self-Knowledge*, edited by Susana Nuccetelli) contains material similar to some parts of chapter 7. I am grateful for permission to use material from these earlier papers.

My work on the book has been generously supported by an AHRB Research Leave Award, a Bristol University Research Fellowship and a Philip Leverhulme Prize. Draft material has been presented at several conferences and departments, including the Joint Session 2001, The European Society for Philosophy and Psychology meetings in 2000 and 2001, and the philosophy departments at The Australian National University in Canberra and at the Universities of Bristol, Birmingham, Cambridge, Glasgow, Stirling, and Sydney. I am grateful for useful comments and stimulating discussion on these occasions. A number of individuals provided helpful feedback on parts of the draft including Helen Beebee, John Campbell, Patrick Greenough, Antti Karlajainen, James Ladyman, Brian McLaughlin, Laura Schroeder, and Daniel Stoljar. During the final stages of the book, I spent a very enjoyable two months at the

Philosophy Program of the Research School of Social Sciences at the Australian National University in Canberra. Many thanks to staff and students who participated in a reading group on the book. Special thanks to Martin Davies who has provided so much help and encouragement over the years and has commented on the whole manuscript. Last, I would like to thank my colleagues here at Bristol, and especially Chris Bertram and Keith Graham, for their warmth and support.

1   Anti-Individualism

In this chapter, I set out distinctions that are crucial for the rest of the book. Although the chapter is designed to be accessible to those unfamiliar with anti-individualism, the terminology established will also be useful to those familiar with the position. In sections 1 through 6, I contrast anti-individualism and individualism, distinguishing three anti-individualist claims, namely, that a subject's thoughts are partly individuated by the natural kinds in her environment ("natural kind anti-individualism"); that a subject's thoughts are partly individuated by the particular objects in her environment ("singular anti-individualism"); and that a subject's thoughts are partly individuated by the linguistic practices of her community ("social anti-individualism"). I make two further distinctions between anti-individualist accounts, between those that accept or reject the idea that a subject may suffer an illusion of thought, and between those that accept or reject the notion of Fregean sense. I use the expression "the illusion version of anti-individualism" for anti-individualist views that accept the possibility of illusions of thought, and "Fregean anti-individualism" for anti-individualist views that accept Fregean sense. I then elucidate the notion of a priori knowledge used throughout the book (sec. 7). I end the chapter by sketching the main lines of argument and conclusions of the book.

1   Content and the Environment

Suppose that you and I are discussing how a mutual friend, Sally, will vote in the upcoming government elections. You point out that Sally wants better state school provision but thinks that the Tories have a poor record on public services. I add that, although many might be put off Labour by high taxes, Sally would welcome higher taxes to pay for better education. We agree that she'll likely vote Labour. Our prediction of her action is based on our views about what Sally believes and wants, or, in philosophical jargon, on the content of her beliefs and desires. In specifying the content of Sally's beliefs and desires, we specify the way she takes the world to be and the way she would like the world to be. More generally, belief and desire are just two examples of a larger class of states—the "propositional attitudes"—that can be construed as composed of an attitude, such as hope, fear, or doubt, and a propositional content, such as that which is hoped, feared, or doubted. For example, a subject might believe that her tax bill will rise, fear that it will rise, doubt that it will rise, or hope that it will rise. In specifying what a subject wants, hopes, fears, expects, doubts, and so on, we specify the content of those attitudes. As the example of Sally illustrates, the content of a subject's propositional attitudes is used in the prediction of her action. In addition, content is used in explaining action. If, as expected, Sally does vote Labour, we may explain this fact by citing her relevant propositional attitudes.

The contents of a subject's propositional attitudes are causally related to her environment. For example, the movement of a cyclist across the road may, via perception, affect my beliefs about the location and velocity of objects in my path. Otherwise, I would hardly be a safe driver. In general, the fact that the content of our attitudes is causally affected by the world enables us to engage effectively with the world. While accepting this, one might also think that types of mental state are to be identified with types of internal state of the subject herself, such as brain states. On this view, the environment may cause a subject to be in a certain type of inner state and hence a certain type of mental state, even though it is inessential to being in that type of mental state. As long as the subject is in, say, the relevant type of brain state, she would have the relevant type of mental state, regardless of what caused her to be in that type of brain state, whether a state of the world, the actions of a neuroscientist, or a Cartesian demon. A range of other views about the nature of mental states makes the environment inessential to being in a certain mental state, for example, behaviorism and functionalism. According to behaviorism, being in a certain type of mental state is a matter of being disposed to make certain bodily movements. According to some versions of functionalism, being in a certain mental state is a matter of having a state that plays a certain role in one's mental economy, that is, one that is disposed to be caused by certain kinds of sensory stimulation and certain other mental states, and that is disposed to cause certain patterns of bodily movement and certain other mental states.[1]

The above conception of the relation of content and the environment is an individualistic one. Like individualists, anti-individualists hold that content is causally affected by the environment. But, in addition, they hold that there is a more intimate connection between the contents of a subject's thoughts and her environment. We can explain the difference between individualism and anti-individualism by using the intuitive distinction between two types of property—relational and nonrelational or intrinsic properties. The property of being taller than the Eiffel Tower, older than the Rosetta Stone, or being a descendant of the Queen are clearly relational properties, properties whose possession by an object requires the existence of other objects to which the first object stands in certain relations. By contrast, nonrelational or intrinsic properties are those that can be possessed independently of the existence of other objects and events. An example of an intrinsic property is the property of having a certain microstructural constitution. Individualists hold that a subject's thought contents are wholly individuated by her intrinsic properties.[2] On this view, any two subjects who are identical in all their intrinsic properties also have the same thought contents. Anti-individualists hold, by contrast, that the contents of a subject's propositional attitudes are partly individuated by her environment. They support this view by arguing that two subjects who are identical in all their intrinsic properties, but who are in different environments, might have different thought contents.[3] We might rephrase the distinction between anti-individualism and individualism by using the notion of supervenience. One family of properties A supervenes on another B if and only if two objects cannot differ in their A-properties without differing in their B-properties. Individualists claim that thought content supervenes on intrinsic properties, whereas anti-individualists deny this.

The classic arguments for anti-individualism are Twin Earth arguments of the kind first suggested in Putnam (1975a). Here, we consider a subject in the same intrinsic state, but in two different environments. It is argued that she plausibly has different thoughts in the two environments.

Since the only difference between the two situations is an environmental difference, it is concluded that a subject's thoughts are partly individuated by the environment. Before looking at the details of such Twin Earth arguments, it is useful to have in mind a distinction between two ways in which a subject can think about, or refer to, particular objects and kinds.

Suppose there has been a series of burglaries in the shops on the High Street. Although we have no idea who is responsible for the various crimes, the evidence points to a single culprit. I might think about the supposed culprit via the description, or general condition, 'the person responsible for the High Street burglaries', where the referent of this description is the unique person, if any, who is responsible for these burglaries. For example, I might think that the person responsible for the High Street burglaries is clever. In such a case, we may say that I (attempt to) *think of a certain object via a description*. Notice that when a subject thinks of an object by description, the content of her thought seems independent of the particular object referred to by the description. Consider the counterfactual situation in which Lightfinger, the actual perpetrator of the crime, does not commit the burglaries, but her rival, Crowbar-Jane, commits a set of burglaries identical except for the perpetrator. In that case, my thought that the person responsible for the High Street burglaries is clever would have the same content as in the actual situation, but it would be about a different person. Similarly, in the counterfactual situation in which no single individual is responsible for the set of burglaries, my thought would have the same content, but would fail to refer to anyone.

Although we sometimes think about individuals by description, it has been argued that such cases are unusual.[4]

According to the *nondescriptive model*, a subject can think of an object not via a description, but rather in virtue of standing in some real relation to that object. For example, suppose that I am looking at an apple, *a*, and I think that that apple is red. Given that I am looking at the particular apple, *a*, my thought refers to that apple. It seems implausible that I refer to apple *a* via a description. A descriptive thought component of the form, the *F*, refers to the unique object, if any, that is *F*. But it is hard to formulate a description that is both uniquely satisfied by apple *a* and plausibly the means by which I think of *a*. Such descriptions as 'the red apple' are not uniquely satisfied by *a*. Other descriptions, such as 'the red apple that is on that table' may be uniquely satisfied by *a*, but they embed demonstrative reference to further objects, and the question arises whether or not I think of these further objects by description. An alternative suggestion is that I think of *a* via the description 'the apple I am currently looking at'. But it is unclear that the concept of looking at something is available to all subjects who are capable of perceptual demonstrative thoughts about objects. For example, is it clear that small children capable of thinking about the particular objects they are seeing have the concept of looking at something? Even for those subjects for whom such a sophisticated thought is available, is it plausible that the original perceptual demonstrative thought involves this level of complexity and so should be treated as equivalent to it? These sorts of considerations have motivated the view that perceiving an object may enable me to refer to it otherwise than by a description.

Singular thoughts that are based on a capacity to recognize a particular object may provide a different type of example of nondescriptive thought. Suppose that I attend a party and talk briefly to an interesting woman. As a result of the encounter, I form the ability to recognize the woman in question. This recognitional capacity enables me to think about the woman even in her absence. For example, I might think that that woman is intelligent. However, it seems implausible that this recognition-based thought involves a descriptive way of thinking of the woman. Suppose that I forget at which party I met the woman and have no other piece of information that uniquely identifies her. For example, I might know only that she lives in Bristol. Although I can recognize her, I might be unable to give a description of her appearance that applies to her uniquely. The terms in which we can describe other subjects (she has blue eyes, brown hair, etc.) usually fail to pick out one unique individual. We are usually much better at recognizing previously presented objects than recalling their features when they are not present. Thus, it might be argued that recognition-based thoughts involve a nondescriptive way of thinking about objects (Evans 1982).

The resulting nondescriptive picture of reference is very different from the descriptive view, according to which thought connects with the objects it is about via a description. On the descriptive view, the singular component of a thought consists in a description, the F, where the object referred to is the object that uniquely fits the description F. The subject has the same thought regardless of which object, if any, fits the description. On the nondescriptive view, a subject's thoughts connect with their objects not via a description but more directly in virtue of the relation in which the subject stands to those objects. On this view, the singular component of the thought is not equivalent to a description that remains constant whatever the state of the world. Rather, the content of the singular component of the thought is individuated partly by the object it is about. Thus, if the subject were counterfactually related to a different object, she would think a different thought. Consider again the example of a subject who sees an apple, a, and thinks that that apple is red. The nondescriptivist conceives of the subject's thought as containing two parts, a singular component whose content is at least partly individuated by the apple, if any, she is looking at, and a predicative component corresponding to the expression 'is red'. If the subject is looking at apple a, then the content of the singular component is individuated partly by the apple a. But, if the subject were looking at a different apple, b, then her thought would be individuated partly by the apple b. As we will see later, nondescriptivists disagree about whether the content of the singular component of the subject's thought is individuated wholly by the object it is about, or whether it contains some other component as well that reflects the way in which the subject thinks of the object.

These two models of reference can be used to illuminate the debate between anti-individualists and individualists. We will see that individualists can use the descriptive model of thought to resist local anti-individualist claims. For instance, they can resist the claim that one's thoughts are individuated partly by the natural kinds in one's environment by arguing that one thinks descriptively of natural kinds. Of course, even if correct, this view would not establish the truth of individualism. The concepts used in the description may be individuated by some feature of the environment, and anti-individualism may be plausible for some other type of thought. So, the debate between anti-individualists and individualists and the debate over the correct account of reference do not line up straightforwardly. Nevertheless, the appeal to the descriptive model of thought is one way in which an individualist may resist particular anti-individualist claims, and this is how we will consider the model. Anti-individualists differ over what conditions are sufficient for a subject to have a thought of a certain type. For example, some have argued that a certain type of causal relation between subject and object is sufficient for a subject to have thoughts about that object (see, e.g., Kripke 1980; Devitt 1980; Fodor 1987). Others argue that a richer set of conditions is required for a subject to have a thought about an object. For example, Evans (1982) argues that a subject can think about an object only if she knows which object is in question, where this amounts to having the ability to distinguish that object from all other things. With this point in mind, the following arguments for anti-individualism aim to describe a subject in a set of conditions sufficiently rich that a range of anti-individualists with divergent views about the conditions sufficient for thought can agree that the subject has the relevant type of thought.

2 Natural Kind Anti-Individualism

According to *natural kind anti-individualism*, a subject's thought contents are individuated partly by the natural kinds in her environment. Paradigmatic examples of natural kinds are chemical substances and biological kinds. Natural kinds are individuated by their fundamental properties, as described by correct scientific theory (Putnam 1975a,b,c; Kripke 1980). It is both necessary and sufficient for an item to be a member of a natural kind that it have the relevant fundamental properties. By contrast, having a certain appearance is neither necessary nor sufficient for membership of a natural kind. For example, it is not sufficient for an item to be made of diamond that it look like diamond, and an animal might be a tiger even if, since it is albino, it lacks the characteristic striped appearance of tigers. There is debate about what kinds are natural kinds, and whether ordinary terms name natural kinds (Zemach 1976; Dupré 1981; Platts 1983; Segal 2000). However, the Twin Earth argument needs only the plausible claim that some ordinary terms, minimally at least one, name a natural kind. I will set up the Twin Earth argument using the standard example of 'water'. Any who question whether 'water' names a natural kind can substitute an alternative example.

Consider an Earth subject Sally at a time when no one knew the correct chemical description of water. Despite this, Sally and her fellows had the term 'water', which they regularly applied to water. At this stage, Sally and her fellows recognized water by its appearance and behavior. However, suppose they held that what makes a sample water is not that it looks and tastes a certain way, but its fundamental, although as yet undiscovered, nature. They intended that the term 'water' express a concept that applies on the basis of these as yet unknown fundamental properties, not on the basis of its appearance. In fact, as we know now, water is H_2O. In virtue of these facts, anti-individualists argue that the concept Sally expresses by 'water' applies to all and only water, that is, H_2O, even though Sally and her community are ignorant of water's correct chemical description.

Now suppose, counterfactually, that instead of being brought up on Earth, Sally was brought up on Twin Earth. Twin Earth is stipulated to be just like Earth, except that wherever there is water on Earth, there is a different substance, twater, on Twin Earth. Twater is stipulated to be a substance that looks, tastes, and behaves just like water but is not water since it has a different chemical formula, XYZ.

On Twin Earth, it is twater that is drunk, comes out of taps, flows in rivers, falls as rain, and to which the term 'water' is applied. In the twin scenario, Sally has exactly the same history of intrinsic or nonrelational states. Thus, for instance, at any time, Sally has exactly the same microstructure; her body performs the same movements, she has the same patterns of stimulation on her retinas, and so on. Further, it seems that Sally would be in subjectively indistinguishable states in the actual and twin situations, for the only difference between the two situations is in the fundamental nature of the stuff called 'water', something of which Sally is ignorant. Nonetheless, natural kind antiindividualists argue that, in the twin situation, the concept Sally expresses by 'water' applies to all and only twater. Thus, they say, Sally has different thoughts in the two situations: in the actual situation, her thoughts involve the concept water, which applies to all and only H_2O; in the twin situation her thoughts involve the different concept twater, which applies to all and only XYZ. Since the only difference between the two situations is in the fundamental nature of the stuff called 'water', natural kind anti-individualists conclude that a subject's thoughts are not individuated wholly by her intrinsic states, but are instead individuated partly by the natural kinds in her environment. (In presenting the argument, I have ignored the fact that Sally's body is largely made up of water. This doesn't significantly affect the debate for, instead, we could have used a natural kind that is not found in human bodies.)

An individualist might try to reply to this argument by arguing that the concept Sally expresses by 'water' is equivalent to a definite description. As we saw above, when a subject thinks about an object or kind by description, her thoughts are independent of the nature of the object or kind, if any, that fits the description. Of course, even if it could be shown that Sally does think of water via some description, this would not establish the truth of individualism. For, it could be that Sally can entertain that description only in virtue of being in the kind of environment she is in. However, if successful, this response at least would show that the content of the thoughts Sally expresses with 'water' are not individuated partly by the nature of the watery stuff in her environment. Consider the suggestion that the concept Sally expresses by 'water' is equivalent to a definite description. The individualist cannot claim that 'water' expresses a description such as 'the stuff that is colorless, clear, tasteless, and falls from skies'; by hypothesis, Sally and her fellows hold that the concept they express with 'water' applies on the basis of fundamental properties, and not just to anything that looks and behaves like water. Further, it cannot be claimed that 'water' expresses the description 'the stuff that has composition H_2O', for it is part of the example that Sally and her fellows are ignorant of the correct chemical description of water.

A final suggestion might be that 'water' expresses the description 'the stuff that is actually tasteless, colorless, and falls from skies around here' (Davies and Humberstone 1980). This description does not involve any theoretical knowledge that Sally and her fellows are stipulated to lack. In addition, it has the intuitively plausible result that, in the actual situation in which Sally is brought up on Earth, 'water' refers to all and only H_2O; but if, counterfactually, she had been brought up on Twin Earth where the lakes and rivers contain XYZ, then 'water' would have referred to all and only XYZ. However, it is implausible that subjects generally think of natural kinds even by descriptions that embed the term 'actually'. Surely we would accept that a community that regularly applies a term to instances of a kind, and has the ability to recognize instances of that kind, has a concept of that kind even if the descriptions they offer of the kind are largely incorrect (Putnam 1975c; Kripke 1980). For example, suppose that a community can recognize instances of a type of bird common in its surroundings and applies a term to instances that type. Surely the concept they express by the relevant term can apply to all and only members of that type even if they have many incorrect beliefs about the bird's way of life. (Note that even if members of the community can recognize instances of this bird type on the basis of its appearance, they may be unable to formulate a description of its appearance that applies uniquely to that kind. As we saw earlier, a subject may have the ability to recognize a particular individual or kind of thing even if the descriptions she would offer of its appearance fail to pick it out uniquely.) If it is generally implausible that subjects think of natural kinds by descriptions embedding 'actually', then individualists cannot provide a general response to Twin Earth arguments for natural kind anti-individualism by suggesting that subjects think of natural kinds in this way.

3 Singular Anti-Individualism

According to *singular anti-individualism*, a subject's thought contents are individuated partly by the particular objects that are in her environment (see, e.g., Perry 1979; Kripke 1980; Evans 1982; Peacocke 1983; McDowell 1986; Salmon 1986; Soames 1987; Kaplan 1989). Suppose that, in the actual situation, Sally is looking at a certain apple, *a*, and she thinks that that apple is red. In this situation, her thought refers to the particular apple, *a*, she is looking at, and its truth value turns on the state of that apple, *a*, and whether it is red. Now consider a counterfactual situation in which everything is the same, but Sally is looking at a distinct apple, *b*, which looks just like *a*. In the counterfactual situation, Sally has exactly the same history of intrinsic, or nonrelational, states. For instance, at any time, Sally has exactly the same microstructure, her body performs the same bodily movements, she has the same patterns of stimulation on her retinas, and so on. However, in virtue of the fact that she is looking at the different apple *b*, her thought refers to *b*, and it is *b*'s state on which the truth value of her thought depends.

Note that if Sally were thinking about the apple by description in the two situations, then, although her thought refers to different apples in the two situations, she would have the same thought content in the two situations. For instance, if she thought of each apple under the description 'the apple I am now looking at', then in each situation she would think the thought that the apple she is now looking at is red. Of course, even if all perceptual demonstrative thoughts were understood on this model, this would not establish individualism even about perceptual demonstrative thoughts. It might be that Sally can entertain the relevant descriptive component only because she is in a certain kind of environment. But, if defensible, this understanding of perceptual demonstrative thought would show at least that a perceptual demonstrative thought is not individuated by the particular object it is about. However, as we saw earlier (sec. 1), the descriptive understanding of perceptual demonstrative thought is implausible.

On the alternative view that Sally thinks of the apple she is seeing nondescriptively, she has different thoughts in the two situations. Now, it is part of the set up that the only

difference between the actual and counterfactual situations is in which apple Sally is seeing. Thus, singular anti-
individualists conclude that a subject's thoughts are not
individuated wholly by her intrinsic states, but are instead
individuated partly by the objects in her environment. I
have sketched the argument for singular anti-individualism
using an example of a perceptual demonstrative thought,
but the argument could be made by using any example
in which the subject plausibly thinks of an object
nondescriptively.

4 Illusions of Thought

In our discussion of natural kind and singular anti-
individualism, we have considered twin cases in which the
counterfactual situation involves a different object or kind
than the actual situation. However, there is a different
possibility: that there is no suitable object or kind in the
counterfactual situation for the subject to refer to. I will
call such cases *no-reference cases*.

One type of no-reference case occurs when a subject
suffers a perceptual illusion. For instance, a subject who
takes herself to be seeing and thinking about an object may
instead be suffering an illusion of seeing such an object. A
different example is provided by the Dry Earth scenario in
which the inhabitants suffer an illusion of there being lakes
and rivers full of a watery liquid (Boghossian 1997, p. 170).
In the second type of no-reference case, the subject does not
suffer a perceptual illusion, but rather takes herself to have
encountered a single object or kind when in fact she has
confused several similar objects or kinds. For instance, on
"Motley Earth," there are lakes and rivers full of watery
liquid, but this liquid is composed of a motley collection of

several different natural kinds that the inhabitants confuse for one natural kind. There are two different views about no-reference cases available to an anti-individualist. First, she could argue that in a no-reference case, the subject thinks about the putative object via a description. For example, it might be suggested that when Sally suffers an illusion of seeing an apple, she thinks that the apple she seems to see is red. In the situation in which there is no dominant natural kind in the stuff called 'water', it might be suggested that Sally thinks that the clear, colorless, liquid called 'water' is wet. Even if Sally thinks a descriptive thought in the no-reference case, this does not entail that she thinks a descriptive thought when things go well, for example, when she does see an apple. So, this understanding of the no-reference case may be adopted by an anti-individualist. Alternatively, the anti-individualist could argue that when there is no suitable object or kind to refer to, the subject fails to think any determinate thought (see Evans 1982; McDowell 1986; Boghossian 1997). For instance, although it may seem to her just as if she is seeing an apple and thinking about it, in fact she is not. Instead, she suffers an illusion of thought. On this view, successful thought sometimes requires there to be a suitable object or kind in the environment so that, when there is no such object or kind, the subject fails to think a thought of the relevant kind at all. I will call an anti-individualism that takes the first of these two options the *descriptive version* of anti-individualism, and an anti-individualism that takes the second the *illusion version* of anti-individualism. It is controversial which of these two views is correct and, in particular, whether a subject can suffer an illusion of thought. I will not attempt to settle this issue here. In the rest of the book, I will consider both illusion and descriptive versions of singular and natural kind anti-individualism.

5 Social Anti-Individualism

According to *social anti-individualism*, a subject's thoughts are individuated partly by the practice of her linguistic community. This form of anti-individualism can be supported by Burge's famous arthritis thought experiment (Burge 1979). Suppose that Sally has suffered arthritis for a number of years. She has been to see her doctor about it on a number of occasions, and she holds various attitudes she would express with the word 'arthritis', such as the attitudes she would express by saying 'I have arthritis in my ankles', 'Arthritis is painful and debilitating', and 'Arthritis is common among the elderly'. In addition, she also has the attitude she would express by saying, 'I fear my arthritis has spread to my thigh'. This attitude indicates that Sally incompletely understands 'arthritis', for, by definition, 'arthritis' applies only to problems of the joints. Despite this, Burge argues, Sally has the concept arthritis. Thus, by her utterance, 'I fear my arthritis has spread to my thigh', she expresses the fear that her arthritis has spread to her thigh. Burge supports this interpretation by saying that it would be natural to report her thoughts in this way, despite her incomplete understanding.

Now consider a counterfactual situation in which Sally is brought up in a different linguistic community in which 'arthritis' has a different definition. Whereas in the actual situation, 'arthritis' is defined to apply to rheumatoid ailments of the joints, in the counterfactual situation, it is defined to apply to rheumatoid ailments of the joints and thighs. Thus, in the counterfactual situation, the term 'arthritis' expresses a different concept, call it 'tharthritis', which applies to rheumatoid ailments of joints and thighs. Despite these environmental differences, Sally is stipulated to have precisely the same history of intrinsic states in the counterfactual situation as she has in the actual situation. At any time, Sally has exactly the same microstructure, she performs the same bodily movements, she has the same patterns of stimulation on her retinas, and so on. As before, she has a number of attitudes that she would express with the term 'arthritis', including the fear she would express with 'I fear that my arthritis has spread to my thigh'. Burge argues that, in the counterfactual situation, Sally lacks the concept arthritis and instead has the concept tharthritis. In support of this interpretation, Burge points out that Sally herself would explain 'arthritis' by saying that it is a rheumatoid condition that occurs in joints and thighs. In addition, experts in the counterfactual community would explain 'arthritis' in this way. Since the only difference between the actual and counterfactual situation is in the way 'arthritis' is defined, Burge concludes that a subject's thoughts are not individuated wholly by her intrinsic states, but are instead individuated partly by the linguistic practices of her community. Unlike the other arguments for anti-individualism, Burge's thought experiment turns on the question of whether a subject can have a concept that she incompletely understands. As a result, Burge's thought experiment applies to a much wider range of terms—terms for natural kinds, and terms for other kinds, as well as verbs, abstract nouns, adjectives, and so on (Burge 1979, p. 79).

Burge's attribution of the concept tharthritis to the subject in the counterfactual situation is relatively uncontroversial. After all, everything seems to point to Sally's having this concept—both the way she would explicate the term herself and her community's linguistic practice. But should we accept that in the actual situation, Sally has the concept arthritis? Although the practice of her linguistic community might support this, the way she herself would explicate the concept seems to count against this attribution. Should we say, perhaps, instead, that in both the actual and counterfactual situations, she has the concept tharthritis?

Burge rejects this individualist conclusion, by appeal both to what others would say about Sally and to what Sally herself would say. Burge argues that it is extremely common for a subject to incompletely understand a term. Furthermore, we routinely ascribe concepts to subjects even despite their incomplete understanding of the relevant term, and we regard them as sharing beliefs with others who fully understand the term. We are happy to do so even when we know of the subject's incomplete understanding (Burge 1979, esp. pp. 79–82, 89–94). Moreover, it seems that the patient herself defers to sources of authority in her linguistic community for the application conditions of the concept she expresses with the term 'arthritis'. Suppose that she visits her doctor and says, 'I'm afraid that my arthritis has spread to my thigh'. The doctor reassures Sally, saying that, by definition, arthritis cannot occur in thighs. It seems likely that Sally would respond with relief, regarding her earlier fear as false, and would go on to ask what might be wrong with her thigh.

This response suggests that it is the public concept arthritis that figures in her belief, not some idiosyncratic concept defined by her own views. If, as Burge suggests, her belief involves the concept arthritis, then her belief is indeed false as a matter of the definition of the concept. However, if her belief had instead involved the concept tharthritis, then her belief might be true, despite what the doctor says about arthritis, for the concept tharthritis is defined so that it applies to rheumatoid problems of the joints and thighs. But, it seems unlikely that Sally would reply to the doctor by saying that although she accepts what the doctor says about the public word 'arthritis', her own belief about what is wrong with her thigh might still be true, since it involves a different concept that does apply to problems of the thighs (ibid., pp. 94–95).

6   Fregean and Non-Fregean Anti-Individualism

We have seen that there is a variety of anti-individualist claims, varying in both the type of thought held to be individuated partly by the environment and in the environmental factors in terms of which those thoughts are individuated. A last difference between anti-individualist positions concerns whether they attempt to combine anti-individualism with the notion of Fregean sense. I will use *Fregean anti-individualism* for the view that combines anti-individualism and Fregean sense, and *non-Fregean anti-individualism* for an anti-individualism that rejects Fregean sense.

Frege famously distinguished between the object, or referent, of a thought, and the way the subject thinks of the object. To take a classic example, assume that an early astronomer makes observations of the planet Venus in both the morning and evening but incorrectly takes the morning and evening observations to be of different stars. She coins two terms—'Hesperus' and 'Phosphorus'—for what she regards as these two distinct stars, one visible in the evening and one in the morning. Although she assents to 'Hesperus is visible in the evening', she denies the truth of 'Phosphorus is visible in the evening'. Further, she fails to put Hesperus and Phosphorus thoughts together in inference. For example, she fails to put together the beliefs she would express by 'Hesperus is visible now' and 'It is important to make as many observations of Phosphorus as possible' to draw the conclusion she would express by 'I should observe Hesperus now'. She would find it informative if told, 'Hesperus is Phosphorus'. Frege explained such examples by claiming that the astronomer thinks of a single object, Venus, in two different ways, or via two different senses.

One could take Frege as suggesting that the subject has two different descriptive ways of thinking of Venus. Thus, for example, the thoughts she would express with 'Hesperus' should be cashed out as thoughts involving some such descriptive component as the star that is visible in the evening and . . .; whereas the thoughts she would express with 'Phosphorus' should be cashed out as involving a different descriptive component, such as the star that is visible in the morning, and. . . . On this understanding of sense, one cannot combine the idea that the subject thinks about an object, say, Venus, in a particular way with the anti-individualist claim that the subject's thoughts are individuated partly by the particular object she is thinking about, here Venus.

However, we need not understand Fregean sense in this descriptive way. Instead, it has been suggested that a sense should be thought of as a way of thinking about an object that would not be available to be thought in the absence of the object (Evans 1982; McDowell 1986). Prima facie, it seems that one can combine this different understanding of the notion of sense with anti-individualism. For example, consider a subject looking at a particular cat and thinking the perceptual demonstrative thought that that cat is sleepy. On the Evans–McDowell view, the demonstrative component of this thought is not exhausted by the particular cat, Tabby, being referred to. Instead, its content is given by the object thought about, Tabby, and an object-dependent sense or way of thinking about Tabby. To say that this sense is object-dependent is just to say that it would not be available to be thought in the absence of Tabby. Thus, on the view that senses are object-dependent, one can combine the view that a subject thinks about an object, x, via a particular sense with the claim that the subject's thoughts are individuated partly by the object, x, that she is thinking about. This second way of understanding Fregean senses might seem highly attractive, appearing to offer us a picture of reference to objects that combines the insights of anti-individualism and the benefits of a Fregean notion of sense. For now, I will leave it open whether it is possible to combine anti-individualism and Fregean sense in this way. However, I will reexamine this issue in chapter 6.

7   A Priori and Empirical

In the rest of the book I consider the epistemic consequences of anti-individualism and, in particular, its consequences for a priori knowledge. It may be useful to explain my use of "a priori" here. The distinction between a priori and empirical truths is an epistemic distinction between the ways in which they can be known. A priori propositions are those that can be known independently of perceptual experience. They include mathematical and logical truths as well as certain definitional truths, such as the propositions that bachelors are unmarried and that red is a color. By contrast, certain propositions cannot be known independently of perceptual experience and are termed *empirical*. These include such propositions as that water is H_2O and my fridge contains two carrots. Correspondingly, a subject knows a proposition a priori if she knows it independently of perceptual experience, whereas she knows it empirically if her knowledge is dependent on perceptual experience.

Notice that a proposition may be known a priori even if it contains a concept that can be acquired only empirically. For instance, some argue that one cannot have the concept red without suitable red experiences. Even if this is correct, someone with the concept can know a priori that red is a color. Even if certain experiences are required to have the concept red, they play no role in the justification of the proposition that red is a color. To deal with the point about empirically acquired concepts, we might say that a proposition is known a priori if it is known without justificatory reliance on perceptual experience. This leaves it open whether the relevant concepts are acquired empirically.

There is wide agreement that the a priori includes mathematical, logical, and certain definitional truths. However, there is disagreement about how far the notion of the a priori extends beyond these core examples. The scope of the a priori depends on how we construe perceptual experience. Perceptual experience could be taken to include only perceptual experience of the external world, or perceptual experience of the external world and the thinker's own bodily states and events, or any conscious state or event, whether perception or conscious thinking (Boghossian and Peacocke 2000, pp. 2–3). These different construals of perceptual experience generate different understandings of the a priori. On the widest construal of the a priori, a subject can have a priori knowledge of her own bodily states and conscious thoughts. For example, she could know a priori that she is in pain and that she thinks that today is Tuesday, for neither need be based on perceptual experience of the external world. On an intermediate construal, she cannot know a priori that she is in pain, but she can have a priori knowledge of conscious thoughts. On the narrowest construal, even her knowledge of her own conscious thoughts is regarded as empirical. Here, I follow many others in taking the moderate position, which allows that a subject can have a priori knowledge of her own conscious thoughts (see, e.g., McKinsey 1991; Boghossian 1997; Warfield 1998; Sawyer 1999; McLaughlin 2000. Others label self-knowledge "nonempirical," including Burge 1988; Davies 1998; Wright 2000).

Although the moderate view is widely accepted, not all endorse it. However, the issues raised in the following chapters are independent of this use of "a priori." To take one example, the first part of the book focuses on whether anti-individualism is incompatible with the claim that a subject can have a priori knowledge of her thought contents. We could restate this putative problem for anti-individualism as follows. According to anti-individualism, what a subject thinks depends on her environment and, in particular, on such facts as the chemical composition of substances and the linguistic practice of her community. This suggests that anti-individualism has the counterintuitive result that a subject can know her own thought contents only by investigating the chemical composition of substances and the linguistic practice of her community. Whether or not one terms a subject's knowledge of her own thoughts "a priori," it is surely implausible that such knowledge requires chemical and linguistic investigation.

8 Outline of the Book

Many have argued that anti-individualism has radical consequences for our knowledge of mind and world and our ability to reason. I investigate whether anti-individualism has such radical consequences in a discussion that weaves together central topics in the philosophy of mind and epistemology. The discussion is divided into three main parts. The book starts with an examination of whether anti-individualism is compatible with the claim that a subject can have a priori knowledge of her thought contents. The second part investigates whether anti-individualism undermines the idea that we are rational subjects. The issues raised concerning rationality turn out to be central to the question of whether anti-individualism is compatible with Fregean sense. In the last part, I discuss whether anti-individualism provides a novel and a priori route to knowledge of the external world. Throughout the book, I include discussion of two versions of anti-individualism that often receive little attention in the literature on these topics: the illusion version of anti-individualism and Fregean anti-individualism.

According to anti-individualism, a subject's thought contents are individuated partly by a variety of features of her environment, such as the fundamental nature of natural kinds in her environment, the particular objects in her environment, and the linguistic practices of her community. This might suggest that, if anti-individualism were true, then a subject could know her thought contents only by using empirical information about her environment and those features of it that partly individuate her thoughts. But, it seems grossly implausible to suppose that to know that I think, say, that water is wet, I need to investigate the chemical composition of the stuff in lakes and rivers, or that to know that I think, say, that arthritis is painful, I need to investigate how medical experts in my community would define 'arthritis'. Indeed, most anti-individualists accept that it would be a serious objection to anti-individualism if it were incompatible with the claim that a subject can have a priori knowledge of her thought contents.

Chapters 2 through 4 discuss two central arguments for incompatibility that I call the *discrimination* and *illusion* arguments, of which only the first has received widespread attention in the literature. The discrimination argument exploits the intuitive link between knowledge and discriminative abilities. We would deny that a subject knows by vision that she is looking at a robin if she cannot visually distinguish the actual situation from an alternative situation in which she is instead looking at another common bird. Similarly, the incompatibilist argues that a subject cannot know a priori that she is thinking, say, that water is wet, when it is a result of anti-individualism that there is an alternative situation in which she lacks this thought that she cannot a priori distinguish from the actual situation. While the discrimination argument applies to all versions of anti-individualism, the illusion argument applies to only the illusion version of anti-individualism. According to the illusion argument, the illusion version of anti-individualism undermines a subject's ability to have a priori knowledge of her thought contents since it allows that a subject may suffer an illusion of thought. For instance, how can a subject know a priori that she thinks, say, that that is a cat, if there is an alternative situation in which she suffers an illusion of thinking about a cat?

There is a certain standard response to the discrimination argument made by those who defend the compatibility of anti-individualism and a priori knowledge of thought contents (*compatibilists* for short). They standardly accept that it is a consequence of anti-individualism that a subject cannot a priori distinguish the actual situation from a counterfactual situation in which she lacks the thought she actually has. Further, they accept that the alternative situation is sometimes relevant and thus potentially undermines knowledge. However, they argue that the alternative situation does not undermine a subject's a priori knowledge of her thought contents, since it does not threaten her reliability about her thought contents. In general, they argue that even if anti-individualism is true, subjects are reliable about their thought contents without using empirical information.

However, it is not clear how this response answers the discrimination argument, according to which knowledge requires discrimination and anti-individualism undermines a subject's ability to a priori distinguish the actual situation from alternative situations in which she lacks the thought she actually has. Prima facie, the compatibilist could answer this argument by showing either that anti-individualism does not undermine a subject's discriminative abilities, or that knowledge requires only reliability and not discriminative abilities. I argue that the compatibilist's (correct) point, that anti-individualism does not threaten a subject's reliability about her thought contents, does not show that it does not threaten her discriminative abilities. Instead, perhaps, the point about reliability is best seen as part of the second type of response. However, I argue that, so far, compatibilists have not provided compelling arguments that knowledge requires only reliability and not discriminative abilities. In the absence of such arguments, it is worth investigating responses to the discrimination argument that might be successful even if knowledge turns out to require discriminative abilities. Such responses would finesse the issue of the requirements for knowledge and could be used both by those who hold that knowledge requires discriminative abilities and those who hold that it requires only reliability.

In chapter 3, I examine whether an anti-individualist could respond to the discrimination argument by building a discrimination requirement into her account of thought. Suppose that knowledge in fact requires discriminative abilities. Nonetheless, the anti-individualist might hope to meet the discrimination requirement for knowledge by building a discrimination requirement into the account of the conditions required for thought. I investigate this strategy by considering Evans's anti-individualist account according to which a subject can have a thought about an object or a kind only if she can distinguish that object or kind from others. I conclude that this strategy is ultimately unsuccessful.

In chapter 4, I develop and defend a different response using the notion of a relevant alternative. I argue that, with one exception, the alternative situations used in the discrimination argument are not normally relevant. Thus, whether knowledge turns out to require discriminative abilities or only reliable belief, these alternative situations do not normally undermine knowledge. The notion of a relevant alternative also provides a response to the illusion argument. I argue that it is hard to answer the illusion argument by focusing on reliability. There are several epistemologically relevant notions of reliability, including local and global reliability. I argue that the illusion version of anti-individualism may threaten global reliability if not local reliability. Instead, I suggest that the possibility of suffering an illusion of thought is not normally relevant.

In chapter 5 I turn to the question of whether anti-individualism undermines the idea that we are rational subjects. According to anti-individualism, a subject's thought contents are individuated partly by the environment. As a result, many have argued that anti-individualism threatens transparency: the claim that a subject can realize a priori whether two thoughts or thought constituents have the same or different contents. If sameness of content is not transparent, then a subject may fail to make simple valid inferences and may fail to notice simple inconsistencies between her beliefs. If difference of content is not transparent, then a subject may make simple invalid inferences. Thus, anti-individualism undermines the concept of a rational agent as one who, at least in simple cases, would not have contradictory beliefs or make invalid inferences or fail to make simple valid inferences. I extend the established literature on this topic by discussing not only non-Fregean anti-individualism but also Fregean anti-individualism. I argue that only non-Fregean anti-individualism is incompatible with transparency of sameness, although both Fregean and non-Fregean varieties of anti-individualism are incompatible with transparency of difference. While I agree that anti-individualism of both Fregean and non-Fregean versions undermines transparency, I argue that this is not a threat to rationality properly understood.

The arguments of chapter 5 lead to the discussion in chapter 6 of whether or not anti-individualism is compatible with Fregean sense. Some have supposed that anti-individualism is incompatible with Fregean sense, but prominent anti-individualists, such as Evans, McDowell, and Peacocke, have developed a sophisticated notion of object-dependent sense that overcomes the standard arguments for incompatibility. Fregeans argue that sense is required to provide a psychological explanation of informative identity judgments, inferences, and belief ascriptions, and to avoid attributing contradictory beliefs to subjects. If anti-individualism were compatible with sense, this would enable the anti-individualist to take advantage of the Fregean explanation of these phenomena. However, I provide new arguments that anti-individualism is in tension with even the sophisticated notion of Fregean sense. I argue that the classic Fregean arguments for sense depend on two key assumptions, the transparency of sameness of content and a related conception of rationality. Further, I argue that it is hard to motivate these key assumptions if one accepts anti-individualism. If one cannot combine anti-individualism with Fregean sense, then there is a stark choice between anti-individualism and the Fregean approach to psychological explanation.

Chapters 7 and 8 examine whether anti-individualism provides a novel and a priori route to knowledge of the world. Suppose, as I have suggested, that anti-individualists can answer the discrimination and illusion arguments for the incompatibility of anti-individualism and the claim that a subject can have a priori knowledge of her thought contents. According to anti-individualism, what thoughts a subject has depends on the environment. So, if anti-individualism is true, a subject might be able to use the philosophical arguments for anti-individualism to gain a priori knowledge that her having a certain thought entails that her environment is some way. Combining this knowledge with her a priori knowledge of her thought contents, she could gain a priori knowledge of her environment. On this basis, some have argued that anti-individualism can provide a new and powerful answer to skeptics who deny that we can have knowledge of the external world. Others have argued that it is absurd to suppose that anyone could gain substantive knowledge of her environment merely by reflecting on her thoughts and a bit of philosophy. They have taken the result to be a reductio of the claim that anti-individualism is compatible with a priori knowledge of one's thought contents. On either understanding, it would be an interesting and important result if anti-individualism did allow subjects to gain a priori knowledge of the nature of the world.

In chapter 7, I consider but reject one response suggested by Wright and Davies. They argue that even if a subject has a priori knowledge of her thought contents and that her thought contents entail some fact about her environment, she cannot thereby gain a priori knowledge of her environment. They claim that, although warrant and knowledge normally transmit across valid inferences, they fail to transmit across a certain subset of valid inferences, including the relevant inference. I reject Davies's and Wright's arguments for a limitation on the transmission of warrant by considering the nature of warrant and justification. Instead, I suggest a different reason to reject the claim that a subject could use anti-individualism and a priori knowledge of her thought contents to gain a priori knowledge of her environment. I argue (in chap. 8) that even if anti-individualism is true, there are no a priori knowable entailments from thought to the world from which a subject could gain a priori knowledge of her environment. It turns out that a priori knowledge of the relevant entailments requires a type of knowledge that anti-individualists deny we have: a priori knowledge of whether or not one is having a thought, of what type one's thought is, or of how to correctly explicate one's thought. If that is right, then anti-individualism fails to provide a novel a priori route to knowledge of the world. The conclusion of the book is that anti-individualism does not have the kind of radical epistemic consequences suggested by many. Certainly, anti-individualism provides a new source of mistakes about the logical properties of thoughts. And this undermines the idea that one can combine anti-individualism with Fregean sense. However, anti-individualism's potential threat to a priori knowledge of one's own thought contents can be largely defused by appeal to the epistemological notion of a relevant alternative. In addition, on a proper understanding of rationality, anti-individualism does not undermine the notion that we are rational subjects. Last, anti-individualism does not provide a new a priori route to knowledge of the world. Many would agree that anti-individualism lacks the radical epistemic consequences it is commonly suggested to have. However, I support this conclusion by a range of new arguments that link central issues in the philosophy of mind, such as rationality, psychological explanation, and the nature of thought, with the epistemological literature on knowledge, warrant, justification, and reliability.

2 Knowledge and Discrimination

1 Privileged Access

One of the most serious objections to anti-individualism is the claim that it is incompatible with the nature of a subject's epistemological access to her beliefs, desires, and other propositional attitudes. A subject's first-person access to her own propositional attitudes is strikingly different from her third-person access to the propositional attitudes of other subjects. To know what someone else thinks, a subject must use empirical evidence about behavior, whether linguistic or nonlinguistic. For instance, I might attribute to you the belief that today is Tuesday, on the grounds that you say that it is, or that your actions fit the activities in your diary for Tuesday. In other cases, the link might be less direct. In your absence I might attribute to you the belief that the government's new education policy is wrong. Here, I haven't used any information about your current behavior. Instead, I use my general knowledge of your political views gained in the past using behavioral evidence. By contrast, a subject can know what she herself thinks without basing this on evidence about her own behavior, whether past or present. For example, I can know that I believe that today is Tuesday

without first observing my behavior, say, hearing myself say
'Today is Tuesday', or noticing myself go about the activities in my diary for Tuesday. Indeed, I can know that I
have this belief without evidencing it in my behavior at all
(perhaps, I have only just woken up). Similarly, I can know
that I believe that the government's new policy is wrong
without inferring this from a general knowledge of my own
political views, gained through observation of my own past
behavior. This distinctive way of gaining knowledge seems
available for a wide range of propositional attitudes. Any
subject has a host of beliefs about mundane matters of fact
that she can know herself to have without using behavioral
evidence, such as beliefs about geographical facts (e.g., that
Paris is the capital of France), beliefs about the properties
of objects and kinds (e.g., that water is wet), beliefs about
numbers (e.g., that $1 + 1 = 2$), and so on. There are numerous examples of other attitudes a subject can know herself
to have without reliance on behavior, including certain
desires (e.g., that this meeting not go on much longer),
hopes (e.g., that I don't buy my grandmother the same
present for Christmas as my brother), and intentions (e.g.,
that I will go shopping later on).

Admittedly, knowledge of one's own propositional attitudes is not always so easy, for example, when an attitude
is unconscious or in cases of self-deception. Here a subject
may need to use empirical evidence from other people or
about her behavior in order to come to know that she has
a certain propositional attitude. For example, it might be
evident from a subject's behavior (her monitoring of his
phone calls, diary, etc.) that she believes that her husband is
having an affair, though she herself might be unaware of this
and might even deny it to herself. She might be able to see
that she indeed has this belief only by using evidence about

her own behavior. However, although such isolated cases exist, self-knowledge seems characterized by the fact that, for a large range of propositional attitudes concerning mundane matters, a subject can know that she is in one of these attitude states without relying on evidence about her behavior.

Of course, subjects often form propositional attitudes, most obviously beliefs, on the basis of empirical evidence. But, once a subject has formed a propositional attitude on the basis of evidence, she does not need to use that evidence to judge that she has the relevant attitude. For example, I might form the belief that lack of exercise is a risk factor for heart disease on the basis of data reported in a newspaper article. But, I need not use the empirical evidence that led me to form the belief in order to know that I have it. Indeed, the belief may persist, and I may know that I have it, even after I have forgotten or lost the evidence on the basis of which it was formed.

It seems, then, that whereas knowledge of others' propositional attitudes is based on empirical evidence concerning behavior, knowledge of one's own propositional attitudes is typically independent of empirical evidence, whether about behavior or the external world in general. In short, a subject can typically have a priori knowledge of her propositional attitudes, that is, she can have such knowledge without basing it in a justificatory way on perceptual experience. Of course, a subject's knowledge of her own conscious propositional attitudes is based on those same conscious attitudes. However, according to a well-established use of "a priori" (which I am following throughout the book), knowledge is a priori if it is justificatorily independent of perceptual experience, where such experience does not include all conscious states and events; rather, it includes only a subject's perceptual experience of the external world and (perhaps) experience of her own bodily states (see chapter 1, section 7). On this view, a subject can have a priori knowledge of her own propositional attitudes.

Notice that a subject can have a priori knowledge of a certain propositional attitude even if some of the concepts that make up its content were acquired in virtue of empirical interactions with the environment. That certain experiences are necessary for having a concept does not entail that those experiences play a justificatory role in knowledge of attitudes containing that concept. More generally, a concept acquired through experience can still figure in a priori knowledge. For example, some definitional truths involving empirically acquired concepts are traditionally regarded as a priori (e.g., 'red is a color'; see chap. 1, sec. 7).

Anti-individualism does not merely stress the role of the environment in acquiring concepts; it also holds that the content of a subject's propositional attitudes is individuated partly in terms of environmental factors about which the subject may be ignorant or mistaken. As a result, anti-individualism may seem intuitively to threaten a subject's a priori knowledge of the contents of her propositional attitudes. As the Twin Earth cases illustrate, a subject may have different thoughts in different environments, say, water thoughts on Earth and twater thoughts on Twin Earth. This raises the worry that, in order to know what thought contents she has, the subject has to investigate those factors that anti-individualists hold partly individuate thought, such as the chemical composition of the substances around her or the practices of her linguistic community. As I will put it from now on, anti-individualism seems to threaten the thesis of *privileged access*, the claim that a subject can have a priori knowledge of her thought contents.

Notice that this objection can be formulated independently of the notion of the a priori. Regardless of one's view about the a priori, it is deeply implausible to suppose that in order to know her thought contents a subject has to investigate the chemical composition of the substances around her or the practices of her linguistic community. For example, it is implausible that in order to know that she thinks that water is wet a subject has to investigate the chemical structure of the stuff in lakes. Indeed, most anti-individualists accept that it would be a serious objection if anti-individualism had the consequence that a subject must investigate her environment in order to know what she thinks (e.g., Davidson 1987; Burge 1988; Heil 1988; Falvey and Owens 1994; Gibbons 1996; McLaughlin and Tye 1998). While the following discussion is framed in terms of the notion of a priori knowledge, those who prefer a different use of this notion could reformulate the discussion accordingly.

The intuitive threat of the incompatibility of anti-individualism with privileged access can be filled out in more detail in two arguments—the discrimination and illusion arguments. The discrimination argument is applicable to any version of anti-individualism and is the focus of this chapter and the next. The illusion argument applies only to the illusion version of anti-individualism, according to which a subject may suffer an illusion of thought. I will discuss this second incompatibilist argument in chapter 4.

2   The Discrimination Argument

According to the discrimination argument, anti-individualism threatens privileged access by undermining a subject's ability to distinguish a priori between the thought contents she actually has and the thought contents she would have in various counterfactual situations. Consider again the Twin Earth thought experiments discussed in the last chapter. In the actual situation, a subject has a certain thought content, p, which is partly individuated by the nature of her environment. The counterfactual situation differs in some factor that, according to anti-individualism, partly individuates thought. As a result, if the subject had been brought up in the counterfactual environment, she would have lacked the thought she has in the actual environment. However, the counterfactual situation is set up in such a way that things would seem subjectively just the same to the subject if she were in that environment. It seems, then, that the subject cannot distinguish a priori between these two situations. To do so, she would need to use empirical information. The incompatibilist takes this to undermine the subject's ability to have a priori knowledge of her thoughts. Suppose that, in the actual situation, the subject not only believes that p, but also believes that she thinks that p. Nonetheless, the incompatibilist argues, her true belief that she thinks that p is not an instance of a priori knowledge, for she cannot distinguish a priori between the actual situation in which she thinks that p, and the counterfactual situation in which she lacks this thought.

The discrimination argument can be applied to natural kind anti-individualism, social anti-individualism, and singular anti-individualism. Further, it can be applied to both descriptive and illusion versions of these views. For example, suppose that in the actual situation, the subject is on Earth and thinks that water is wet. To set up the discrimination argument, we need a counterfactual situation in which everything would seem the same to the subject, but she would lack the thought that water is wet. This could be a twin environment in which she thinks a different thought, say, that twater is wet. Or it could be a no-reference situation in which there is no single liquid in the rivers and lakes, either because the stuff in rivers and lakes forms a motley collection of natural kinds, or, more radically, because the subject suffers an illusion of seeing rivers and lakes. On both the descriptive and illusion views, if the subject had been brought up in either of these counterfactual situations, she would lack the thought that water is wet. On the descriptive view, she would instead think of the supposed liquid via a description. On the rival illusion view, she would suffer an illusion of thought. So, the discrimination argument could use either a twin or no-reference situation and can be applied to both descriptive and illusion versions of anti-individualism.

Here I concentrate on one instance of the discrimination argument formulated using a "slow switch" case involving thoughts about natural kinds. Suppose that Sally is initially on Earth where the stuff in rivers and lakes has chemical composition H_2O, and this is known by some members of the Earth community, although Sally herself is ignorant of this fact. After living there for many years, she is unwittingly switched to Twin Earth where she spends the rest of her life. Twin Earth is just like Earth, except that the stuff in rivers and lakes has chemical composition XYZ, and the term 'water' is applied to this different stuff. Twin Earth chemists and some, but not all, Twin Earth layfolk know that the chemical composition of the stuff in their lakes and rivers is XYZ.

An anti-individualist would accept that the switch from Earth to Twin Earth affects the content of Sally's thoughts. For example, according to the anti-individualist, when Sally is initially on Earth, she expresses the belief that water is wet

with an utterance of 'Water is wet'. But, the anti-individualist would argue that once Sally has been on Twin Earth for
a sufficiently long period,[1] she would no longer express the
same belief by this utterance. As a result of the switch,
Sally is now related to a different substance and a different
linguistic community in which 'water' has a different
extension. Anti-individualists differ over what effect these
new environmental relations have on Sally's thought contents. For simplicity, I will assume that, after the switch,
Sally's utterance of 'Water is wet' expresses a thought
involving the concept of twater.[2] However, the discrimination argument applies regardless of which concept, if any,
Sally expresses by 'water' after the switch. All the discrimination argument requires is that, after the switch, Sally no
longer expresses the belief that water is wet by her utterance
of 'Water is wet'.

Although Sally's thought contents change as a result of
the switch, it seems that she would fail to notice the change
in her environment or her thoughts. It is part of the case that
Sally is switched unwittingly and that the two environments
appear exactly the same to her. If we were to ask Sally
whether her thoughts have changed in content after they
have in fact done so, it seems likely that she would say
they have not. Sally could know that her thought contents
have changed only by learning that she has been switched
between different environments. The incompatibilist concludes that Sally cannot distinguish a priori between the
actual situation in which she thinks that water is wet and
the alternative situation in which she lacks this thought. As
a result, she argues that Sally's actual belief that she thinks
that water is wet fails to be an instance of a priori knowledge. How, she asks, can Sally know a priori that she thinks
that water is wet when she cannot distinguish a priori the

actual situation in which she has this thought from the alternative situation in which she lacks it?

The incompatibilist argument exploits the idea that intuitively knowledge is connected to the notion of a discriminative ability. Consider a subject in good perceptual conditions who forms the correct perceptually based belief that the bird on her lawn is a crow. Her belief that the bird is a crow is both true and caused by the fact that it is a crow. But we would deny that her belief is knowledge if she cannot distinguish a crow from another kind of bird that is abundant in her area, say, a rook, on the basis of perception. By contrast, consider a keen bird-watcher looking at the same scene. She too forms the correct perceptually based belief that the bird is a crow. However, unlike the first subject, the second can visually distinguish crows from other birds that are abundant in the area, and also from similar birds rarely found in the area. We would judge that the bird-watcher does know that the bird is a crow. Such intuitions have led a number of philosophers to suppose that it is not sufficient for the belief that p to be knowledge that it is true and caused by the fact that p. In addition, knowledge requires a certain discriminative ability (see e.g., Goldman 1976, 1986; McGinn 1984).

A compatibilist might try to respond to the discrimination argument by pointing out that, on pain of skepticism, knowledge that p cannot require that one can distinguish the actual situation in which p from every possible alternative situation in which p is false. Consider a subject who is looking at a rose and having a perceptual experience as of seeing a rose. She could have a subjectively indistinguishable experience had she just become a brain in a vat (BIV) being stimulated to make it seem as if she is seeing a rose. So, if knowledge that p required that one can distinguish the actual situation in which p from every possible alternative, then, in the actual situation, she could not know that she is seeing a rose. More generally, if knowledge that p required that one can distinguish the actual situation in which p from every possible alternative, perceptual experience could not provide any knowledge of the world. To avoid this skeptical conclusion, the idea that knowledge requires discriminative abilities needs to be formulated as the idea that knowledge that p requires the ability to distinguish the actual situation in which p from a subset of the alternative situations in which p is false—those that are relevant or nearby (see, e.g., Dretske 1970; Nozick 1981; Goldman 1986; DeRose 1995; Lewis 1996).

So, a compatibilist could respond to the discrimination argument by arguing that the alternative situation in which Sally lacks the thought that water is wet is not a relevant alternative to the actual situation. After all, there is no such planet as Twin Earth, and speakers are not transported unawares from Earth to other planets while asleep. Nonetheless, most compatibilists have not taken this line of response,[3] for, as they admit, there are subjects for whom such an alternative situation is relevant. First, even though ordinary subjects are not transported between planets while asleep, the slow switch subject, Sally, is stipulated to be a subject who is actually so transported. Thus, for Sally, the possibility that she is on Twin Earth thinking twin thoughts is relevant (see, e.g., Falvey and Owens 1994, p. 115). Second, and more important, the possibility that a subject is in a twin environment is a relevant possibility even for some ordinary subjects (ibid.; Ludlow 1995a; Gibbons 1996; McLaughlin and Tye 1998). There are many examples of a word that has different meanings in different linguistic groupings. For example, the words 'chicory', 'chips', 'pavement', 'profes-

sor', 'public school', and 'football' all have different meanings in British and American English (Segal 2000, chap. 4).
Further, a word may have different meanings within different subgroupings of a single linguistic community. For
example, within UK English, the word 'pragmatist' has both
a philosophical and an ordinary meaning (Ludlow 1995a).
A subject who is ignorant of such differences could travel
between the relevant linguistic groupings, effectively under-
going a slow switch. For such a subject, the possibility of
being in a twin environment is a relevant alternative. We
will return to the issue of the relevance of such alternative
situations in chapter 4. But, for now, I will follow compatibilists in holding that, for some subjects, such alternative
situations are relevant.

Instead of challenging the relevance of the alternative
situation, compatibilists have standardly responded to the
discrimination argument by stressing the reliability of a
subject's judgments about her thought contents (e.g., Burge
1988; Heil 1988; Falvey and Owens 1994; Gibbons 1996).
They argue that even the subject who is switched between
Earth and Twin Earth does not make a mistake about what
she thinks. First, a subject's environment individuates
not only her first-order thoughts, but also her second-order
thoughts, her thoughts about her thoughts. If her environment makes it the case that it is the concept water, rather
than twater, that figures in her first-order thoughts, then
this concept figures in her second-order thoughts as well.
Second, Burge (1988) points out that there is a special kind
of second-order thoughts, "cogito" thoughts, that are self-
verifying. Cogito thoughts are beliefs of the form: I believe
that I think that *p*. Such beliefs ascribe to a subject no particular attitude toward a thought content, but only that the
subject entertains the thought content via some attitude or

other. If a subject believes that she thinks that *p*, she thereby entertains the thought content that *p*, and thus makes her belief true. As a result, even if Sally is unaware that she has been switched and that her thought contents have changed, her cogito thoughts cannot be mistaken. Even after the switch, and while being ignorant of it, Sally cannot believe falsely that she thinks that there is water in front of her. Instead, she ascribes correctly to herself what thoughts she has. For example, if she thinks that there is twater in front of her, then she believes that there is twater in front of her.[4]

We might wonder how stressing the reliability of the subject's beliefs about her thought contents constitutes a reply to the discrimination argument. That argument focuses on the notion of a discriminative ability, and it is not obvious that this notion can be equated with the notion of a reliable ability to form true beliefs. The incompatibilist questions how the subject can have a priori knowledge of her thought contents given that she cannot distinguish a priori between the actual situation in which she thinks that water is wet and the nearby alternative situation in which she lacks this thought. In raising this question, the incompatibilist uses the intuitive connection between knowledge and discrimination. Some might suggest that a reliable ability to form true beliefs is sufficient for having a discriminative ability. If that were so, then it would be clear how stressing the reliability of cogito thoughts could answer the discrimination argument. I will consider but reject this compatibilist strategy in the next section. If having a reliable ability to form true beliefs is not sufficient for having a discriminative ability, then the compatibilist has two options. First, she might argue on other grounds that the slow switch subject can distinguish a priori between the actual situation and the relevant twin situation. Second, she might accept with the incompatibilist that the slow switch subject cannot distinguish a priori the actual from the twin situation, but argue that such a discriminative ability is not required for knowledge of thought. I consider these options below.

3   Discrimination and Reliability

We may start our investigation of the relation between discriminative abilities and reliability by looking at the work of Goldman. Goldman was a key figure in bringing out the intuitive connection between knowledge and discrimination, but he used this connection to motivate a reliabilist account of knowledge. In his classic (1976) paper, Goldman rejects his earlier causal account of knowledge and argues that knowledge requires certain discriminative abilities. He suggests that the notion of propositional knowledge is closely connected with the notion of knowing one thing from another, where this involves the ability to distinguish these two things (Goldman 1976, p. 772; 1986, p. 47).

He further motivates this view by the now famous barn case (Goldman 1976, pp. 772–773). Suppose that a subject is driving through ordinary countryside, in good visual conditions, observing her surroundings. She says, looking at what is in fact a barn, 'That's a barn'. In the ordinary case, Goldman says, this belief would constitute knowledge. However, now suppose counterfactually that the subject is driving through an area in which there are numerous fake barns that she cannot distinguish visually from real barns. As it happens, the subject is in fact looking at a barn and truly believes that it is a barn. In this second case, Goldman suggests, we would deny that the driver knows that that is a barn.

Goldman argues that this pair of cases supports the idea that knowledge requires certain discriminative abilities. In the first situation, the driver can distinguish barns from the other kinds of objects in her environment, such as cows and tractors. But, in the second, she cannot do so because of the presence of the fake barns. Notice that these two cases do not suggest that knowledge requires that the subject be able to distinguish the actual situation from every possible situation. If this were required, then even in the first situation the driver would not count as knowing that the object she is looking at is a barn, for, of course, she would not be able to distinguish real barns from possible fake barns (which as it happens are not present in her environment). This leads Goldman to suggest that knowledge requires the ability to distinguish the actual situation from a subset of alternative situations—the "relevant" ones:

A person knows that p, I suggest, only if the actual state of affairs in which p is true is distinguishable or discriminable by him from a relevant possible state of affairs in which p is false. If there is a relevant possible state of affairs in which p is false and which is indistinguishable by him from the actual state of affairs, then he fails to know that p. (Goldman 1976, p. 774)

Goldman reiterates his commitment to the idea that knowledge requires discriminative abilities in his (1986) book, *Epistemology and Cognition*, where he again endorses the view that "propositional knowledge that p involves discriminating the truth of p from relevant alternatives" (p. 47).

A similar view has been defended by McGinn. McGinn endorses the principle that "one can know that p only if one can tell whether p" (1984, p. 26), and he argues that telling whether p involves having the ability to distinguish the actual state of affairs in which p from relevant alternative states of affairs: "Can I tell whether there is a table there? I think that in the ordinary use of the phrase 'tell whether', what this requires is that I can distinguish there being a table there from there being a chair, or a dog, or some such" (ibid.). However, he adds that "the possession of the capacity to tell whether there is a table does not require that one be able to tell whether one is a brain in a vat" (p. 27).

The notion of a discriminative capacity figures explicitly in McGinn's final analysis of knowledge: "S knows that p just if his (true) belief that p is acquired by the exercise of a capacity to discriminate truth from falsehood within some relevant class R of propositions" (1984, p. 17). McGinn explicitly denies that the notion of the ability to discriminate truth from falsehood can be reduced to the notion of the tendency to believe true propositions and refrain from believing false ones, although he fails to provide much elucidation of the notion of a discriminative ability (p. 23).

By contrast, Goldman's final statement, of his view in both his (1976) paper and his later book, makes no mention of discriminative abilities. Instead he uses the notion of a reliable belief-producing process: "[A] true belief that p fails to be knowledge if there are any relevant alternative situations in which the proposition p would be false, but the process used would have caused S to believe that p anyway" (Goldman 1986, p. 46; see also 1976, p. 786). It may seem, then, that at least for a subject who is capable of having beliefs and who possesses the requisite concepts, Goldman interprets the notion of a discriminative ability as amounting to a reliable ability to form true beliefs. (For a creature without the capacity to have beliefs, the notion of a discriminative ability would have to be understood in a different way.) If this equation were correct or, more minimally, if having a reliable ability to form true beliefs were sufficient for a discriminative ability, then it would be easy for the compatibilist to answer the discrimination argument. For, as we have seen, a subject's cogito thoughts cannot be mistaken. Even the slow switch subject cannot believe falsely that she thinks that water is wet. But, in fact, I will argue that the slow switch case itself shows us that the reliable ability to form true beliefs about which of two types is instantiated is not sufficient for the ability to distinguish those two types.

Recall why the incompatibilist held that Sally cannot distinguish a priori the actual situation in which she thinks that water is wet from the relevant alternative situation in which, as a result of the switch to Twin Earth, she instead thinks that twater is wet. It is part of the example that the switch is carried out in such a way that Sally is unaware that she has been switched. In addition, the only differences between Earth and Twin Earth are ones she is ignorant of, such as the chemical composition of the stuff in lakes and the views of chemical experts. She would fail to notice the change in her environment and her thoughts. Furthermore, if we were to ask her whether her thoughts have changed content after they have done so, she would deny that they have done so. Thus, it seems intuitively plausible that Sally cannot distinguish a priori between the actual and twin situations. This has been accepted by leading compatibilist anti-individualists such as Burge, who writes, "[The slow switch subject] would have no signs of the differences in his thoughts, no difference in the way things feel. . . . the person would be unable to discriminate between different mental events under the stated switching conditions" (1988, p. 653. For similar comments see Burge 1996, p. 95; Boghossian 1989, p. 160; Falvey and Owens 1994, p. 111). However, we have already seen that the subject's cogito thoughts cannot be mistaken, even after the switch. Thus, it seems that the slow switch example shows us that a reliable ability to form true beliefs is not sufficient for a discriminative ability. We may fill out the intuition that the slow switch subject lacks the ability to distinguish a priori the actual from the twin situation by noting the connection between discriminative abilities and several other abilities—the abilities to notice change, to make reliable judgments of sameness and difference, and to act differentially. For instance, suppose that a subject has the ability to distinguish yellow and blue. If she does, then we would expect not only that she can reliably judge whether objects are yellow or blue, but also that she has certain other abilities. In particular, we would expect that she is able to notice if an object changes from yellow to blue. We would also expect that she can reliably say of any pair of objects from a collection of objects, all of which are either blue or yellow but not both, whether or not they are the same color. Last, we would expect that her ability to distinguish the two colors could be manifested in an ability to act differentially with respect to samples of those colors. Suppose that we show her objects some of which are yellow and some of which are blue (but none of which is both), and ask her to carry out these instructions:

Press button A iff the object is blue.

Press button B iff the object is yellow.

As long as the subject can press the relevant buttons (e.g., she is not paralyzed, and they are not out of her reach) then, if she can distinguish the two colors, she should be able to manifest this by passing our simple test.

We have already seen that the slow switch subject, Sally, cannot make correct judgments about whether her thought contents have changed unless she is given the empirical information that she has been switched to a different environment. In addition, it seems that her judgments about sameness and difference of type of thought are not reliable: after the switch, she would judge falsely that she expresses the same thought by 'Water is wet' as she used to.[5] Further, she cannot pass some simple tests that require her to act differentially with respect to the two kinds of thought. Suppose that before she is switched, we introduce her to the philosophical arguments for anti-individualism and explain that she will undergo a slow switch that will change her thought contents. In addition, we tell her that the switch will affect the concept she expresses with 'water': although she now expresses one concept with this term, she will later come to express a different concept with the term. We do not tell her at what time the switch will take place. We ask her to carry out the instruction to press a certain button A if and only if she notices that she has come to express a different concept with the term 'water'. We set things up so that she is able to press this button easily at any time (perhaps it is carried on a small transmitter that she carries around with her). It seems clear that, without empirical information about the time of the switch, our subject will fail this simple test even though she can press the relevant button. If by some fluke she manages to press the button when she starts to have twater thoughts, then this will be a matter of chance, and she will be unable to repeat the feat in further trials. Nor will it help if we offer her a large incentive to correctly follow the instructions, such as a million pounds. It seems that she cannot respond differentially to water and twater thoughts by pressing the button when and only when she has twater thoughts.

While accepting that possession of a discriminative ability requires more than merely the reliable ability to form true beliefs, someone might try to argue that the slow switch subject can meet the more stringent requirements for possession of a discriminative ability. First, she might argue that the slow switch subject can act differentially with respect to water and twater thoughts even if she is ignorant of when the switch takes place. One way to do this would be to suggest that the very environmental conditions that individuate the content of Sally's thoughts also individuate the content of her utterances. If that is right, then the environmental conditions that determine that Sally's post-switch thoughts involve the concept of twater also determine that Sally's post-switch utterances of 'water' express the concept of twater. On this view, although Sally uses the same word-form, 'water', to report the contents of her water and twater thoughts, in doing so she ascribes different contents to them. When she is on Earth, causally connected to water and part of the Earth linguistic community, she has thoughts involving the concept of water and correctly reports them as involving the concept of water. However, when she is on Twin Earth, causally connected to twater and a member of the Twin Earth linguistic community, she has thoughts involving the concept of twater, which she correctly reports as involving the concept of twater.[6]

A second way of filling out the idea that Sally acts differentially in response to water and twater thoughts uses the intentional way of typing actions. When we type actions intentionally, we type them in terms of the reasons for which the agent performed the action. For example, consider someone waving her arm. This action could be typed as an instance of (attempting to) greet a friend if, say, it is motivated by the subject's desire to greet a friend and her belief that waving her arm like this is a way of doing that. Two actions that involve exactly the same type of body movements may differ in their intentional descriptions. For example, a second agent might move her arm in just the same way as the first, but for the different reason that she wants to stretch a certain muscle and believes that waving her arm in this way stretches the relevant muscle. In this case, her action would count as a case of (attempting to) stretch the relevant muscle, not a case of greeting.

The anti-individualist may exploit the intentional way of typing actions to argue that Sally does act differentially with respect to water and twater thoughts. For example, consider two occasions on which Sally reaches out toward a glass of colorless, clear liquid. On the first occasion, she is on Earth, and her action is caused by the desire that she drink some water. On the second occasion, she is on Twin Earth, and her action is caused by her desire that she drink some twater. Although her arm moves in just the same way on each occasion, her actions are of different intentional types in virtue of their different intentional causes: one is an action of reaching for water; the other of reaching for twater. (That Sally's actions have different intentional descriptions on Earth and Twin Earth has also been noted in the different debate about whether anti-individualism threatens the causal efficacy of content; see, e.g., Burge 1986a, p. 11.)

Even if we allow that the slow switch subject can act differentially with respect to water and twater thoughts, this does not show that she has the other abilities associated with possession of a discriminative capacity—the ability to notice change and the ability to make correct same/different judgments. This may cast doubt on the claim that she can distinguish a priori the two types of thought. In addition, I think we should query the claim that the slow switch subject can act differentially with respect to water and twater thoughts. Ordinarily, when a subject has the ability to distinguish between two kinds of thing, she can manifest this in a wide range of ways. For instance, if a subject can distinguish yellow and blue, then, for a wide range of actions she can perform, she can act differentially with respect to items of these two colors, whether it is by clapping her hands, stamping her feet, blinking, wiggling her ears, and so on. But we have already seen that there is one action type, pressing button A, that is within Sally's behavioral repertoire, but which she cannot use to respond differentially to twater thoughts. Nor is this an isolated case. There are numerous actions that she can perform, such as singing, shouting, stamping her feet, pressing bells, but which she cannot perform when and only when she has twater thoughts unless she is given empirical information about when the switch takes place. So, Sally does not have the kind of general ability we would expect if she could genuinely distinguish water and twater thoughts.

I suggest that Sally's ability to act differentially is so limited because her abilities to report the contents of her water and twater thoughts differently and to act differently with respect to those thoughts when intentionally described do not require her to tell the difference between water and twater thoughts. By contrast, for a wide range of other action types within her behavioral repertoire, acting differentially with respect to water and twater thoughts requires that she can tell the difference between these kinds of thoughts. For instance, the claim that Sally reports her water and twater thoughts as involving different contents is grounded in the view that the intentional content of Sally's utterances is determined by environmental factors of which she may be ignorant. Thus, Sally counts as acting differentially even if she does not realize that her environment and her thoughts have changed. Indeed, it seems plausible that she would deny that either her environment or her thoughts have changed and would also deny that the contents of her reports have changed. Similarly, Sally's nonverbal actions would have different intentional descriptions in virtue of their different intentional causes even if Sally does not realize that her environment and her thoughts have changed. Plausibly, she would deny that either her environment or her thoughts have changed, and she would further deny that she is acting differently from how she did before. By contrast, for a large range of action types, such as pressing buttons, acting differentially with respect to water and twater thoughts does require the subject to be able to tell the difference between water and twater thoughts. But, as we have seen, Sally cannot make correct judgments of sameness and difference between water and twater thoughts unless she is told when the switch occurs.

In summary, the anti-individualist's action argument fails to motivate the view that Sally can distinguish a priori between water and twater thoughts. First, she does not have the ability to act differentially with respect to these thoughts that we would expect if she could genuinely distinguish a priori between water and twater thoughts. Second, the explanation of this failure is plausibly that Sally cannot tell the difference a priori between water and twater thoughts. But she ought to have this latter ability if she could distinguish a priori the two kinds of thoughts.

Despite these problems, the anti-individualist may offer one final argument for the claim that Sally can distinguish a priori between water and twater thoughts. As mentioned earlier, anti-individualists disagree about the effect of a slow switch on thought content. One disagreement concerns what new concepts a subject acquires as a result of a slow switch. A different disagreement concerns whether a subject can recall her old thoughts after the switch. Some have argued that, after a switch, a subject still retains the concept of water and that it figures in those of her thoughts that are based on memories of Earth experiences, even if she also acquires a new concept, say, the concept of twater, that figures in other thoughts, such as thoughts based on interactions with her new Twin Earth environment (see Boghossian 1992, pp. 19–20; Gibbons 1996, pp. 302–303; Burge 1998, pp. 356–357).[7] However, others have argued that, as a result of the switch, the subject would lose the concept water and the ability to recall her old Earth thoughts (e.g., Ludlow 1995b; Tye 1998; Heal 1998).

One might support the latter view by arguing that, after the switch, all the thoughts that Sally would express with 'water' are connected at least in part to the new environment. For example, in explaining her thoughts, she would defer to experts in her current (Twin Earth) environment and would take the nature of substances in her current (Twin Earth) environment to be relevant. Suppose for now that, as a result of the switch, Sally loses the concept water. This may help explain away Sally's apparent inability to distinguish a priori between water and twater thoughts. Her apparent inability might be explained not by her lacking this ability, but rather by an inability, post-switch, to remember the thoughts she used to express with 'water'. A subject cannot judge correctly whether a currently presented object, or kind, is the same as, or different from, a previously presented one, unless she can remember the previously presented one. For example, I would be unable to judge correctly whether the wallpaper I am now looking at is the same color as the carpet at home if I could not now remember what color the carpet at home is. It may be suggested that the reason Sally cannot make correct judgments of sameness or difference between water and twater thoughts is that, after the switch, she can no longer remember the thoughts she used to express with 'water'. If that is right, then it may also explain why, for a large range of actions that Sally can perform, Sally cannot act differentially with respect to water and twater thoughts without being told that she has been switched between environments. As I argued above, for a large range of different action types, such as pressing different buttons, acting differentially with respect to water and twater thoughts requires the ability to judge correctly whether water and twater thoughts have the same or different content.

I will not attempt to resolve the question of whether, as a result of the switch, Sally loses the concept water. But, we should examine whether the appeal to memory loss constitutes a good response to the discrimination argument. First, since many anti-individualists deny that, as a result of the switch, Sally loses the concept of water, the memory response is not available to all anti-individualists. Further, advocates of the memory strategy need to defend their interpretation of the slow switch case as one in which the subject loses her old concept. But, this may be difficult given the current controversy about what thought contents a subject has after a slow switch.

The memory strategy faces a second problem too: even if, after the switch, Sally can no longer remember the thoughts she used to express with 'water', it may also be the case that she lacks the ability to distinguish a priori between water and twater thoughts. The key question, then, is whether the advocate of the memory strategy can add any further evidence to show that Sally lacks only the ability to remember the thoughts she used to express with 'water', rather than also lacking the ability to distinguish a priori between water and twater thoughts. Usually, when a subject

appears to lack the ability to distinguish between two kinds
or items, there are various ways in which we could seek to
establish whether her failure is due to problems with
memory, or an inability to distinguish the relevant kinds or
items, or both.

For example, imagine that we are testing a subject's ability
to distinguish between types of birds. During the training
period of the test, we show her exemplars of one particular
species. Then, in the test period, we show her a sequence of
exemplars of various species of bird, including the target
species and some others, and ask her to say of each exem-
plar whether it is of the same or different type of bird as the
target species. Suppose the subject fails the test. Nevertheless, we could argue that this result is due to a failure of
memory alone if there is other evidence that she possesses
the relevant discriminative ability. For example, perhaps we
ask her to describe the birds she sees in the later part of the
test. She may describe them so accurately that this provides
evidence that she can distinguish between the target species
and the others. Perhaps for every type of bird shown (other
than the target) her description includes mention of some
feature, such as red legs, that distinguishes that type from
the target species. A different way of seeing if her failure to
pass the test is due to memory failure alone would be to set
up a second test in which there is no possibility of memory
failure and see whether she can then distinguish the different types of birds. A simple way to do this would be to
present exemplars of the target species and the other species
simultaneously, rather than sequentially, and see if she
can make correct judgments of sameness and difference. If
she can, then the original failure is plausibly explained by
failure of memory alone, rather than lack of a discriminative
ability.

Unfortunately, the advocate of the memory strategy cannot appeal to either sort of evidence to show that Sally's apparent inability to distinguish a priori between water and twater thoughts is explicable by memory failure alone. If, before and after the switch, we ask Sally to describe her thoughts, this would yield no evidence that she can distinguish a priori between them. Whereas the different types of bird may produce different visual experiences, water and twater thoughts are not associated with different phenomenologies. Further, Sally would give the same explanations of her concepts of water and twater; she would say of each that it is the concept of the odorless, colorless liquid common to lakes and rivers. She is ignorant of the fact that distinguishes these two concepts, namely that they apply to substances with different chemical compositions, H_2O and XYZ.[8] So, the way Sally describes her thoughts provides evidence that she cannot distinguish a priori between water and twater thoughts. In addition, one cannot support the memory strategy by using cases in which Sally simultaneously has water and twater thoughts, for the memory strategy is based on the view that a slow switch involves a subject gaining new concepts while losing her original concepts.

Let us summarize the dialectical position. The discrimination argument poses the following challenge to compatibilism: how can Sally have a priori knowledge that she is thinking that water is wet when she cannot distinguish a priori the actual situation in which she thinks that water is wet from an alternative situation in which she lacks this thought? Compatibilists have replied by accepting that the alternative situation is relevant, but arguing that Sally is reliable about her thought contents, even after the switch. As we saw earlier, it is not clear how this point about reliability is supposed to answer the incompatibilist challenge, which is based on a point about discrimination. The notion of a reliable ability to form true beliefs is not obviously equivalent to the notion of a discriminative ability, and, indeed, we have seen that the reliable ability to form true beliefs is not sufficient for a discriminative ability. A compatibilist could answer the discrimination argument by showing either that, contrary to initial appearances, Sally can in fact distinguish a priori between the actual and relevant alternative situations, or that knowledge requires only reliability and not the ability to discriminate between actual and relevant alternative situations. In the first part of the chapter, we considered but rejected the first of these options in detail. The second part of the chapter considers the second option: can the compatibilist show that knowledge requires only the reliable ability to form true beliefs, rather than a discriminative ability?

One way to show that knowledge requires only reliability would be to adopt a reliabilist account of knowledge. In broad terms, reliabilism holds that a true belief that p is knowledge if and only if it was produced by a reliable process. On this view, Sally's true belief that she thinks that water is wet would constitute a priori knowledge, for Sally's cogito thoughts are reliable although these thoughts are not based in a justificatory way on empirical information. So, we start our investigation of the compatibilist's second option by considering some of the key motivations for a reliabilist account of knowledge. We do so by reconsidering Goldman's classic argument for reliabilism.

4   Knowledge and Reliability

Recall Goldman's classic fake barn argument for reliabilism. In the first case, a subject is driving through ordinary

countryside in good visual conditions and says, looking at
what is in fact a barn, 'That's a barn'. Goldman argues that
this belief constitutes knowledge. In the second case, the
subject is driving through an area in which there are numerous fake barns that look exactly like real barns from the
road. Again the subject looks at a barn and correctly judges
that it is a barn. In this second case, Goldman suggests, we
would deny that the driver knows that that is a barn.

Goldman uses this pair of cases to support a reliabilist
account of knowledge by linking knowledge and discriminative abilities. In the first situation, in which we credit the
driver with knowledge, she can distinguish barns from the
other kinds of objects in her environment. Thus, she is reliable about whether or not an object is a barn. In the second case, in which we judge that she lacks knowledge, she
cannot distinguish barns from the many fakes present in the
region. Thus, in this different situation, she is not reliable
about whether or not an object is a barn. Goldman concludes
that a subject knows that p only if there is no relevant alternative state of affairs in which p is false that is indistinguishable by her from the actual state of affairs. As we saw
earlier, he goes on to use this to motivate a reliabilist account
of knowledge in which a true belief that p is knowledge only
if there is no relevant alternative state of affairs in which p
is false but the process used would have caused the subject
to believe that p anyway.[9]

Notice that in this classic argument for reliabilism, the
possession of a reliable belief-forming process goes hand in
hand with the possession of a discriminative ability. In particular, it goes together with the ability to notice if an object
changes from one type to another, the ability to make correct
judgments of sameness and difference of type, and the
ability to respond differentially to objects of the two relevant

types. Consider the first case, in which the subject is driving through normal countryside and correctly judges that she is looking at a barn. In this normal situation, the subject possesses the ability to distinguish barns from the other types of object in the countryside, such as houses, cars, cows, or pigs. The subject can make correct judgments of sameness and difference of type between barns and instances of other kinds in her environment. For example, on being presented with, say, a car and a barn, and being asked whether they are of the same or different type, the subject would say correctly that they are of different types. In addition, the subject can act differentially with respect to barns and nonbarns. For example, the subject could carry out instructions to blow her horn once if and only if she is looking at a barn. She also possesses a reliable process for generating beliefs about whether an object she sees is a barn or some other kind of thing, such as a cow.

Now consider the second case, in which the subject is in fake barn country. Here she lacks a reliable process for generating beliefs about whether an object she sees is a barn. For example, every time she sees what is in fact a fake, she would judge incorrectly that she is looking at a barn. In addition, she lacks the ability to distinguish barns and fakes. For example, she would mistakenly take what are in fact fake barns to be of the same type as barns. And, she could not correctly carry out the instruction to blow her horn once if and only if she is looking at a barn, for she will blow the horn once not only when seeing real barns, but also when seeing fakes.

Given this, it seems that the barn case that motivated Goldman to adopt a reliabilist account of knowledge could equally be used to motivate a different account of knowledge, one according to which knowledge requires

discriminative abilities. Like Goldman's own account, this
alternative account would draw a distinction between those
counterfactual situations that are relevant to knowledge and
those that are not. In particular, it would state that knowledge requires the ability to distinguish the actual situation
from only a subset of alternative situations, the relevant
ones. Since the possession of a reliable belief-producing
process and the possession of a discriminative ability go
hand in hand in the barn case, it hardly supports one of
these accounts of knowledge over the other. Rather, it
supports both equally.

Reliabilism has been motivated not only by cases such as
the fake barn case but also by its ability to deal with skepticism about the external world. Suppose that a subject has
an experience as of seeing a table as a result of seeing a table
in good visual conditions. Nonetheless, the skeptic argues
that the subject does not know she is seeing a table on the
basis of this experience, for the subject could be in a subjectively indistinguishable state if she had just become a
BIV. The reliabilist replies that an alternative situation
undermines knowledge only if it is relevant. Since the BIV
situation is not normally relevant, it does not normally
undermine perceptual knowledge. Notice that an analogous
response can be made on the view that knowledge that p
requires one to be able to distinguish the actual situation in
which p from relevant alternative situations in which p is
false. On this view, the subject would lack knowledge that
she is seeing a table if she were a BIV, or if the BIV possibility were relevant. However, so long as the BIV possibility is not relevant, perceptual experience can provide one
with knowledge of the world.

It seems, then, that in some of the key cases used to
support reliabilist accounts, possession of a reliable belief-

forming process goes hand in hand with possession of a relevant discriminative ability. This is no accident: in these cases, the fact that a subject has a reliable belief-forming process can be explained by the fact that the subject can distinguish the relevant kinds. From this perspective the slow switch case is quite peculiar in that the subject possesses a reliable belief-forming process even though she lacks the relevant discriminative ability. This may lead us to wonder whether many of the classic arguments given for reliabilism have overlooked the distinction between two possible types of account of knowledge—one based on the notion of a reliable belief-forming process, the other on the notion of a discriminative ability. Certainly, Goldman seems to have assumed that there is no difference between these two kinds of account. And, this is a natural assumption given that these different accounts would make the same claims about the fake barn and BIV cases. Furthermore, the difference between these accounts would not be apparent in many other cases discussed in the epistemological literature. If the classic literature motivating reliabilism has overlooked the distinction between these two types of account, then this literature cannot be relied on to settle the question of whether knowledge requires only reliability or the possession of discriminative abilities. To see which account is correct, one needs to discuss a case, such as the slow switch case, where the two abilities—the ability to form reliable beliefs and the ability to discriminate—come apart. But, I suggest, the standard literature motivating reliabilism has not considered such cases, and so it does not show whether knowledge requires discriminative abilities or only reliable belief.

Even if the classic arguments for reliabilism have not distinguished between an account of knowledge in terms of reliable belief and one in terms of discriminative abilities, two recent articles that focus on the slow switch problem are sensitive to the distinction—Falvey and Owens 1994 and McLaughlin and Tye 1998. Before concluding this chapter, I want to examine the compatibilist solutions they recommend. The key question for us is whether they show that Sally can know a priori that she thinks that p even if she cannot distinguish a priori between the thought that p and other relevant alternative thoughts.

5   Other Compatibilist Responses—Falvey and Owens, and McLaughlin and Tye

Falvey and Owens consider the following principles about when a relevant alternative prevents a belief from being knowledge:

RA) If i) q is a relevant alternative to p, and ii) S's belief that p is based on evidence that is compatible with its being the case that q, then S does not know that p.

RA') If i) q is a relevant alternative to p, and ii') S's justification for his belief that p is such that, if q were true, then S would still believe that p, then S does not know that p. (p. 116)

According to (RA'), a relevant alternative undermines knowledge that p if it would lead to a false belief that p. By contrast, according to (RA), a relevant alternative undermines knowledge that p if it is compatible with the evidence for the belief that p. Whether anti-individualism undermines privileged access depends on which of these two principles is correct.

To see this point in more detail, suppose that Sally is on Earth and believes correctly that she thinks that water is wet. Given that Sally is subject to a slow switch, it is a relevant alternative that she is on Twin Earth thinking that twater is wet. Falvey and Owens argue that if (RA) is correct, then Sally's belief does not constitute a priori knowledge. We might wonder how to apply (RA) to the case of self-knowledge. It seems implausible that knowledge of one's thought contents is based on evidence; certainly, it is not based on empirical evidence. But, from other comments, it seems that Falvey and Owens's talk of evidence is designed to capture the idea that knowledge that p requires the ability to distinguish the actual situation from relevant alternatives. They argue that Sally's belief that she thinks that water is wet does not constitute a priori knowledge on the grounds that she "cannot point to evidence in her experiential history that rules out the hypothesis that she is on Twin Earth. . . . Such a situation would be evidentially indistinguishable from her actual situation" (p. 117). However, if (RA') were true but (RA) were not, then Sally could know a priori that she thinks that water is wet regardless of her inability to distinguish water and twater thoughts. As we have already seen, if Sally were on Twin Earth thinking that twater is wet, then she would not believe that she thinks that water is wet, but instead that she thinks that twater is wet.

Falvey and Owens argue for the rejection of (RA) in favor of (RA') by appeal to a case we have already considered at length—Goldman's barn case. They consider a subject, Tom, in fake barn country where there are numerous barns that he cannot distinguish visually from real barns. As it happens, Tom is looking at a barn and forms the correct belief that there is a barn in front of him. However, the evidence on which he bases this belief, namely his visual experience, does not rule out that he is looking at a fake barn. As we have already agreed, Tom's belief is not knowledge. Falvey and Owens use their diagnosis of this judgment to argue for (RA') and against (RA):

Why does Tom's failure to possess evidence ruling out the possibility that the object is a facsimile undermine his claim to knowledge? Intuitively, the answer is that given the presence of the facsimiles in Tom's vicinity, Tom could easily be deceived into thinking that a facsimile was a genuine barn. In particular, since Tom's belief that the object is a barn is based on the object's visual appearance, if the object were a facsimile, Tom would still believe that it was a genuine barn. It seems, then, that the plausibility of RA) is grounded in a more basic principle, namely RA'). . . . We think that it is this condition [RA'] which best captures the importance of the notion of relevant alternatives in refuting putative claims to knowledge. One who knows is, as Plato taught us, reliable about what he knows. If a person's belief is insensitive to alternative possibilities to the extent that he is prone to error, then he is unreliable. (1994, pp. 116–117)[10]

However, we have already seen that there are two different hypotheses about why Tom's belief fails to be knowledge—(1) the hypothesis that Tom's belief fails to be knowledge because it was produced by an unreliable process; and (2) the hypothesis that Tom's belief fails to be knowledge because he cannot distinguish visually between the actual situation in which there is a barn in front of him and the relevant alternative situation in which there is a fake in front of him. Falvey and Owens do not provide any real argument for their endorsement of hypothesis (1) as against (2). The passage quoted above constitutes the whole of their reasoning in support of (RA'). Let us grant Falvey and Owens's claim that knowledge requires reliability and, hence, that if a subject is insensitive to relevant alternative possibilities to the extent that she is prone to error, her belief fails to constitute knowledge. It does not follow that this is the only condition in which a relevant alternative undermines knowledge. In particular, it might still be the case that a subject's true belief that p is knowledge only if she can distinguish the actual state of affairs in which p from relevant alternative states of affairs. Perhaps Falvey and Owens are assuming the stronger claim that it is both necessary and sufficient for a subject's true belief to constitute knowledge that it has been produced by a reliable process, regardless of the subject's discriminative abilities. If this were correct, then Sally could know a priori that she thinks that water is wet, for her cogito thoughts are reliable, even on Twin Earth. But Falvey and Owens have given no argument for this stronger claim. And I have suggested that it would be tendentious to appeal to the standard epistemological literature on reliabilism to support such a view, since that literature seems to overlook the distinction between an account of knowledge in terms of reliable belief and an account in terms of discriminative abilities.

In any case, McLaughlin and Tye (1998) have shown that Falvey and Owens are wrong to hold that a relevant alternative undermines knowledge "only in those cases where it supports the judgment that the subject is liable to error in her beliefs" (p. 118). In McLaughlin and Tye's case, a subject, Oscar, believes correctly that he has a brain. However, it is a relevant alternative that Oscar's head is full of sawdust: there is a widespread rumor in his community that a wizard has removed some people's brains and replaced them with sawdust. Now Oscar comes to hear of the rumor and begins to doubt that he has a brain. In order to decide the issue, he removes the entrails of a chicken and gets the reading that he has a brain. As a result, he again believes that he has a brain. We should surely deny that Oscar's belief, which is based on the chicken reading, constitutes knowledge. However, the case does not meet Falvey and Owens's condition for a relevant alternative to undermine knowledge, for here we have a relevant alternative that would not lead the subject to have false beliefs. If Oscar's head were full of sawdust he would not have any beliefs, whether true or false (p. 356, n. 15). In conclusion, Falvey and Owens fail to show that Sally can know a priori that she thinks that p even if she cannot a priori distinguish the thought that p from other relevant alternative thoughts. They provide no argument for the claim that a relevant alternative prevents a true belief from constituting knowledge only if that alternative would lead the subject to have a false belief. In addition, this principle is incorrect.

In contrast to Falvey and Owens, McLaughlin and Tye attempt to show how, compatibly with anti-individualism, a subject's second-order beliefs about her thought contents may constitute knowledge even if (RA) is correct (a subject's true belief that p is not knowledge if it is based on evidence that is compatible with some relevant alternative q). Although they endorse the view that second-order beliefs are based on evidence, they reject the idea that such beliefs are inferentially based. Instead, they endorse an "externalist" understanding of the relevant evidence relation, holding that the evidence for a subject's second-order belief is the relevant first-order thought, where second-order beliefs are reliably caused by the relevant first-order thoughts. Thus, the evidence for Sally's second-order belief that she thinks that water is wet is her first-order thought that water is wet. The fact that Sally thinks that water is wet is incompatible with the possibility that she is instead thinking any alternative thought. So, on McLaughlin and Tye's view, the evidence for Sally's belief that she thinks that water is wet, namely the fact that she thinks that water is wet, rules out the possibility that she is instead thinking a twin thought.

Although McLaughlin and Tye present an account of evidence on which a subject's evidence for her second-order beliefs about her thought contents is incompatible with relevant alternative situations, I argue that, even on their account, subjects lack the discriminative abilities that incompatibilists think are required for privileged access.[11] McLaughlin and Tye's key claim is that a subject's second-order beliefs about her thought contents are reliably caused by her first-order thoughts, where the cause of a particular second-order belief, namely the relevant first-order thought, is incompatible with the subject's instead having some other first-order thought. We saw in the earlier discussion of the slow switch that the fact that a subject's second-order beliefs about her thought contents are reliable does not show that she has the ability to distinguish a priori between the actual situation and alternative situations in which, owing to different environmental conditions, she has different thoughts. Nor does the causal element in McLaughlin and Tye's account show that the subject has this discriminative ability. Even if Sally's belief that she thinks that water is wet is caused by her thought that water is wet, where her thinking this latter thought is incompatible with the possibility that she is instead thinking some other thought, this does not entail that she can distinguish a priori water from twater thoughts.

It may help to put the point in a more general form. Suppose that a subject believes that p, where this belief is caused by the fact that p. That the cause of this belief, namely p, is incompatible with every alternative not-p possibility does not show anything about the subject's ability to distinguish the actual situation from relevant alternative situations. For instance, suppose that a subject's true perceptually based belief that that fruit is an apple is caused by the fact that that fruit is an apple. Since the fact that that fruit is an apple is incompatible with any alternative, if the cause of the belief counts as the "evidence" for it, then the evidence for the belief is incompatible with any alternative. But the fact that the subject's belief that that fruit is an apple was caused by the fact that that fruit is an apple is compatible with the possibility that the subject cannot distinguish visually between apples and another common fruit, say, nectarines (her vision is that poor). So, on McLaughlin and Tye's view, Sally's having evidence that rules it out that she is having a twater thought does not show that she can distinguish a priori between water and twater thoughts. It seems, then, that McLaughlin and Tye do not show that anti-individualism is compatible with the discriminative abilities that incompatibilists think are required for privileged access.

Let me summarize the discussion in this section. Falvey and Owens formulate two possible conditions for a relevant alternative to prevent the true belief that p from being knowledge, that it is compatible with the evidence on which the belief that p is based, or that it would lead to a false belief that p. Given our earlier discussion of how Falvey and Owens apply the first condition to the slow switch case, one might think that this condition amounts to the claim favored by incompatibilists, that a relevant alternative prevents the true belief that p from being knowledge if the subject cannot distinguish the actual situation in which p from that alternative situation. I have argued that Falvey and Owens do not show that only the second of their two conditions is correct. McLaughlin and Tye argue that, compatibly with anti-individualism, a subject's second-order beliefs about her thought contents may constitute knowledge even if the first of Falvey and Owens's conditions is correct. However, I have argued that this does not show that anti-individualism is compatible with the discriminative abilities that incompatibilists think are required for privileged access, namely that a subject can distinguish a priori the actual situation in which she thinks that p from relevant alternative situations in which she lacks this thought. Thus, we have yet to be shown either that knowledge does not require discriminative abilities or that anti-individualism does not undermine discriminative abilities.

6 Conclusion

In this chapter, we have examined one of the key arguments for incompatibilism—the discrimination argument. According to this argument, anti-individualism threatens privileged access since it undermines a subject's ability to distinguish a priori between the actual situation and alternative situations in which she lacks the thought she actually has. Compatibilists standardly have responded to this argument by admitting that, in some cases, such alternative situations are indeed relevant and thus potentially knowledge undermining. Nevertheless, they argue, the slow switch subject is reliable about what she thinks. However, it is unclear how this point about reliability answers the discrimination argument, which exploits the intuitive connection between knowledge and discriminative abilities, a connection acknowledged by prominent reliabilists such as Goldman. I have argued that possession of a reliable ability to form true beliefs is not sufficient for a discriminative ability. Given this, a compatibilist could provide a satisfactory response to the discrimination argument either by showing on independent grounds that anti-individualism does not undermine a subject's discriminative abilities, or by showing that knowledge requires only reliability and not discriminative abilities.

In the first part of the chapter, we rejected several reasons for thinking that the slow switch subject can distinguish a priori between the actual situation, in which she thinks that water is wet, and the relevant alternative situation, in which she does not. In the second part of the chapter, we saw that in the key cases used to motivate reliabilism, reliable belief and discriminative abilities go hand in hand. Thus, these cases fail to decide between an account of knowledge in terms of reliable belief and one in terms of discriminative abilities. Indeed, the distinction between these two types of account may have been missed by much of the standard literature motivating reliabilist accounts. The distinction between these two kinds of account has come to the fore in recent discussions of the discrimination argument. However, I argued, these discussions have failed to show either that knowledge requires only reliable belief and not discriminative abilities, or that the anti-individualist can meet the discrimination requirement. Of course, nothing that has been said rules out the possibility of such a demonstration being given. In particular, it may be that compatibilists can find further considerations to show that knowledge does not require discriminative abilities. However, in the absence of such arguments, it is worth considering other strategies for responding to the discrimination argument, which may be successful even if knowledge turns out to require discriminative abilities. Such strategies would finesse the issue of the correct account of knowledge and could be used both by those who hold that knowledge requires discriminative abilities and those who hold that it requires only reliability. In the next two chapters, I consider two such strategies.

A compatibilist might hope to meet a putative discrimination requirement for knowledge by building a discrimination requirement into the conditions for having a thought. I examine this idea in the next chapter by considering Evans's anti-individualist view, according to which a subject can think about an object only if she can distinguish the object of her thought from all other things. In chapter 4, I explore another strategy of responding to the discrimination argument, namely, by arguing that the alternative situations are not normally relevant. Thus, whether knowledge requires discriminative abilities or only reliability, such alternative situations are not normally knowledge undermining.

3   Thought and Discriminative Abilities—Evans

1   Introduction

In this chapter I examine a response to the discrimination argument that takes seriously the incompatibilist's claim that knowledge requires discriminative abilities. According to the discrimination argument, anti-individualism threatens privileged access because it undermines a subject's ability to distinguish a priori between the actual situation and relevant alternative situations in which she lacks the thought she has in the actual situation. The incompatibilist accepts that knowledge that p does not require the ability to distinguish the actual situation in which p from every alternative situation no matter how bizarre. Instead, she holds that a subject knows that p only if she can distinguish the actual situation in which p from relevant alternative situations in which p is false.

Suppose that the incompatibilist conception of knowledge is correct and a subject knows a priori that she thinks that p only if she can distinguish a priori the actual situation in which she thinks that p from relevant alternative situations in which she lacks this thought. A compatibilist anti-individualist might hope to meet this discrimination requirement for knowledge of thought by building a discrimination requirement into the conditions required for having a thought. If having a certain discriminative ability is required for having a certain first-order thought, then someone who meets the conditions for having that thought may thereby meet the discrimination requirement for knowledge of that thought.

Evans has developed an anti-individualist account of singular thought according to which a subject can have a thought about an object only if she can distinguish it from every other object. It may be suggested that a subject who has the ability to distinguish the object of her thought from every other object can also distinguish the actual situation in which she thinks about that object from alternative situations in which she instead thinks about a different object. For example, consider a subject who is looking at an apple, a, and thinks the perceptual demonstrative thought about a that it is red. To clarify that it is a that the subject is thinking about and that partly individuates her thought, we may say that she thinks that that apple (a) is red. (Clearly, the subject need not think of the relevant apple as a; we just use this tag to specify which object she is thinking about.) Suppose that there is a relevant alternative situation in which the subject is instead looking at a distinct apple, b, and thinks the different thought that that apple (b) is red. According to the discrimination argument, the subject can know a priori that she is thinking that that apple (a) is red only if she can distinguish a priori the actual situation from the relevant alternative situation in which she instead thinks that that apple (b) is red. On Evans's account, the subject can think about apple a only if she can distinguish apple a from every other object, including apple b. It might be suggested that if the subject can distinguish apple a from apple *b*, then she can distinguish the actual situation in which she sees and thinks about *a* from the alternative situation in which she sees and thinks about *b*. If this move could be generalized, then a subject who meets Evans's conditions for thinking about *a* can distinguish the actual situation in which she sees and thinks about *a* from any relevant alternative in which she instead sees and thinks about a different object.

Thus, Evans's account of thought may offer a solution to the discrimination argument at least for the case of singular anti-individualism. Indeed, it may seem that a subject meeting Evans's conditions for having a thought about an object meets a discrimination requirement stronger than even that which the incompatibilist places on knowledge of thought, for such a subject can distinguish the object of her thought not only from other relevant objects, but from every other object. I begin my assessment of this proposal by considering what Evans's discrimination requirement for thought amounts to.

2 Evans's Account of Singular Thought

Evans (1982) provides a sustained defense of singular anti-individualism, according to which a subject's thoughts are individuated partly by the objects they are about. For instance, suppose that in the actual situation, a subject is looking at apple *a* and thinks about it nondescriptively, thinking that that apple (*a*) is red. Evans holds that if the subject had counterfactually been looking at a different apple, *b*, then she would have had the different thought that that apple (*b*) is red. Evans defends the illusion version of singular anti-individualism, arguing that if the subject had counterfactually suffered an illusion of seeing an object, she would have suffered an illusion of thought. In addition, Evans's view is Fregean: he holds that the content of the singular component of the subject's thought is individuated not only by the object it is about, but also by the way the subject thinks of the object (chap. 1, sec. 6). However, the most distinctive feature of Evans's view, which will be our focus here, is his conception of the conditions necessary to think about an object. Evans argues that a subject can think about an object only if she can distinguish that object from all other objects (p. 90 and passim).

To clarify Evans's view, it is useful to contrast it with a rival view about the conditions required for thought. According to the causal view, for a subject to think about an object it is sufficient that she stand in a certain causal relation to it, whether or not she can distinguish it from other objects (see, e.g. Kripke 1980; Devitt 1980; Fodor 1987). To bring out the difference between Evans's view and the causal view, consider Evans's steel ball case in which a subject has a certain causal relation to an object but lacks the ability to distinguish that object from others (1982, pp. 90–91). On a certain day in the past, a subject sees a steel ball suspended from and rotating about a point. On the next day, the subject sees a second steel ball also suspended from and rotating about a point. Although the two steel balls are distinct, they are exactly alike in their qualities. The subject then suffers localized amnesia that removes all memories of the first episode, although she retains memories from the second. Last, suppose that years later, the subject reminisces about 'that shiny ball' she saw many years ago. Given the subject's amnesia, her memories are in fact causally related to only one steel ball. Thus, on the causal view, the subject is thinking about the second ball. Although Evans agrees that the subject's memories are causally related to just one ball, he denies that the subject can think about that ball. For, he points out, the subject cannot do anything to discriminate the two balls and show that it is just that second which she is thinking of (assuming that she does not think of distinguishing the ball she is thinking of as the ball from which her current memories derive). He argues that we should reject the claim that a subject is thinking about a particular object when she can do nothing to show that it is that object which she is thinking of.

Even if we have sympathy with Evans's rejection of the pure causal view, we may wonder whether Evans's own discrimination requirement for thought is too demanding. The Twin Earth arguments show that a subject may have a thought about an object or a kind even if she cannot distinguish it from actual or possible duplicates merely by appearance. For example, a subject may think about water even if she cannot distinguish water from twater by its appearance and behavior; and, a subject may think about one can of beer (that beer is tempting) even if there are hundreds of indistinguishable cans of beer in the local supermarket. But in fact, we will see that Evans's requirements on thought are not as demanding as they may initially appear. It is no part of his view that a subject can think about an object only if she can distinguish it from all others by appearance alone. Instead, Evans allows that a subject can distinguish an object from all others by exploiting her environmental relation to it.

Evans argues that there are three main ways in which a subject may distinguish one object from another and thus think about an object: by perception, by having a recognitional capacity, and by description (1982, p. 90 and passim). Knowing an individuating description of an object straightforwardly allows one to distinguish that object from all other things, as the object fitting that description. For instance, a subject can distinguish a particular crown from all other things by description as the crown that was worn by Elizabeth I of England at her coronation. Of course, a descriptive thought of the form the *F* is *G* is not individuated by the object it is about, so this type of thought is not our concern here. Instead, the discussion will focus on the other two types of thought that Evans distinguishes: perceptual demonstrative and recognition-based.

Evans argues that currently perceiving an object allows one to distinguish it from all other things since perception standardly enables one to locate the object perceived and discover what type of thing it is (1982, chap. 6, secs. 4, 5). A spatiotemporal object is distinguished from every other object by the type of thing it is and by its location. For example, a statue is distinguished from every other thing, including the lump of matter of which it is made, by its location and the fact that it is a statue. So a subject who can locate an object and discover its type can distinguish it from all other things. Suppose that a subject sees a lamp on a nearby table. On the basis of her perception, she can discover what kind of thing it is (a lamp) and where it is located (there).[1] Thus, she can distinguish the lamp from every other object. On Evans's account, it is not necessary that the subject have actually located the lamp and identified its type. Thought requires merely that the subject can distinguish the relevant object from others, rather than that she has distinguished it. So, perception enables one to think about an object so long as it enables one to locate the object and discover its type, even if one has not yet done so (ibid. pp. 172, 178–179). Notice that it is no part of Evans's account that, in order to think of the lamp, the subject must be able to distinguish it from every other object merely by its appearance. Indeed, there may be hundreds of identical lamps that the subject cannot distinguish from the target lamp on the basis of appearance alone. Instead, the subject can exploit her perceptual relation to the lamp to gain spatial information about the lamp that distinguishes it from other duplicate lamps.

Evans's account of how a recognitional capacity for an object enables one to distinguish it from every other thing is rather more complex. But we'll see that, as in the perceptual case, his account exploits both the object's appearance and the subject's spatial relation to it. Evans plausibly argues that a subject cannot have a recognitional capacity for an object unless she has some appreciation of the role of spatiotemporal considerations in the reidentification of objects (1982, pp. 278–279). In particular, the subject must appreciate that the mere fact that a currently perceived object looks just like a previously encountered object does not guarantee their identity. Rather, she must realize that an object is identical to a previously encountered object only if it bears the right spatiotemporal relation to that object. Unless a subject has some appreciation of the role of spatiotemporal considerations in the reidentification of objects, there is nothing to show that the subject has a recognitional capacity for a particular object a as oppose to the type of look that a has: in an environment in which only one object a has a certain appearance, there is no difference between the objects that would trigger a recognitional capacity for a and the objects that would trigger a recognitional capacity for the appearance type that a instantiates.

Suppose, then, that a subject perceives an object at a certain time and grasps the role of spatiotemporal considerations in the reidentification of objects. At some later time, the subject can make an estimate of the area within which the object can be found, which Evans calls "the area of search." This area is a function of "the subject's estimate of the probability and speed of movement, and the time that has elapsed since the last sighting, and it will centre upon the estimated position of the last sighting" (1982, p. 279). Evans argues that the subject has a recognitional capacity for the previously encountered object a only if "i) she is disposed to identify [a] as the relevant [object] on the basis of its appearance; ii) there is no other [object] within the area of search which she is disposed to identify as the relevant [object] on the basis of its appearance; and iii) a is the right [object], i.e. the [object] from which the information saturating her thought was derived" (ibid., p. 280). To take Evans's example, suppose that a subject encounters a particular sheep, s, at a certain time. Some time later, say, ten minutes later, she can form an estimate of the area in which the sheep is likely to be. This area of search might be a certain part of the hillside. The subject has a recognitional capacity for s and can think about s only if s is the only sheep within the area of search that she would be disposed to regard as the relevant sheep.

Notice again that, on Evans's view, having a recognitional capacity for an object does not entail that one can distinguish it from every other object by its appearance. Rather, one distinguishes it from other objects by exploiting both its appearance and spatiotemporal facts. Thus, one can have a recognitional capacity for a particular object even if there is a duplicate of that object indistinguishable in appearance. For example, in Evans's sheep case, there may well be another sheep that the subject would mistake for the relevant sheep, say, a sheep on the other side of the valley. But that does not undermine her recognitional capacity so long as the duplicate is not within the area of search. Despite this point, on Evans's account, recognitional capacities are absolutely discriminating: a recognitional capacity for an object enables one to distinguish that object from all other objects. It is part of his definition of a recognitional capacity that there is only one object within the area of search that the subject is disposed to identify as the relevant object. In addition, the subject is disposed to identify an object as the relevant object only if it is within the area of search. As Evans puts it, the subject "would not be considering sheep on the other side of the valley" (1982, p. 279).[2]

3 Evans and the Discrimination Argument

Having examined Evans's discrimination requirement for thought, let us examine whether the requirement could provide an answer to the discrimination argument. Recall that the discrimination argument exploits the intuitive link between knowledge and discriminative abilities and, in particular, the intuition that a subject knows that p only if she can distinguish the actual situation in which p is true from relevant alternative situations in which p is false. Applied to the case of thought, a subject can know a priori that she thinks that p only if she can distinguish a priori the actual situation in which she thinks that p from relevant alternative situations in which she lacks the thought that p. The incompatibilist uses the discrimination argument to argue that one cannot have a priori knowledge of the contents of externally individuated thoughts. Given this, we should focus on those types of thought that Evans takes to be externally individuated, namely perceptual demonstrative and recognition-based thoughts.

Suppose that Sally thinks the externally individuated thought that that object (x) is F, where this thought is based on either the current perception of x, or a recognitional capacity for x. The incompatibilist argues that Sally cannot know a priori that she thinks that that object (x) is F, for, she says, Sally cannot distinguish a priori the actual situation from a relevant alternative situation in which she lacks this thought. In the last chapter, we saw that, typically, compatibilist anti-individualists have not challenged the claim that there are relevant alternative situations in which the subject lacks the thought she actually thinks. Could the compatibilist instead use Evans's account of singular thought to argue that Sally does have the ability to distinguish a priori between the two situations? Recall that on Evans's view, a subject can think about an object only if she can distinguish that object from every other object. For example, she can think that that object (x) is F only if she can distinguish x from every other object, including any duplicate y. As a result, it might be suggested that Evans's view has the consequence that Sally can distinguish a priori the actual situation in which she thinks that that object (x) is F from relevant alternative situations in which she has a different thought.

A first problem for this suggestion emerges when we remember that the discrimination argument can exploit any relevant alternative situation in which the subject lacks the thought she has in the actual situation. Such situations include twin situations in which she is so related to a twin object that she thinks the different thought that that object (y) is F, and no-reference situations in which she is not suitably related to an object to have thoughts about it. A no-reference situation might involve her suffering an illusion of seeing an object, or mistakenly supposing that she has a recognitional capacity for a single object when, in fact, she is confusing several objects. In such cases, Evans argues that she would suffer an illusion of thought. But, even on Evans's account, the subject cannot distinguish a priori between a situation in which, being suitably related to a single object x, she thinks that that object (x) is F, and one in which she suffers an illusion of thought.

Notice that the problem does not depend on Evans's endorsement of the illusion version of anti-individualism and would arise even if, instead, he endorsed the descriptive version. Although Evans makes it a condition of thinking about an object that one can distinguish that object from all other things, it is no part of his view that a subject can think about an object only if she can distinguish the actual situation in which she has a certain external relation to an object and so can think about it from one in which she suffers the illusion of being in such a relation. For example, Evans does not claim that a subject can have a perceptually based thought about an object only if she can distinguish perceiving it from suffering an illusion of seeing such an object, or that a subject can have a recognition-based thought about an object only if she can distinguish having a recognitional capacity for an object from the illusion of having such a capacity. Indeed, it would be implausible to place such a requirement on thought. Thus, Evans's discrimination requirement for thought does not provide a full solution to the discrimination argument. Even on his account, there is one class of alternative situations—no-reference situations—in which the subject lacks the thought she actually has and which she cannot distinguish a priori from the actual situation. If such an alternative is relevant then it undermines the subject's knowledge of her thought in the actual situation.[3]

Despite this limitation on Evans's view, it is worth considering whether his account of thought enables a subject to distinguish a priori the actual situation from some other types of alternative situations. It would be a substantive and interesting result if Evans's view had the consequence that a subject can distinguish a priori between the actual situation in which she thinks that that object (x) is F and alternative situations in which, being related to a twin object, y, she thinks the different thought that that object (y) is F. This more limited claim will be the focus of the remaining discussion. I will start by discussing perceptual demonstrative thoughts before considering recognition-based thoughts.

4   Perceptual Demonstrative Thoughts

Suppose that in Sally's neighborhood there are two identical twins Anya and Tanya. Sally doesn't know their names and the twins are so similar that Sally cannot distinguish them visually. One day, Sally sees Anya. Sally's perceptual relation to Anya enables her to discover what type of thing Anya is (a person) and locate her. Anya's location and the fact that she is a person distinguishes her from every other thing, including her identical twin Tanya. Thus, Sally meets Evans's condition for being able to think about Anya—she can distinguish Anya from all other things. Suppose, then, that Sally thinks the perceptual demonstrative thought that that girl (Anya) is happy. Suppose, too, that Sally correctly believes that she thinks that that girl (Anya) is happy. Does Sally's belief constitute a priori knowledge?

According to the discrimination argument, Sally can know a priori that she thinks that that girl (Anya) is happy only if she can distinguish a priori between the actual situation and relevant alternative situations in which she lacks this thought. Given that Anya has an identical twin, Tanya, in the neighborhood, it seems a relevant alternative that Tanya might have occupied the very position that Anya is in fact occupying so that Sally thought about Tanya rather than Anya. But, it seems clear that Sally cannot distinguish a priori between the actual situation in which she sees Anya and thinks that that girl (Anya) is happy and the relevant alternative situation in which she instead sees Tanya and so thinks the different thought that that girl (Tanya) is happy. Given that the twins look exactly alike, everything would seem the same were Sally looking at and thinking about Tanya rather than Anya. Admittedly, when Sally is looking at Anya she can distinguish Anya from all other things, since perception enables her to discover the type of thing Anya is and her location. But the fact that, in the actual situation, Sally can exploit her actual spatial relation to Anya to distinguish her from other things doesn't help her distinguish the actual and counterfactual situations in which objects have different spatial relations to her. In particular, she cannot use Anya's actual location to distinguish the actual situation from the counterfactual situation in which Tanya occupies that very position rather than Anya.

We can illustrate Sally's inability to distinguish a priori between the two situations by considering a switch case. Suppose that Sally is watching Anya play in the garden. In virtue of the perceptual relation, Sally can discover that Anya is a person and can locate her. Thus, she meets Evans's requirements for thinking about Anya. Sally thinks that that girl (Anya) is happy. Then, while Sally's attention is distracted, Tanya is subtly switched for Anya in such a way that Sally doesn't notice. It may be that during the switch itself, and for a limited time after, Sally's failure to notice the switch undermines her ability to think about either girl. However, it seems that Evans should accept that, after a

time, Sally's new perceptual relation with Tanya enables her
to think about Tanya; this perceptual relation enables her to
identify what type of thing Tanya is and where she is
located, and these facts distinguish Tanya from every other
thing, including her twin, Anya. Thus, it seems that, after
the switch, Sally can think about Tanya, say, that that girl
(Tanya) is happy.

We have now described a case in which Sally initially
meets Evans's discrimination requirement for thinking
about Anya and thinks that that girl (Anya) is happy and
later meets his discrimination requirement for thinking
about Tanya and thinks that that girl (Tanya) is happy. But,
despite this, I will argue that Sally lacks the discriminative
ability required for a priori knowledge of her thoughts.
In particular, she lacks the ability to distinguish a priori
between the situation in which she thinks about Anya and
the situation in which she thinks about Tanya. Sally would
fail to notice the switch in her thoughts just as she fails to
notice the switch between Anya and Tanya. On being asked,
Sally would falsely judge that she is thinking the same
thought as she thought earlier.[4] In order to know that her
thought contents have changed, it seems that she needs to
have empirical information about the switch in the girls.
Moreover, it seems that Sally not only fails to notice the
change in her thought contents and would make incorrect
judgments of sameness and difference of content, but also
lacks the ability to act differentially with respect to the two
thoughts. (Recall that these were the three tests for possession of a discriminative ability outlined in chapter 2.)
Suppose that Sally is forewarned that the girls will be subtly
switched but not told when the switch will occur. Sally is
asked to press a button when the thought she would express

with 'That girl is happy' changes its content. If the girls are switched in such a way that Sally fails to notice the switch, then she will fail to press the button in line with the change in her thoughts. Or, if she does so, this would be a fluke unrepeatable in later trials.[5] Thus, Sally lacks the discriminative ability intuitively required for a priori knowledge of her actual thought. In particular, she cannot distinguish a priori between the actual situation in which she thinks that that girl (Anya) is happy and a relevant alternative situation in which she thinks the twin thought that that girl (Tanya) is happy.

It seems, then, that Evans's discrimination requirement for having a perceptual demonstrative thought about an object fails to answer the discrimination argument. A subject could meet Evans's discrimination requirement for having a perceptual demonstrative thought about an object and yet fail to meet the discrimination requirement for a priori knowledge of that thought. Even if a subject can distinguish an object x from every other thing and so think about it, it doesn't follow that she can distinguish a priori between the actual situation in which she is looking at and thinking about x and relevant alternative situations in which she is instead looking at and thinking about a duplicate.

At this point, many readers will be satisfied that a subject can meet Evans's discrimination requirement for having a perceptual demonstrative thought about an object without satisfying the discrimination requirement for knowledge of that thought. Such readers can immediately move on to the discussion of recognition-based thoughts in section 6. However, other readers may wish to read section 5, where we consider some possible compatibilist objections to the argument of this section.

5   Possible Compatibilist Responses

According to the slow switch argument of the last section, one can switch Sally between a situation in which she is seeing and thinking about Anya and one in which she is seeing and thinking about Tanya, although she fails to notice the switch. The incompatibilist concludes that Sally cannot distinguish a priori between these two situations in which she has different thoughts. I want to consider three compatibilist replies to this argument. According to the first, Sally's failure to notice the switch leads her to suffer an illusion of thought, rather than having two different thoughts that she cannot discriminate. The second response focuses on the fact that there is no time at which Sally both thinks that that girl (Anya) is happy and that that girl (Tanya) is happy; rather, she has these thoughts at different times. The third response attempts to exploit Evans's notion of discrimination by description to argue that, in fact, Sally can distinguish a priori between the actual situation and one in which she instead thinks a twin thought.

A compatibilist who holds the illusion version of singular anti-individualism may dispute the description of the slow switch case as one in which Sally first has thoughts about Anya, and then has thoughts about Tanya, but cannot distinguish a priori between these two situations. Instead, she may argue that Sally's failure to notice the switch between Anya and Tanya undermines her ability to think about either of the girls so that Sally suffers an illusion of thought. Thus, Sally would not meet the discrimination requirement for thinking about, say, Anya, but fail to meet the discrimination requirement for knowledge of this thought. Rather, she would fail to meet the discrimination requirements for both thought and knowledge of thought. The idea that Sally suffers an illusion of thought might be supported by thinking of perceptual demonstrative thoughts as grounded in the ability to track objects perceptually. Although one can form perceptual demonstrative thoughts on the basis of a momentary perception, such thoughts are usually connected with perceptual tracking of objects over (short) periods of time. Thus, when one tries but fails to track an object perceptually, it is arguable that one fails to have a perceptual demonstrative thought about that object (see, e.g., Evans 1982; Campbell 1987).

However, even if one accepts the tracking conception of perceptual demonstrative thought, this response is inadequate. Even on that conception, having a perceptual demonstrative thought about x at a time cannot plausibly require that there is no later time at which one loses track of x. For instance, if I track a runner in a marathon for 10 minutes then, plausibly, I can have perceptual demonstrative thoughts about her even if I later lose track of her. So, we could avoid this objection by extending the periods of time before and after the switch during which Sally successfully tracks Anya and, subsequently, Tanya. Thus, even on the tracking conception, Sally first has a perceptual demonstrative thought about Anya and, at a later time, a perceptual demonstrative thought about Tanya, even if there is an intervening period in which she suffers an illusion of thought. But, it would still remain the case that Sally cannot distinguish a priori between the actual situation in which she thinks that that girl (Anya) is happy and the relevant alternative situation in which she instead thinks that that girl (Tanya) is happy. Thus, the case would still show that a subject can satisfy Evans's discrimination requirement for thought without satisfying the discrimination requirement for knowledge of thought.

A second response starts from the fact that, in the switch example, there is no time at which Sally thinks that that girl (Anya) is happy and thinks that that girl (Tanya) is happy; rather, she has these different thoughts successively. Indeed, this is a nonaccidental feature of the case. Of course, it could be that Sally simultaneously sees the girls at different locations and thinks both that that girl (Anya) is happy and that that girl (Tanya) is happy. But then she would be able to distinguish the two girls by their different locations; and she could also distinguish the two thoughts. However, she cannot see Anya at a certain location and think a perceptual demonstrative thought about Anya and simultaneously see Tanya at that very location and think a perceptual demonstrative thought about Tanya. Rather, she first sees Anya at a certain location and thinks that that girl (Anya) is happy; then the girls are switched so that she instead sees Tanya at that very location and thinks that that girl (Tanya) is happy. As the case is originally described, after the switch, Sally no longer sees Anya, so, it seems, she cannot have perceptual demonstrative thoughts about Anya. This feature of the case might lead the compatibilist to attempt to explain away Sally's apparent inability to distinguish a priori between the two situations as the result of a memory failure rather than a discriminative failure.

It is sometimes possible to explain away an apparent discriminative failure as resulting from a memory failure alone. For instance, my apparent inability to distinguish the color of some wallpaper in a shop from the color of the carpet at home may be explained wholly by my inability to recall the color of the carpet now that I'm in the shop. Similarly, Sally's apparent inability to distinguish a priori between the situation in which she thinks that that girl (Anya) is happy and the situation in which she thinks that that girl (Tanya) is happy might be explained as a result of the fact that, after the switch, she can no longer remember her earlier thought about Anya.

We encountered this kind of response to the discrimination argument in chapter 2 and can object to it here just as we did there. First, there is controversy among anti-individualists about what thoughts a subject has after a switch. Some might claim that, after the switch, Sally can remember her earlier thought. So, this response would be available only on some anti-individualist positions. Second, even if Sally cannot remember her earlier thought after the switch, this is compatible with her lacking the ability to distinguish a priori between the situations. And surely this is the most plausible view, for everything would seem the same to Sally in the actual and relevant alternative situations.

The compatibilist might use the fact that there is no time at which Sally thinks both that that girl (Anya) is happy and that that girl (Tanya) is happy to raise a different query. She might suggest that for Sally to know a priori that she is thinking that that girl (Anya) is happy, she need only be able to distinguish a priori between this thought and other thoughts she could have simultaneously with this thought. If that were the case, then, her inability to distinguish a priori between the thought that that girl (Anya) is happy and the thought that that girl (Tanya) is happy would not undermine her a priori knowledge that she thinks that that girl (Anya) is happy. However, in fact, a failure to distinguish two states may undermine knowledge even if one cannot be in both states simultaneously. For example, suppose that I have been trying to learn how to monitor and regulate my heart rate without equipment just by using biofeedback. I claim to know that my heart is now beating irregularly. My claim to knowledge would be undermined if it is shown that I fail to notice the change between periods when my heart is beating irregularly and periods when it is not, even though my heart cannot beat irregularly and regularly at the same time.

The compatibilist might suggest one last response to the argument that Evans's account of perceptual demonstrative thought fails to answer the discrimination argument. This last response uses Evans's notion of discrimination by description.[6] In particular, the compatibilist might suggest that Sally has a description-based ability to discriminate the actual situation from relevant alternative situations. For instance, she might suggest that Sally can distinguish the actual situation from the relevant alternative situation indexically, by thinking of the actual situation as one in which she thinks a thought of the type she is actually thinking, where the description, 'the type she is actually thinking', is understood rigidly. Since in the relevant alternative situation she thinks a different type of thought, this indexical description distinguishes the actual situation in which she thinks that that girl (Anya) is happy from the relevant alternative situation in which she thinks instead that that girl (Tanya) is happy. However, this method of distinguishing the two situations is insufficient to defend the view that, in the actual situation, Sally can know a priori that she thinks that that girl (Anya) is happy. At best, it could be used to defend the different claim that, in the actual situation, Sally can know a priori that she thinks a thought of the type that she actually thinks. But, this is a trivial piece of knowledge, which Sally can have even if she is completely ignorant of the content of her thought. Compare the fact that, even when lost, a subject can know that she is where she actually is.

The compatibilist might suggest instead that Sally can distinguish the two situations by using a description that exploits the very content of Sally's thought. Consider Sally in the actual situation in which she thinks that that girl (Anya) is happy. It is part of the case that Sally believes that she thinks that that girl (Anya) is happy; the question is whether this belief constitutes a priori knowledge. Given this belief, it seems that Sally can distinguish the actual situation from any relevant alternative situation by thinking of it as the situation in which she thinks that that girl (Anya) is happy. After all, in any relevant alternative situation, by definition, she would not be thinking that that girl (Anya) is happy, but would be having some other kind of thought. Further, it might be argued that Sally's ability to distinguish the two situations in this way is a priori, for, as we saw in chapter 2, Sally does not need to use any empirical evidence to form her second-order belief that she thinks that that girl (Anya) is happy. Rather, she just reuses the same concepts used in the relevant first-order thought.[7]

However, the notion of discriminating two situations by description in this way cannot be the notion of discrimination that intuitively seems linked to knowledge. Consider the fake barn case, in which a subject is looking at a barn and correctly believes that there is a barn in front of her. It is agreed on all sides that the subject's belief is not knowledge given the prevalence of fake barns. Those impressed by the thought that knowledge requires discriminative capacities put the point by saying that the subject cannot distinguish the actual situation in which there is a barn in front of her from a relevant alternative situation in which there is a fake. However, someone could attempt to say that the subject can after all distinguish the actual situation from the relevant alternative situation by description. In particular, the subject can think of the actual situation as one in which there is a barn in front of her. This distinguishes the actual situation from any relevant alternative situation since, in any such relevant alternative situation, there is no barn in front of her. But, intuitively, it would be quite wrong to suppose that in the actual situation the subject knows that there is a barn in front of her. It seems clear, then, that the notion of discrimination by description cannot be the notion of discrimination that is intuitively tied to knowledge.

In conclusion, it seems that, in the case of perceptual demonstrative thoughts, Evans's discrimination requirement for thought comes apart from the discrimination requirement for knowledge of thought. Even on Evans's view, a subject may meet the discrimination requirement for having the perceptual demonstrative thought that that (x) is F while being unable to distinguish a priori between the actual situation in which she thinks that that (x) is F and a relevant alternative situation in which she thinks the twin thought that that (y) is F.

6   Recognition-based Thoughts

Now let us consider the other main category of genuine singular thoughts that Evans identifies: recognition-based thoughts. Can a subject who satisfies Evans's requirement for having a recognition-based thought about an object distinguish a priori between the actual situation and an alternative situation in which she instead encounters and thinks a recognition-based thought about a distinct object? This issue plausibly turns on whether the alternative situation can involve an exact duplicate of the object actually encountered. If the alternative situation were to involve the subject encountering and thinking a recognition-based thought about an exact duplicate, then everything would seem the same to her in the two situations. Thus, it seems, she could not distinguish a priori between the two situations.

I will argue that, on Evans's own account, a subject's having a recognition-based thought about an object is compatible with there being a relevant alternative situation in which the subject instead encounters and thinks a recognition-based thought about an exact duplicate. However, I will defend a modified version of Evans's account on which it follows from a subject's having a recognition-based thought about an object that there is no relevant alternative situation that involves an exact duplicate. As a result, on the modified view, a subject who has a recognition-based thought about an object can distinguish a priori between the actual situation in which she has this thought and relevant alternative situations in which she instead encounters and thinks a recognition-based thought about a different object.

Of course, this result does not offer a full solution to the discrimination argument even in the case of recognition-based thoughts. We have already seen that a subject who actually thinks a recognition-based thought about an object cannot distinguish a priori between the actual situation and an alternative situation in which she merely seems to have a recognitional capacity for, and a recognition-based thought about, an object (sec. 3). Nevertheless, it is interesting to show that a subject who thinks a recognition-based thought about an object can distinguish a priori between the actual situation and relevant alternative situations in which she instead encounters, and thinks a recognition-based thought about, a different object. This result will be used as part of a full response to the discrimination argument in chapter 4.

As we saw earlier, central to Evans's account of recognitional capacities is the notion of the area of search, the area within which the subject estimates the encountered object to be. He explains that this area is a function of "the subject's estimate of the probability and speed of movement, and the time that has elapsed since the last sighting, and it will centre upon the estimated position of the last sighting" (1982, p. 279). On Evans's account, a subject has a recognitional capacity for a previously encountered object x only if x is the only object within the area of search that she would take to be the relevant object. This is compatible with the possibility that there is a duplicate that she would mistake for the relevant object, as long as it is outside the area of search. Nevertheless, on Evans's account, a subject's recognitional capacity for an object is absolutely discriminating: it enables the subject to distinguish the object from every other object. The subject would not be disposed to regard an object outside the area of search as the relevant object, and x is the only object within the area of search that she is disposed to identify as the relevant object.

The notion of the area of search will be crucial to the discussion of whether a subject satisfying Evans's conditions for having a recognition-based thought about an object can distinguish a priori between the actual situation and relevant alternative situations in which she instead encounters, and thinks a recognition-based thought about, a different object. In setting up the argument, it is useful to introduce two new expressions: the *estimated area of search* and the *actual area of search*. The estimated area of search is the area within which the subject estimates the object to be. This corresponds to what Evans calls "the area of search." By contrast, the actual area of search is the area within which the object could be correctly estimated to be. The actual area of search is a function of the correct estimate of the probability and speed of movement and the correct estimate of the time that has elapsed since the last sighting, and it centers on the actual position of the last sighting. The argument concerns a case in which the actual and estimated areas of search diverge and in which there is an exact duplicate in the actual area of search but not in the estimated area of search. Given Evans's focus on the estimated area of search, his account has the result that a subject's having a recognitional capacity for an object is compatible with there being a relevant alternative situation in which she instead encounters and forms a recognitional-capacity for an exact duplicate. However, I use the case to motivate a modified version of Evans's view that instead uses the notion of the actual area of search. I argue that, on this account, a subject's having a recognitional capacity for an object is incompatible with there being a relevant alternative situation in which she instead encounters and forms a recognitional capacity for an exact duplicate.

Suppose that two subjects encounter a single cat, Tabby, at the same time, from almost identical positions. Then, distracted by something else, they stop watching Tabby. The question now arises whether either of the subjects can recognize Tabby and thus think about him. It is assumed that each subject knows that she has not moved from the position of the original sighting. One of these subjects, Naive, does not know much about cats. She underestimates the speed at which cats can move, and, hence, her estimated area of search for Tabby, A_N, is much smaller than the actual area of search. The other subject, Sage, knows a lot about cats; her estimated area of search is the larger area, A_S, which coincides with the actual area of search. Within the smaller area A_N, there is only one cat, Tabby, that would trigger each subject's recognitional capacity. But, there is a second indistinguishable cat, Kitty, within the larger area A_s (the actual area of search) that would trigger each subject's recognitional capacity. On Evans's account, a subject has a recognitional capacity for an object x only if x is the only object within the estimated area of search that she is disposed to take as the relevant object. Thus, his account has the result that Naive, whose estimated area of search is smaller than the actual area of search, can recognize and think about Tabby: Tabby is the only object in Naive's estimated area of search that Naive is disposed to identify as the cat in question. However, Evans's account delivers the result that Sage, whose estimated area of search coincides with the actual area of search, cannot think about Tabby: there is more than one cat within Sage's estimated area of search that Sage is disposed to recognize as the cat in question.

Although Evans's account may seem implausible, let us go along with it for the moment and consider its consequences for the discrimination argument. Suppose that Naive can think about Tabby and thinks, say, that that cat (Tabby) is friendly. The crucial question for the discrimination argument is whether Naive can distinguish a priori between the actual situation in which she thinks this thought and relevant alternative situations in which she instead encounters a different object and thus thinks a different recognition-based thought. Given the details of the case, it seems implausible that the relevant alternative situations are restricted to those in which Naive encounters only objects from within her estimated area of search for Tabby, for, her estimated area of search is much smaller than the actual area of search, the area in which Tabby could be correctly estimated to be. Instead, I suggest that the relevant alternative situations include those in which Naive encounters objects from within the actual area of search. But, there is a look-alike cat in this area, Kitty, which Naive would mistake for Tabby. Thus, there is a relevant alternative situation in which Naive encounters the look-alike cat instead of Tabby and, as a result, thinks the different recognition-based thought that that cat (Kitty) is friendly. It seems that Naive cannot distinguish a priori between the actual situation in which she thinks about Tabby and the relevant alternative situation in which she instead thinks about Kitty, for everything would seem the same in the two situations. So, on Evans's account, a subject who thinks the recognition-based thought that that (x) is F may not be able to distinguish a priori between the actual situation in which she thinks this thought and all relevant alternative situations in which she thinks the twin thought that that (y) is F, since the relevant alternative situations may involve a duplicate that looks exactly like x.

However, I think that the Tabby case gives us independent reason to modify Evans's account of the area of search. We will later see that, on this modified account, if a subject has a recognition-based thought about an object, then there is no relevant alternative situation in which she instead encounters and thinks about a duplicate of that object. Evans's account of the area of search as the area within which the subject estimates the object to be has implausible consequences for both recognitional abilities and knowledge. We have already seen that Evans's account has the consequence that Naive but not Sage can recognize and think about Tabby. But, this is to claim that Naive has a recognitional capacity for and thoughts about Tabby in virtue of the fact that her estimated area of search is incorrect, whereas Sage fails to have a recognitional capacity for and thoughts about Tabby in virtue of the fact that her estimated area of search for Tabby is correct. It is surely counterintuitive that having a false belief about the area in which Tabby is likely to be can enable one to have thoughts about Tabby that one would be unable to have if one had a true belief about the area in which Tabby is likely to be.

This view is supported by the link between recognitional capacities and knowledge. When a subject recognizes an object, she can be regarded as having knowledge about the object, to the effect that it is the same object as the object she previously encountered. Imagine that Naive and Sage come across Tabby again. On the view that Naive but not Sage recognizes Tabby, Naive but not Sage has knowledge about Tabby. But, this is to suppose that Naive has knowledge about Tabby in virtue of the fact that her estimated area of search for Tabby is incorrect, whereas Sage fails to have knowledge about Tabby in virtue of the fact that her estimated area of search for Tabby is correct. But, it is implausible to claim that, in virtue of having a false belief about the area in which Tabby is likely to be, a subject can have a certain piece of knowledge about Tabby that she would lack if she had a true belief about the area in which Tabby is likely to be.

Hence, Evans's own account of the area of search is implausible. Instead, the case suggests that we should identify the area of search with what I have called the actual area of search—the area within which the object could be correctly estimated to be. On this view, a subject has a recognitional capacity for an object x only if there is only one object, x, within the actual area of search that she would take to be the object in question. This has the intuitively correct result that neither of the subjects has a recognitional capacity for Tabby, or knowledge about him, for there is a duplicate within the actual area of search that each would mistake for Tabby.

Let us now consider how this modified version of Evans's account of recognitional capacities affects the discrimination argument. Suppose that Sally has a recognitional capacity for x and thinks the recognition-based thought that that (x) is F. We saw that, on Evans's account of recognitional capacities, Sally cannot distinguish a priori between the actual situation in which she thinks that that (x) is F and relevant alternative situations in which she thinks a twin thought. For a relevant alternative situation could involve Sally encountering and thinking about an exact duplicate of x. However, it turns out that, on the modified account, a relevant alternative situation cannot involve an exact duplicate. The relevant alternative situations are plausibly constrained by the actual area of search. This is the area in which x could be correctly estimated to be, the only area in which x can be. So it seems that a relevant alternative situation must involve the subject encountering a different object that is within the actual area of search for x. According to the modified account, a subject has a recognitional capacity for an object x only if there is only one object, x, within the actual area of search that she would take to be the object in question. Thus, if the relevant alternative situations are constrained by the actual area of search, then a subject's having a recognitional capacity for x entails that there is no relevant duplicate that she would mistake for x. Thus, there can be no relevant alternative situation in which she encounters an exact duplicate of x.

This result is reinforced if we consider the link between recognitional capacities and knowledge. As we saw earlier, possession of a recognitional capacity is naturally regarded as possession of a method for gaining knowledge about the world; and, the process of recognizing an object plausibly yields some knowledge about that object, that it is the object previously encountered. So, an account of recognitional capacities should enable a subject to meet the conditions for having knowledge. However, it turns out that a recognitional capacity would not be knowledge yielding if possession of such a capacity were compatible with the existence of a relevant duplicate. Suppose that Sally has a recognitional capacity for a person, Lucy. On reencountering Lucy, she forms the belief that she is the person previously encountered. But, this belief would not be knowledge if there is a relevant duplicate that Sally would mistake for Lucy. If there were such a duplicate, there would be a relevant alternative situation in which Sally encounters the duplicate rather than Lucy, a situation she cannot distinguish from the actual situation and in which she would falsely believe that the person she is seeing is the person previously encountered. Thus, epistemic considerations provide independent support for the view that if Sally has a recognitional capacity for x, then there is no relevant duplicate that she would mistake for x.[8]

I have defended a modified account of recognitional capacities according to which Sally has a recognitional capacity for x only if there is no object within the actual area of search that she would mistake for x. This account of recognitional capacities helps provide a partial solution to the discrimination argument applied to recognition-based thoughts. According to that argument, a subject can know a priori that she thinks that p only if she can distinguish a priori between the actual situation in which she thinks that p and relevant alternative situations in which she does not. In the case of recognition-based thoughts, the relevant alternative situations include those in which she instead encounters, and thinks recognition-based thoughts about, a distinct object. We have seen that the subject would be unable to distinguish a priori the actual situation from such a relevant alternative situation if it were to involve her encountering and thinking about an exact duplicate of the object actually encountered. However, on the modified account, the relevant alternative situations cannot involve the subject encountering a duplicate object. On the modified account, S has a recognitional capacity for x only if there is no object within the actual area of search that she would mistake for x. I have argued that, on this view, if a subject has a recognitional capacity for x, then there is no relevant duplicate that she would mistake for x. Thus, if a subject thinks the recognition-based thought that that (x) is F, there is no relevant alternative situation in which everything seems the same but she instead encounters a duplicate of x and thinks a recognition-based thought about this duplicate. So, on the suggested conception of recognitional abilities, having the recognition-based thought that that (x) is F does enable the subject to distinguish a priori this situation from relevant alternative situations in which she thinks the different recognition-based thought that that (y) is F.

This result does not provide a complete solution to the discrimination argument even in the case of recognition-based thoughts. As we saw earlier, a subject cannot distinguish a priori between the situation in which she has the recognition-based thought that that (x) is F and a situation in which she suffers an illusion of having such a thought. However, the modified account does produce the limited result that a subject can distinguish a priori between the actual situation in which she thinks the recognition-based thought that that (x) is F and relevant alternative situations in which she encounters and thinks recognition-based thoughts about a different object.

   Despite the advantages of the modified account, it may be objected that it accords less well with Evans's views about the conditions for thinking about an object. I consider this objection in the next section. My reply involves applying the modified account of recognitional capacities to thoughts about kinds. This extended account is used in the final response to the discrimination argument in chapter 4.

7   Comparison of Evans's Account and the Modified Account

Evans holds that a subject can think about an object only if she can distinguish it from every other object. We will see that although, on Evans's own account, recognition-based thoughts meet this requirement, this is not so on the modified account. Recall that, on Evans's original account, a subject has a recognitional capacity for x only if there is only one object, x, within the area of search that the subject would take to be the object in question. Evans argues that so defined, a recognitional capacity for an object is absolutely discriminating, that is, it enables the subject to distinguish the object from every other thing. This is because (1) the subject would be disposed to regard an object as the object in question only if it is within the area of search; and, (2) as a matter of definition, a subject possesses a recognitional capacity for x only if x is the only object within the area of search that she is disposed to regard as the relevant object (see note 2 above).

   However, the fact that on Evans's account recognitional capacities are absolutely discriminating depends on Evans's identification of the area of search with the estimated area of search. To see this, consider the modified view, that a subject has a recognitional capacity for x only if there is only one object, x, within the actual area of search that she would be disposed to regard as the object in question. There is no reason to suppose that a subject would restrict her attention to objects within the actual area of search, for, as in the Tabby example, this may diverge substantially from the area within which she estimates the object to be. So, she might be disposed to regard an object as the right object even if it is outside the actual area of search. Thus, the fact that there is only one object, x, that she would take to be the right object within the actual area of search is compatible with the possibility that she would take some other object, y, to be the right object. So, on the modified account, a recognitional capacity for an object may not be absolutely discriminating. However, the modified account does support a weaker claim, namely that if a subject has a recognitional capacity for an object, then she can distinguish that object from every other relevant object, where the relevant objects are identified as those within the actual area of search.

Given that, on the modified account, recognitional capacities are not absolutely discriminating, Evans would deny that, so understood, possession of a recognitional capacity is sufficient for thought about an object. Evans holds that a subject can think about an object only if she can distinguish the object of her thought from all other things. However, I will suggest that this is not a reason to reject the modified account. First, I have argued that Evans's own account gives counterintuitive results in the Tabby case and undermines the link between recognitional capacities and knowledge. Second, notice that there is no easy way to extend Evans's account of recognitional capacities to the case of kinds while retaining the idea that recognitional capacities are absolutely discriminating. Evans's account of how recognitional capacities for objects are absolutely discriminating exploits the metaphysical nature of objects. In particular, it exploits the fact that similarity of two objects does not guarantee their identity and that two objects are identical only if they bear the right spatiotemporal relations to each other. On this basis Evans introduces the notion of the area of search, the area within which an object can be estimated to be given where it was last sighted.

However, as Evans himself notes, the metaphysical nature of kinds imposes no spatiotemporal restrictions on the positions where a single kind may be instantiated. There is no analogy in the case of kinds to the notion of the area of search for an object. Consequently, if we allow that subjects have recognitional capacities for kinds, then we must allow that these recognitional capacities are not absolutely discriminating. Just as in the case of objects, it is plausible that a subject who has a recognitional capacity for a kind would be fooled by a duplicate. But we cannot make recognitional capacities for kinds absolutely discriminating by using the notion of the area of search as Evans did in the case of objects. However, if we should anyway accept that recognitional capacities for kinds are not absolutely discriminating, why should we require that recognitional capacities for objects are?

Unlike Evans's account of recognitional capacities for objects, the modified account can easily be applied to the case of kinds (Brown 1998). Just as a subject has a recognitional capacity for an object only if she can distinguish it from other relevant objects, so a subject has a recognitional capacity for a kind only if she can distinguish it from other relevant kinds. In the case of objects, I suggested that an object is relevant only if it is within the actual area of search.

In the case of kinds, I suggest that a kind is relevant only if it is within the local, actual environment of the subject. Thus, for example, if a subject can distinguish swallows from every other kind in her local, actual environment, she has a recognitional capacity for swallows, even if there is, far away in Australia, a kind of bird she would mistake for a swallow. Alternatively, if a subject cannot distinguish swallows and swifts, which are both present in her environment, then she lacks a recognitional capacity for swallows. Admittedly the notion of the local actual environment of the subject is rather vague. But, this is no objection if, as seems likely, the notions of a recognitional capacity and knowledge embed a similar vagueness.

Although, on the modified account, possession of a recognitional capacity does not meet Evans's requirements for having a thought about an object, epistemological considerations may lead us to reevaluate Evans's view about the requirements for thought. Evans motivates his requirement by appeal to Russell's epistemological principle that "a subject cannot make a judgement about something unless she knows which object her judgement is about" (1982, p. 89). Evans interprets this as requiring that the subject can distinguish the object of her judgment from all other things. But, we might wonder whether this is the correct interpretation of the epistemic principle once we accept that knowledge would be undermined not by all possible alternative situations, but only by a subset, those that are relevant. This suggests a more relaxed discrimination requirement: a subject can think about an object only if she can distinguish it from other relevant objects. If this more relaxed view is correct, then of course the recommended view of recognitional capacities is indeed sufficient for thought about an object.

These brief remarks are of course insufficient to settle the debate about the requirements for thought. However, I hope I have said enough to motivate a modified version of Evans's account of recognitional capacities that can be applied to both objects and kinds. On this account, a subject has the ability to recognize an object x (or kind k) only if she can distinguish it from every other relevant object (or kind), that is, x (k) is the only relevant object (kind) that she is disposed to regard as the previously encountered one. So, on this account, a subject who has a recognition-based thought that that (x or k) is F can distinguish a priori the actual situation from relevant alternative situations in which she instead encounters a different object (kind) and thus thinks a different recognition-based thought.

8   Conclusion

We have been considering a response to the discrimination argument that takes seriously the incompatibilist's claim that knowledge requires discriminative abilities. According to the discrimination argument, anti-individualism under-mines a subject's ability to know her thought contents a priori since it undermines her ability to distinguish a priori between the actual situation and relevant alternative situations in which she has different thoughts. Suppose that knowledge does require discriminative abilities, and so a subject knows that p only if she can distinguish the actual situation in which p from relevant alternative situations in which p is false. Applied to thought, a subject knows a priori that she thinks that p only if she can distinguish a priori between the actual situation in which she thinks that p and relevant alternative situations in which she lacks this thought. One might hope to meet the discrimination requirement for knowledge of thought by building a discrimination requirement into one's account of the conditions for thought, say, Evans's discrimination requirement. In fact, Evans's discrimination requirement for thought is not sufficient to meet the discrimination requirement for knowledge. The potentially knowledge-undermining alternative situations include no-reference situations, in which the subject lacks the thought that that object (x) is F because she suffers an illusion of perception or of having a recognitional capacity for an object. But Evans's account of having a thought about an object requires only that one can distinguish it from all other objects. It does not require that one can distinguish, say, perceiving an object from suffering an illusion of perceiving such an object. Thus, there is no reason to suppose that, on his account, a subject can distinguish a priori the actual situation from one kind of relevant alternative situation, no-reference situations.

However, it might be thought that on Evans's account, a subject would have a more limited ability, the ability to distinguish a priori the actual situation from a different kind of relevant alternative situation, those in which she is so related to a different object y that she instead thinks the different thought that that object (y) is F. Even this more limited claim is incorrect. In the case of perceptual demonstrative thoughts, a subject who thinks that that object (x) is F may be unable to distinguish a priori the actual situation in which she thinks this thought from relevant alternative situations in which she sees a duplicate object and thinks the different thought that that object (y) is F (see sec. 4). Further, on Evans's own account of a recognitional capacity, a subject who thinks the recognition-based thought that that object (x) is F may be unable to distinguish a priori between the actual situation in which she thinks this thought and relevant alternative situations in which she thinks the different recognition-based thought that that object (y) is F (see sec. 6).

I ended the chapter by arguing for a modified version of Evans's account of recognitional capacities. On this account, a subject has a recognitional capacity for an object x only if x is the only relevant object that she would take to be the previously encountered object. It is part of her having a recognitional capacity for x that there is no relevant duplicate that she would mistake for the previously encountered object. Thus, on this view, if a subject thinks the recognition-based thought that that object (x) is F, then there is no relevant alternative situation in which she encounters an exact duplicate of x, y, and thinks the different recognition-based thought that that object (y) is F. So, there is no relevant alternative situation in which she thinks a different recognition-based thought but everything seems the same to her. Thus, on the recommended account, if Sally thinks the recognition-based thought that that object (x) is F, then she can distinguish a priori between the actual situation in which she thinks this thought and relevant alternative situations in which she encounters some other object and thinks a different recognition-based thought. Although this limited result does not in itself provide an answer to the discrimination argument, we will see in the next chapter how a compatibilist anti-individualist might use this result as part of her answer to that argument.

4 The Illusion Argument

1 Introduction

In the previous two chapters, we have been examining one argument for the incompatibility of anti-individualism and privileged access: the discrimination argument. According to this argument, anti-individualism undermines privileged access by undermining a subject's ability to distinguish a priori between the actual situation in which she thinks some thought and relevant alternative situations in which she lacks this thought. As we have seen, the discrimination argument can be applied to any version of anti-individualism (chap. 2, sec. 2).

In this chapter, we will examine an incompatibilist argument that applies to just one version of anti-individualism: the illusion version.[1] The distinctive nature of this view emerges in no-reference situations, situations in which the subject is not suitably related to an object or kind to think about that object or kind. One type of no-reference situation occurs when a subject suffers a perceptual illusion. For instance, a subject who takes herself to be seeing and thinking about an object may instead be suffering an illusion of seeing such an object. A different example is provided by

Boghossian's Dry Earth scenario in which the inhabitants suffer an illusion of there being lakes and rivers full of a watery liquid. In the second type of no-reference situation, the subject does not suffer a perceptual illusion, but rather takes herself to have encountered a single object or kind when in fact she has confused several similar objects or kinds. For instance, on Motley Earth, there are lakes and rivers full of watery liquid, but this liquid is composed of a motley collection of several natural kinds that the inhabitants confuse for one natural kind.

What thoughts should an anti-individualist attribute to a subject in a no-reference situation? Suppose that a subject suffers an illusion of seeing a vase and, attempting to refer to the vase, says 'That vase is beautiful'. According to the descriptive view, her utterance expresses a thought about the putative vase, where she thinks of the vase via a description, say 'the vase that I am seeing'. By contrast, according to the illusion view, the subject's utterance fails to express any thought. Rather, she suffers an illusion of thought; although it seems to her just as if she is having a thought, she is not (see, e.g., Evans 1982; McDowell 1986; Boghossian 1997). Notice that the illusion view accepts that the subject may have some other relevant thoughts including, perhaps, thoughts about the putative vase she sees under the description, 'the vase that I am seeing'. Nevertheless, according to the illusion view, the subject also suffers an illusion of thought. Thus, on the illusion view, unlike the descriptive view, the subject makes a radical error about her thoughts: she takes herself to be thinking a thought when she is not. This type of radical error about one's thoughts may seem to undermine privileged access. How can one know a priori, say, that one thinks that p if one can be so wrong about one's thoughts as to suppose that one is thinking a thought when one is not, but only suffering an illusion of doing so?

To fill out this intuition, let us use an example involving perceptual demonstrative thoughts. Suppose that Sally is actually hearing a particular wasp, w, and thinks the perceptual demonstrative thought that that wasp (w) is near. However, suppose also that Sally has been sensitized to wasps as there is a nest near her office and, as a result, she frequently imagines that she hears a wasp when she does not. Thus, there is a nearby counterfactual situation in which she suffers an illusion of hearing a wasp. According to the illusion version of anti-individualism, in this counterfactual situation, Sally suffers an illusion of thought and makes a mistake about her thoug. ts: she falsely takes herself to have a thought about the wasp she thinks she hears. The incompatibilist argues that the counterfactual situation undermines Sally's a priori knowledge of her actual thoughts. She argues that Sally cannot have a priori knowledge of the content of her actual thought, for she is not reliable about whether she is having a thought at all. In particular, in the actual situation, Sally cannot know a priori that she thinks that that wasp (w) is near, for there is a nearby situation in which she suffers an illusion of thought and mistakenly believes that she is thinking about a wasp to the effect that it is near, when she is not. (Although this example and the following discussion concentrate on an example of a singular thought, the illusion argument could also apply to thoughts about natural kinds.)

The putative threat raised by this illusion argument is distinct from the threat raised by the discrimination argument, even when the latter is applied to the illusion version of singular anti-individualism. According to the discrimination argument, a subject who actually thinks the externally individuated thought that p cannot know a priori that she thinks that p, for there is a relevant alternative situation in which she lacks this thought that she cannot distinguish a priori from the actual situation. The alternative situation might be a twin situation in which she is so related to a distinct object or kind that she has a twin thought. Alternatively, it might be a no-reference situation in which she is not related to any single object or kind in such a way as to think about that object or kind. What thoughts she has in such a situation depends on whether the illusion or descriptive version of anti-individualism is correct. But, whichever view is correct, in the no-reference situation, the subject lacks the thought she has in the actual situation. Thus, the discrimination argument takes the twin and no-reference situations as raising a common concern: how can S know a priori that she thinks that p if there is a relevant alternative situation in which she lacks the thought that p that she cannot distinguish a priori from the actual situation? The discrimination argument exploits the intuitive idea that knowledge that p requires the ability to distinguish p from relevant alternative situations in which p is false. By contrast, the illusion argument exploits the different idea that knowledge requires reliability. According to the argument, the illusion version of anti-individualism undermines privileged access, since, on this view, a subject may suffer an illusion of thought and thus make a mistake about whether she is thinking a thought. By contrast, on the descriptive view, the subject does not suffer an illusion of thought.

There has been little discussion of the illusion argument in the literature. (An exception is my earlier article, Brown 2000c, on which part of the following discussion is closely based.) However, compatibilists may be tempted to reply to the illusion argument as they do to the discrimination argument, namely by accepting the relevance of the alternative situations but stressing the reliability of a subject's judgments about her thought contents. Does this response answer the illusion argument?

2 Relevance and Reliability

In responding to the discrimination argument, compatibilists typically accept that alternative situations are sometimes relevant, but stress the reliability of a subject's judgments about her thoughts. In particular, they note that such an alternative situation would not lead a subject to make false cogito judgments about her thoughts (see chap. 2). For example, consider a subject who is slowly switched between Earth and Twin Earth. On Earth, she thinks that there is water in front of her, and she believes that she thinks that there is water in front of her. On Twin Earth, she thinks that there is twater in front of her, and she believes that she thinks that there is twater in front of her. In each case, her second-order belief is correct. There is no possibility that the subject may mistakenly believe, say, that she thinks that there is water in front of her when she lacks this thought. Such cogito thoughts are self-verifying: in believing that one thinks that p, one thereby entertains the content p and thus makes the second-order belief true.

A compatibilist might try to apply the same strategy to the illusion argument. Certainly, there are circumstances in which an illusion situation is relevant. In our example, the possibility that Sally is merely suffering an illusion of hearing and thinking about a wasp is relevant because of her hypersensitivity to wasps, which leads her to regularly think she is hearing one when she is not. For a different example, consider a city dweller alone at night in a wood.

She may be so spooked by the darkness that she frequently imagines that she hears something coming toward her when in fact there is nothing there.

However, the compatibilist may try to argue that even if illusion situations are sometimes relevant, they do not undermine a subject's reliability about her thought contents, for they do not lead her to make false cogito judgments about what thoughts she is having. Take Sally, who actually thinks that that wasp (w) is near and believes that she thinks that that wasp (w) is near. Her belief that she thinks that that wasp (w) is near is self-verifying, for, in virtue of having this belief, she entertains the thought content that that wasp (w) is near. Now consider the illusion situation in which it seems to Sally as if she is hearing and thinking about a wasp although, in fact, she is not. In the illusion situation, Sally is not suitably related to w to have thoughts, at any level, whose semantic value partly depends on w. Thus, in that situation, Sally cannot misattribute to herself the thought that that wasp (w) is near. But she can attribute to herself the thoughts she actually has, such as the thought that the wasp she is hearing is near. Of course, in the illusion situation, Sally falsely believes that she is thinking about a wasp. But this belief is not of the cogito form. Thus, the anti-individualist may argue that Sally's cogito thoughts are self-verifying even in the illusion situation.

The incompatibilist may not be wholly convinced by this response. She will agree that, in the illusion situation, Sally cannot incorrectly attribute to herself the thought that that wasp (w) is near. But she will note that, in the illusion situation, Sally does make a mistake about her thoughts: she falsely supposes that she is having a thought about a wasp that she hears to the effect that it is near. Although this false second-order belief is not a cogito thought, it is nonetheless a second-order belief about the type of thought content she is having. Moreover, on the illusion version of anti-individualism to which the argument is addressed, Sally's mistake in the illusion case is not about the external relations her thoughts have, but rather about the thoughts themselves (see McDowell 1977, pp. 173–175; Evans 1982, p. 73). Suppose that in the illusion situation, she attempts to express herself by saying, 'That wasp is near'. On the illusion view, it is not the case that Sally's utterance expresses a thought but she is mistaken about whether it has a reference. Rather, her utterance fails to express a thought at all. Thus, in the illusion situation, Sally makes a mistake about what thoughts she has. The incompatibilist may suggest that the fact that Sally makes a mistake about her thought contents in the illusion situation undermines her ability to have a priori knowledge of her thought contents in the veridical situation. In the next section, we will see how the incompatibilist could support this claim by appeal to epistemological work on reliabilist accounts of knowledge.

3   Two Notions of Reliability

The core idea of the reliabilist approach to knowledge is that a true belief is knowledge only if it is produced by a reliable process. Intuitively, if a belief is produced by such a process, then it is not an accident that it is true and it could not easily have been false. One way to fill out the idea that knowledge requires reliability is to say that the true belief that p is knowledge only if it was produced by a process that wouldn't easily have produced a false belief in that very proposition, p.[2]

For instance, Nozick (1981, p. 176) argues that the true belief that p is knowledge only if the following conditionals are true:

(1) If p weren't true, then S wouldn't believe that p; and

(2) If p were true, then S would believe that p.

(See 1981, p. 179, for the version of these conditionals adjusted for the method of belief-formation.) These subjunctive conditionals can be fleshed out by using the notion of a possible world. On this understanding, S's true belief that p is knowledge only if (1) in nearby or close possible worlds in which p is false, S does not believe that p, and (2) in nearby or close possible worlds in which p is true, S believes that p. Goldman (1986) places a condition on knowledge similar to Nozick's first condition, saying that "a true belief that p fails to be knowledge if there are any relevant alternative situations in which the proposition p would be false, but the process used would cause S to believe p anyway" (p. 46).

Following McGinn and Goldman, we may describe Nozick's and Goldman's conditions as examples of "local reliability" conditions for knowledge (McGinn 1984, p. 16; Goldman 1986, pp. 44–46). The process M that produces the subject's belief that p is *locally reliable* if and only if M is reliable with respect to the particular proposition p. More precisely, I will say that the process M that produces the subject's belief that p is *locally reliable* if and only if:

(1) there is no nearby (or relevant) possible situation in which p is false, and M produces the belief that p; and,

(2) there is no nearby (or relevant) possible situation in which p is true, and M fails to produce the belief that p.

A different way of filling out the idea that knowledge requires reliability focuses on what McGinn and Goldman call "global reliability." As we have seen, the belief that p was produced by a locally reliable process only if it is reliable with respect to that very proposition, p. By contrast, "[g]lobal reliability is reliability for all (or many) uses of the process, not just its uses in forming the belief in question" (Goldman 1986, p. 45). Thus, global reliability requires that the process is reliable with respect to not only the particular proposition p but also a larger range of propositions. As Goldman explains it, the notion of global reliability is a "statistical or dispositional property of a belief-forming process type." A type of belief-forming process is globally reliable if and only if it produces, or tends to produce, a high ratio of true beliefs for a range of uses of the process (ibid., p. 49).

The distinction between local and global reliability grounds a distinction between two reliabilist approaches to knowledge. On what we may call the *local reliabilist* approach, a true belief is knowledge if and only if it was produced by a process that is locally reliable (see, e.g., Nozick 1981). By contrast, on what we may call the *global reliabilist* approach, global reliability is a necessary condition for knowledge (see, e.g., McGinn 1984; Goldman 1986). (Those defending the global reliability approach disagree about whether local reliability is required for knowledge in addition to global reliability: Goldman thinks that it is, whereas McGinn denies this.)

We can use these epistemological distinctions to clarify the issue of whether the illusion version of anti-individualism threatens privileged access. Consider Sally in the actual situation in which she thinks that that wasp (w) is near and self-ascribes this thought. The compatibilist argues that Sally's second-order belief is knowledge since it was produced by a reliable process. She points out that, in the illusion situation, Sally would not incorrectly self-attribute the thought that that wasp (w) is near. Rather, she would self-ascribe such first-order thoughts as she actually has, say, the thought that the wasp that she is hearing is near. In effect, then, the compatibilist has shown that the process that produces Sally's second-order belief (her belief that she thinks that that wasp [w] is near) is locally reliable. In particular, the compatibilist has shown that the illusion situation provides no problem for condition (1) for local reliability, that there is no nearby possible situation in which p is false, and M produces the belief that p. Applied to Sally's second-order belief, condition (1) amounts to the requirement that there is no nearby possible situation in which Sally does not think that that wasp (w) is near, but M still produces the belief that she thinks that that wasp (w) is near. The compatibilist's point is that the illusion situation is no counterexample to this condition for knowledge. Although, in the illusion situation, Sally no longer thinks that that wasp (w) is near, she no longer self-ascribes this thought either.

If the local reliabilist approach to knowledge is correct, then the compatibilist has shown that Sally's actual belief that she thinks that that wasp (w) is near constitutes knowledge.[3] And, given that this piece of knowledge is not based in a justificatory way on any empirical information, it is a priori. Some anti-individualists accept reliabilist accounts of self-knowledge, such as Gibbons (1996) and McLaughlin and Tye (1998). In addition, even some of those who reject reliabilist accounts of self-knowledge accept that reliability is necessary for knowledge (e.g., Falvey and Owens 1994, p. 117; Peacocke 1998, pp. 219–220). On this view, the compatibilist response amounts to demonstrating that Sally's second-order belief meets a necessary condition for knowledge that might have seemed threatened by the illusion version of anti-individualism. Thus, if it is local reliability that is necessary for knowledge, then there is no reason to suppose that the illusion version of anti-individualism and privileged access are incompatible.

However, if it is global reliability that is necessary for knowledge, then it is less clear whether the compatibilist response to the illusion argument is successful.[4] Whether the process that produces Sally's belief that she thinks that that wasp (w) is near is globally reliable depends on whether it is reliable with respect to propositions other than the proposition that she thinks that that wasp (w) is near. But we have already seen that, in the illusion situation, Sally makes a mistake about her thought contents: she mistakenly believes that she is thinking about a wasp that she hears. Further, given her hypersensitivity, she frequently suffers illusions of hearing and thinking about a wasp. If such illusions of thought are sufficiently frequent, then Sally's actual belief that she thinks that that wasp (w) is near may not be produced by a globally reliable process.[5] Thus, if global reliability is required for knowledge, her actual belief may not constitute knowledge, and the illusion version of anti-individualism may threaten privileged access.

The next two sections examine the two issues that are crucial for the success of this incompatibilist line of argument: (1) whether global reliability is necessary for knowledge; and (2) what would be required for the process that produces Sally's actual second-order belief to be globally reliable. The second issue involves examining the most appropriate way to type the process that produces Sally's actual belief and the range of uses of the process relevant to global reliability.

4   Local or Global Reliability?

There are well-known objections to the idea that knowledge is true belief plus local reliability. One important objection, due to McGinn and endorsed by Goldman (1986, p. 48, n. 18), concerns Gettier-style cases involving necessary truths, whether a priori or a posteriori. To set up the problem, first consider a Gettier-style case involving a contingent proposition. For example, consider the case in which I have much evidence that my colleague, Jones, owns a Ford, although in fact she does not. On this basis, I form the (false) belief that Jones owns a Ford from which I infer the belief that someone in my office owns a Ford. As it happens, another person in the office, Smith, whom I've never met, does own a Ford. Given these facts, my belief that someone in the office owns a Ford is justified and true, but intuitively it is not a case of knowledge. The local reliabilist approach would deal with this case by invoking the first condition for local reliability:

(1)   there is no nearby possible situation in which p is false, and M produces the belief that p.

In the nearby situation in which no one in my office owns a Ford, say, because Smith sold hers, I would still believe that someone owns a Ford on the basis of my evidence about Jones. So, I fail the first condition for local reliability. (See Nozick 1981, p. 173.)

Now consider a Gettier-style case in which I come to believe a necessary truth but in a way that prevents it from constituting knowledge. For example, I come to believe a mathematical truth on the basis of the testimony of another person who (unknown to me) is trying to deceive me but happens to tell me a truth. The local reliabilist approach cannot deal with this case in the same way as it deals with

Gettier-style cases concerning contingently true propositions, that is, by using condition (1). In the case of necessary
truths, this condition is trivially met since there is no possible situation in which the believed proposition is false.[6] So,
the local reliabilist approach can deal with these cases only
by using the second condition:

(2)   there is no nearby possible situation in which p is
true, and M fails to produce the belief that p.

However, the fact that the local reliabilist approach would
use condition (1), rather than (2), to deal with Gettier-style
cases involving contingent truths may make us doubt
whether condition (2) alone can deal with Gettier-style cases
involving necessary truths. Indeed, McGinn argues that condition (2) is not adequate for this task: it may be that a
subject believes that p, where p is a necessary truth and this
belief is not intuitively a case of knowledge, but the subject's
belief nonetheless meets condition (2). For example, in the
case of the deceitful informant, the facts of my situation
might make it the case that, in nearby possible situations, I
would still believe the relevant mathematical truth. This
could happen if, for example, I am disposed to trust my
deceitful informant, who herself is disposed to believe that
the mathematical truth in question is not a truth. (McGinn
1984, p. 14.)

The case of the deceitful informant shows that it is not
sufficient for the belief that p to constitute knowledge that
it is true and formed by a locally reliable process, that is, a
process that is reliable with respect to just that proposition. A
natural reliabilist response, made by both McGinn and
Goldman, attempts to deal with the case by making global
reliability a necessary condition for knowledge.[7] After all, the
method of forming beliefs on the basis of the testimony of

another person who is deliberately attempting to deceive me is likely to lead to many false beliefs. Although in the case described the process is locally reliable with respect to the mathematical truth in question, it is not globally reliable. For a range of propositions other than that mathematical truth, reliance on the process will lead me to false beliefs. So, a reliabilist about knowledge may argue that the case shows us that global reliability is a necessary condition for knowledge (McGinn 1984, pp. 16–17; Goldman 1986, pp. 48–49).

A further argument against the local reliabilist approach arises from singular anti-individualism, whether in the illusion or descriptive version. The argument uses a modification of the standard fake barn example in which a subject, say, Laura, is in an area in which, unknown to her, there are numerous fake barns that are visually indistinguishable from real ones. As it happens, Laura is actually looking at a real barn, b. As a result, she forms the true perceptual demonstrative belief that that object (b) is a barn, where the content of this belief depends partly on barn b. As is widely agreed, Laura's belief is not a case of knowledge. Given the number of fakes around, Laura might easily have been looking at a fake, say, f. And, if she were looking at the fake, f, then she would believe it to be a barn. Thus, it seems Laura's true belief that that object (b) is a barn is not a case of knowledge.

However, it is not clear whether the local reliabilist approach would agree with this judgment. On this approach, whether Laura's belief that that object (b) is a barn is knowledge depends on the following conditionals:

(1*)   there is no nearby possible situation in which b is not a barn, and M produces the belief that that object (b) is a barn; and

(2*)   there is no nearby possible situation in which *b* is a
barn, and *M* fails to produce the belief that that object (*b*)
is a barn

(where *M* is the process that produces Laura's belief that
that object (*b*) is a barn). It seems that the presence of fakes
does not prevent Laura's belief from meeting condition (2*).
In nearby situations in which *b* is a barn, and Laura is
looking at it, she would still believe that that object (*b*) is a
barn. Now, consider condition (1*). Our original intuition
was that Laura's actual belief is not a case of knowledge
because she might easily have been looking at a fake, and
she cannot distinguish fakes from barns. But the situation in
which Laura is looking at a fake, say, *f*, does not constitute
a counterexample to (1*). First, it is not obviously a situation
in which *b* is not a barn; to say that Laura is looking at the
fake, *f*, leaves it entirely open what properties the object *b*
has. Second, if Laura were looking at the fake, *f*, then she
would form the perceptual demonstrative belief that that
object (*f*) is a barn, but not the belief that that object (*b*) is
a barn.

What we need to provide a counterexample to (1*) is a
nearby possible situation in which the object, *b*, that is actually a barn, is not a barn, and in which Laura continues to
believe that that object (*b*) is a barn. So, on the local reliabilist approach, whether Laura's actual belief is knowledge
depends on whether there is a nearby possible situation in
which the barn *b* is not a barn. However, it is unclear
whether there is any such possible situation, never mind one
that is near the actual situation. Whether there is a situation
in which the object, *b*, that is actually a barn is not a barn
depends on the complex issue of what properties, if any, are
essential to objects. Kripke has maintained that the origin

and composition of an object are essential to that object. For example, he argues, a particular table that was in fact originally made out of a certain block of wood could not have been made out of any other block of wood, or any other substance; and that a particular person who in fact has biological parents x and y could not have had any other biological parents (Kripke 1980, pp. 113–114). Further, Kripke suggests that being a table is an essential property of a particular table (ibid., p. 114, n. 57). If that is right, then perhaps the particular barn, b, could not exist while being a fake.

However, it seems clear that whatever the outcome of this contentious metaphysical issue and, thus, whether or not Laura's actual belief is produced by a locally reliable process, her belief is not a case of knowledge. Given the presence of numerous fakes, Laura might easily have been looking at a fake, and she would mistake a fake for a real barn. In addition, the case shows that the local reliabilist approach to knowledge is incorrect. This approach makes knowledge a function solely of truth and local reliability. As we saw above, the factor that clearly prevents Laura's belief from being knowledge is that Laura would mistake a fake for a barn. But this does not undermine any of the conditions in the local reliabilist account of knowledge. Thus, the barn case shows that there is some necessary condition for knowledge not mentioned in the local reliabilist account.[8]

If we wish to remain within a broadly reliabilist approach to knowledge, the obvious suggestion for the necessary condition is global reliability.[9] The reason Laura does not know on the basis of vision that that object (b) is a barn is clear: there are numerous fake barns in the vicinity and she would mistake a fake for a real barn. In other words, the process that produces the belief that that object (b) is a barn is not reliable over the range of propositions of the form: s is a barn, where 's' is replaced with a singular referring expression. So, reliabilists should accept that global reliability is necessary for knowledge. The barn case is also important for those who reject reliabilist accounts of knowledge but claim that reliability is necessary for knowledge, for the case suggests that the relevant notion of reliability involves global as well as local reliability.

5 The Illusion Argument Reconsidered

Let us now reconsider whether the compatibilist can respond to the illusion argument by emphasizing the self-verifying nature of cogito thoughts. Some compatibilists hold a reliabilist account of self-knowledge; others hold that reliability is necessary for self-knowledge. However, we saw in the last section that those who hold that reliability is necessary for knowledge should accept that global reliability is necessary for knowledge. But, if global reliability is required for knowledge, then whether Sally's belief that she thinks that that wasp (w) is near constitutes a priori knowledge depends on whether it was produced by a process that is reliable with respect to a range of propositions, not merely the proposition that she thinks that that wasp (w) is near. We saw earlier that, without using empirical information, Sally is not reliable about such propositions as that she is thinking about a wasp: in the illusion situation, she would believe that she is thinking about a wasp, even though she is not. In addition, she frequently suffers an illusion of hearing and thinking about a wasp owing to her hypersensitivity. So, if the range of propositions relevant to global reliability includes the proposition that she is thinking about a wasp, then the process that produced Sally's actual second-order belief is not globally reliable, and hence, Sally lacks a priori knowledge that she thinks that that wasp (w) is near.

A compatibilist may try to argue that the range of propositions relevant to global reliability does not include such propositions as that she (Sally) is thinking about a wasp. Instead, she may suggest that the relevant range includes only cogito thoughts, but not other second-order thoughts. On this view, whether the process in question is globally reliable depends on whether it would produce second-order beliefs of the form: I believe that I think that p in all and only those nearby situations in which the subject thinks that p. Since cogito thoughts are self-verifying, the process that produced Sally's second-order belief does meet this condition. We have seen that, even in the illusion situation, Sally does not make false judgments of the relevant form. In particular, since in the illusion situation she is not suitably related to w to have perceptual demonstrative thoughts about him, she does not falsely attribute to herself the thought that that wasp (w) is near. Rather, she attributes to herself the first-order thoughts she actually has, such as the thought that the wasp that she hears is near. Of course, in the illusion situation, she does judge falsely that she is thinking about a wasp. But this thought is not of the cogito form.

The compatibilist might try to defend her restricted conception of the range of propositions relevant to global reliability by using certain claims of McGinn's. He suggests that the propositions relevant to global reliability are those that are "in some intuitive sense 'at the same level' as the given proposition—they are propositions 'of the same kind' as the given one" (1984, p. 27). For example, he suggests that the proposition that there is a dog is of the same kind as the proposition that there is a table, whereas the proposition

that I am a brain in a vat is not. Elsewhere, he suggests that
relevance is determined by subject matter, suggesting that
propositions about others' mental states are not relevant to
knowledge of a proposition about a material object (ibid., n.
48). Using these remarks, the compatibilist may claim that
the first-person proposition that she (Sally) is thinking about
a wasp has a different subject matter than the first-person
proposition that she (Sally) is thinking that that wasp (w) is
near. For example, the compatibilist might be tempted to say
that the proposition that she (Sally) is thinking about a wasp
is not one about what type of thought content Sally has, but
rather one about the external relations Sally's thought
content bears to the world.

However, this objection cannot be coherently made as
a defense of the illusion version of anti-individualism. As
we saw earlier (sec. 2), according to this version of anti-
individualism, Sally's mistake in the illusion situation is not
one about how some thought she has relates to the world;
rather, in the illusion situation, Sally's utterance of 'That
wasp is near' fails to express any thought at all. Thus, in the
illusion situation, Sally makes a mistake about what type of
thought she has and, indeed, about whether, in essaying a
thought, she manages to have a thought at all.

Could a defender of the illusion version of anti-
individualism use any other argument to defend her
restricted conception of the relevant range of propositions?
She could point out that Sally's belief, in the illusion situation, that she is thinking about a wasp is not of the cogito
form (I believe that I think that p). However, it is not clear
why this difference in form should outweigh the other sim-
ilarities between the two second-order beliefs. In each case,
Sally thinks about herself in a first-person way and attributes a certain type of thought content to herself. Given this,

it seems quite reasonable to say that the two beliefs are "of the same type," "at the same level," and concern "the same subject matter."

The problem of specifying the range of propositions relevant to global reliability is related to one of the standard problems facing global reliabilist accounts of knowledge: the generality problem. Global reliability is a feature of types of process. But there are many different ways of typing the process that produces a given belief, where these different types may be associated with different levels of reliability. The generality problem is the problem of determining which type should be used to fix the reliability of the process (Goldman 1986, p. 49). For example, imagine that a subject forms the correct belief that there is a crow in front of her on the basis of a fleeting visual experience in poor light. If we type the process that produces this belief as one of producing beliefs on the basis of fleeting visual experiences in poor light, then it is not very reliable. But if we type it as the process of producing beliefs on the basis of visual experience, then it is highly reliable.

Different ways of typing processes sometimes affect the range of propositions relevant to global reliability.[10] Imagine a subject who forms the correct belief that there is a magpie nearby on the basis of her visual experience. We could type the process that produces the belief as one of forming beliefs about the current state of the environment on the basis of visual experience. If we do so, then certain propositions become irrelevant in assessing global reliability, for example, the proposition that someone lit a fire here last night, or the proposition that I now have a headache. By contrast, if we type the process as one of forming beliefs on the basis of experience, then both of the above propositions may be relevant.

Returning to the discussion of the illusion argument, the question of whether the process that produces Sally's second-order belief is globally reliable could be viewed as an instance of the generality problem. We could type the process as one that takes first-order beliefs as inputs, and outputs cogito thoughts, that is, thoughts of the form: I believe that I think that p. If we do, then the process is globally reliable. Alternatively, we could type the process as one that produces first-person beliefs about the type of thought content the subject herself is having. So construed, the process would not be globally reliable, since in the illusion situation Sally believes falsely that she is thinking about a wasp and she frequently suffers such an illusion.

Unfortunately for the compatibilist, there is no generally agreed-on method for solving the generality problem. Indeed, it constitutes one of the main objections to global reliabilist accounts of knowledge. Given this, it is hard for the compatibilist to argue that there is just one correct way of typing the process that produces Sally's belief, namely as a process that takes first-order beliefs as inputs, and outputs cogito thoughts. Thus, it is hard for the compatibilist to answer the illusion argument by arguing that Sally's mistake about her thoughts in the illusion situation is not relevant to global reliability.

6 Conclusion of the Illusion Argument

I have been examining whether one can defend the compatibility of privileged access and one version of anti-individualism: the illusion version. The distinctive claim of this type of anti-individualism is that a subject can suffer an illusion of having a thought. The argument centered on the case of Sally. In the actual situation, Sally hears a certain wasp, w, and thinks that that wasp (w) is near. Prima facie, her ability to have a priori knowledge of this thought content seems to be undermined by the fact that she frequently suffers an illusion of hearing and thinking about a wasp. In such a situation, Sally would judge mistakenly that she is thinking about a wasp that she hears when she is not.

Given that Sally frequently suffers wasp illusions, the compatibilist cannot deny the relevance of the illusion situation for Sally. I have been examining whether the compatibilist can instead reply to the illusion argument by stressing the reliability of Sally's cogito thoughts. Certainly, in the illusion situation, Sally does not believe falsely that she thinks that that wasp (w) is near: in that situation, she is not suitably related to wasp w to have thoughts about w, whether first- or second-order. Thus, Sally's actual belief that she thinks that that wasp (w) is near is produced by a locally reliable process, a process that is reliable with respect to that particular proposition. However, we saw that knowledge that p requires not only local reliability but also global reliability, that is, reliability with respect to a range of propositions other than p. But Sally is not reliable about the proposition that she is thinking about a wasp that she hears, for she would believe mistakenly that she is thinking about a wasp that she hears in the illusion situation, and she frequently suffers such illusions. We have seen that it is hard for a compatibilist to show that the proposition that she (Sally) is thinking about a wasp that she hears is not relevant to global reliability. It seems, then, that a focus on reliability fails to provide the compatibilist with a clear-cut answer to the illusion argument.

Although the discussion has concentrated on an example of a subject suffering a perceptual illusion, the argument can be applied more widely. It can apply to any anti-individualist view that accepts that a subject can suffer an illusion of thought in a no-reference situation. Such a situation may involve either perceptual illusion or a subject confusing several objects or kinds for one. Thus, the illusion argument applies to a variety of thoughts about objects, including perceptual demonstrative and recognition-based thoughts, as well as thoughts about natural kinds.

7 The Illusion and Discrimination Arguments

The illusion argument is the second of the two incompatibilist arguments we have looked at in this first part of the book. In chapters 2 and 3, we examined the discrimination argument for the incompatibility of anti-individualism and privileged access. Let us summarize our discussion of these two arguments. The illusion argument targets the illusion version of anti-individualism. We have seen that no clear-cut reply to the illusion argument is provided by accepting the relevance of the illusion situation but stressing the reliability of cogito thoughts. By contrast, the discrimination argument applies to all versions of anti-individualism. According to the discrimination argument, anti-individualism undermines privileged access, since it undermines a subject's ability to distinguish a priori between the actual situation in which she thinks a certain thought and relevant alternative situations in which she lacks this thought. Just as we have seen that one cannot provide a clear-cut reply to the illusion argument by accepting the relevance of the alternative situation but stressing the reliability of cogito thoughts, so we saw earlier that this response does not fully answer the discrimination argument. Recall that it is unclear how emphasizing reliability is

supposed to answer the discrimination argument, which
turns on a point about discrimination: how can a subject
know a priori that she thinks that *p* if there is a relevant alternative situation in which she lacks this thought that she
cannot distinguish a priori from the actual situation? The
compatibilist could respond to the discrimination argument
by showing either that the subject can distinguish a priori
the actual from relevant alternative situations, or that such
a discriminative ability is not required for knowledge. In
chapters 2 and 3, I argued that the subject cannot distinguish
a priori the actual from relevant alternative situations. This
is so even on Evans's anti-individualist view, which builds
a discrimination requirement into the account of thought. In
chapter 2, I argued that compatibilists have not yet shown
that knowledge does not require discriminative abilities.

The discussion of the illusion and discrimination arguments suggests that it would be worthwhile pursuing a different strategy. Perhaps, instead of granting the relevance of
the alternative situation and stressing reliability, the compatibilist should instead challenge the relevance of the alternative situations.[11] Even if there are some cases in which
there is a relevant alternative situation, perhaps this is not
normally so. But if alternative situations are not normally
relevant, then the compatibilist could show how, normally,
subjects can have a priori knowledge of their thought contents even if anti-individualism is true. This relevant alternatives strategy finesses the issue of the correct account of
knowledge. If the alternative situations are not normally relevant, then they are not normally knowledge undermining
regardless of whether knowledge requires discriminative
abilities or merely reliable belief. Thus, this strategy could
be used both by those who think that knowledge requires

discriminative abilities and by those who think that it requires only reliable belief. I examine this strategy for solving the illusion and discrimination arguments in the remainder of the chapter.

To set up the discussion, it will be useful to recap the nature of the alternative situations used in the discrimination and illusion arguments. The discrimination argument can exploit any relevant alternative situation that the subject cannot distinguish a priori from the actual situation and in which she lacks the thought she has in the actual situation. Such an alternative situation may be a twin situation in which the subject is related to a duplicate object (kind) in such a way that she thinks a different thought partly individuated by this duplicate. Or, the alternative situation may be a no-reference situation in which the subject is not related to any object (kind) in such a way as to have a thought about it. For example, she may suffer an illusion of seeing an object (kind) or of having a recognitional capacity for an object (kind). What thoughts the subject has in such a situation depends on the version of anti-individualism at issue: on the descriptive version, she has a thought of the form, the F is G; on the illusion version, she suffers an illusion of having a thought. Whereas the discrimination argument can exploit either type of alternative situation and applies to both the illusion and descriptive version of anti-individualism, the illusion argument exploits just the no-reference type of alternative situation and applies only to the illusion version of anti-individualism. I will now consider in detail whether the kinds of alternative situation exploited by the discrimination and/or illusion arguments are normally relevant, starting by considering whether twin situations are normally relevant for socially individuated thoughts.

8   Social Anti-Individualism and Twin Situations

Suppose that, in the actual situation, a subject thinks that p, where her thought is individuated partly by the practices of her linguistic community. The incompatibilist argues that the subject lacks a priori knowledge of her thought in the actual situation if she cannot distinguish a priori the actual situation from a relevant twin situation, in which everything seems the same but she thinks a different thought since she is related to a different linguistic community. In chapter 2, we saw that such twin situations are relevant for someone who is slowly switched between two linguistic communities in which a single word has a different meaning.

For example, suppose that Sally is a slow switcher who spends the early part of her life in the U.K. and then lives for many years in the United States, before finally returning to retire in the U.K. Sally fails to realize that 'chicory' applies to different kinds of salad vegetable in U.K.- and U.S.-English. She would explicate 'chicory' by saying that it applies to a leafy green salad vegetable, although she is not sure what precise kind. Before the switch, a social anti-individualist would claim that, despite her incomplete understanding, Sally has various thoughts involving the concept chicory$_{UK}$, for example, the thought that chicory$_{UK}$ is healthy. But a social anti-individualist would claim that, as a result of the switch, Sally later loses this thought and instead comes to have a different thought. There is controversy about exactly what thought she comes to have. This controversy doesn't affect our argument and so, for simplicity, suppose that she comes to think that chicory$_{US}$ is healthy. Take Sally at a time when she in the U.K. thinking that chicory$_{UK}$ is healthy. It seems that Sally cannot distinguish a priori this situation from the twin situation in which she is instead in the United States thinking the different thought that chicory$_{US}$ is healthy. Everything seems the same in the two situations. Sally wouldn't notice the change in her thoughts as she is switched between the U.K. and the United States. To know that her thoughts have changed she needs to use empirical information about the switch.

Let us focus on those features of the slow switch case that make it plausible that the switch leads to a change in thought that Sally cannot notice without making use of empirical information. I will argue that these features are: (1) Sally is slowly switched between two linguistic communities that share a single word but define it slightly differently; (2) Sally is ignorant of this linguistic difference; and (3) nonetheless, she is a competent speaker of both languages and a competent user of the target word in both languages. Condition (3) is essential. Social anti-individualists hold that a subject's thought is individuated by a language only if the subject is a competent speaker of that language. For example, Burge accepts that the conventions of English do not individuate the thoughts of a monolingual speaker of French even if she utters some English sentence (Burge 1979, pp. 89–92). Further, the social anti-individualist claim that a subject's thoughts are partly individuated by the way a term is used in her linguistic community is increasingly implausible the greater the subject's incomplete understanding of that term (ibid., pp. 89–91). Where a subject wholly misunderstands a word, it is implausible that her thoughts are partly individuated by the public meaning of the word. So, the claim that Sally's thoughts change content as a result of the switch is plausible only if Sally is competent with both U.K.- and U.S.-English and is a competent user of 'chicory' in both languages.

For Sally to count as a competent user of 'chicory' in both languages, it must have only a slightly different meaning in the two languages (condition 1). If the difference in meaning were great, it is hard to see how Sally could count as competent with the word in both languages. Furthermore, it is essential that Sally is a slow switcher (condition 1). By definition, a slow switch is one in which the subject spends long enough in each environment that an anti-individualist would accept that the switch affects thought contents. Condition (2), that the subject is ignorant of the difference between the two languages, is crucial for the claim that she would not notice the change in her thoughts as she is switched between the two communities. Suppose that Sally were aware of the different meaning of 'chicory' in the two languages and acquires some beliefs involving the U.K. concept and some involving the U.S. concept. If she were aware of the difference in the meaning of 'chicory' then she would distinguish the two types of thought and would not treat them as having the same content.

We have now isolated the key conditions that make it plausible that a slow switch leads to a change in thought content that the switched subject cannot notice without using empirical information. I will argue that those conditions are not, and indeed cannot be, normally jointly met. As a result, for a subject who thinks the socially individuated thought that p it is not normally a relevant alternative that she is instead in a twin situation in which everything seems the same but she thinks a different thought. Conditions (1)–(3) are not normally jointly met. Despite the increasing popularity of travel, most subjects are not slow switchers, that is, most subjects do not spend significant periods living in another country, becoming competent in its language. Many travelers do no more than pick up a few words of the languages of the countries to which they travel, and spend only a few weeks there. It is no accident that conditions (1)–(3) are not normally jointly met. If slow switching became the norm, this would undermine the conditions that the relevant word has different meanings in the two languages, and that the subject is ignorant of this difference (conditions 1 and 2). Consider the example of U.K.- and U.S.-English. At the moment, despite the interaction between speakers of U.K.- and U.S.-English, there are still many speakers who almost wholly interact only with speakers of their national variant. More important, most speakers of each variant still defer to national experts for correct usage. Thus, there are still two distinct languages, with different conventions for correct usage. However, if most inhabitants of the U.K. and the U.S. came to spend half of their lives in one country and half in the other, these linguistic differences would start to break down. Words that previously had different meanings in the two languages would tend to settle on a single meaning. More important, speakers would tend to consult common authorities for correct linguistic practice. Thus, over time, the two languages would become one. To the extent that differences between the two languages remain, it seems that the frequent exchange between the two communities would make it less likely that the differences would remain unknown. Indeed, one might think that, if slow switching were to become the norm, linguistic differences could persist only if most of the subjects in the two communities were aware of these differences. If they were not, then they would equally defer to U.K. and U.S. linguistic experts to explicate the meanings of a given word in all its uses. As a result, the word would no longer have distinct meanings in different uses.

In conclusion, the key features of the slow switch would be undermined if slow switching became the norm. Thus, it cannot be the case that an alternative situation in which one thinks a different thought in virtue of being related to a different linguistic community is normally relevant for most speakers.

9 Natural Kind Anti-Individualism and Twin Situations

Having argued that twin situations are not normally relevant for socially individuated thoughts, let us consider thoughts that are individuated partly by natural kinds. Suppose that a subject thinks that water is wet where this thought is individuated partly by the fact that her environment contains water, that is, the substance with composition H_2O. In a twin situation, everything would seem the same to the subject, but, because she is related to a different natural kind, she would think a different thought, say, the thought that twater is wet. It is standardly argued that such a twin situation is relevant for a subject who is slowly switched between one environment and another, say, living the first part of her life on Earth before being whisked unawares to Twin Earth, where the lakes and rivers contain twater, not water. Clearly this slow switch story is merely imaginary: ordinary subjects are not whisked off unawares to far-flung planets, and there is no twater or Twin Earth. So, this fictional story does nothing to make twin situations relevant for ordinary subjects. Further, I will argue that such twin situations are not normally relevant.

Consider the classic Twin Earth argument for natural kind anti-individualism. To avoid confusing arguments for natural kind and social anti-individualism, let us focus on a single subject, rather than a community. Central to the Twin Earth argument is the claim that a subject can have a concept of a natural kind even while being ignorant of the kind's fundamental nature. Suppose that a subject has come across samples of a natural kind, say, gold, and so has developed the ability to recognize instances of gold. As a result, she applies a term to instances of gold. In such circumstances, it is plausible that she has the concept of gold, even if she is ignorant of its chemical composition. Notice that the claim that the subject has the ability to recognize gold seems central to making it plausible that she has the concept of gold: it is her possession of a recognitional capacity for gold that enables her to apply the term to instances of gold.[12] So, it seems reasonable to treat her thoughts about gold as based on a recognitional capacity for gold. However, I will now argue that if a subject thinks a recognition-based thought about a kind then there is no relevant twin situation in which she instead encounters a duplicate kind and thus thinks a twin thought. I defend this claim by first defending the different claim that if a subject has a recognitional capacity for a natural kind, then there is no relevant duplicate kind.

In chapter 3 I argued that the notion of a recognitional capacity is tied to the concept of knowledge: if someone has a recognitional capacity for an object or a kind, then she can gain knowledge when she reencounters that object or kind to the effect that it is the object or kind previously encountered. However, this link between recognitional capacities and knowledge constrains the correct account of recognitional capacities. Suppose that S has a recognitional capacity for a kind and, on encountering a further instance of the kind, thinks that it is an instance of the kind she previously encountered. This belief would not constitute knowledge if

there were a relevant alternative situation in which everything seems the same but in which she encounters an
instance of a duplicate kind: she would be unable to distinguish this duplicate situation from the actual situation and
thus would believe mistakenly of the instance of the duplicate that it is an instance of the previously encountered kind.
Thus, if her recognitional capacity is to be knowledge-
yielding in the way described, it cannot be the case that there
is a relevant alternative situation in which everything is the
same but she encounters a duplicate. In consequence, and
as I argued in chapter 3, a subject has a recognitional capacity for an object or kind x only if there is no relevant duplicate for x.

This result about recognitional capacities for kinds has
consequences for recognition-based thoughts about kinds.
Suppose that a subject thinks the recognition-based thought
that that (x) is F. It is part of her having a recognitional
capacity for x that there is no relevant duplicate. Thus, there
is no relevant alternative situation in which she encounters
a duplicate instead of x. A fortiori, there is no relevant
alternative situation in which she encounters a duplicate,
develops a recognitional capacity for that duplicate, and so
thinks a recognition-based thought about the duplicate. For
instance, if a subject thinks a recognition-based thought
about water, there is no relevant alternative situation in
which instead of encountering water, she encounters a
duplicate, say, twater, and thinks a twater thought rather
than a water thought. (Notice that, although the account of
recognitional capacities and recognition-based thoughts
used here was developed during the earlier discussion of
Evans, it could be adopted without endorsing his discrimination requirement for thought.)

So far, I have argued that for both social anti-individualism and natural kind anti-individualism, if a subject actually thinks the externally individuated thought that p, then there is no relevant twin situation. I now turn to consider singular anti-individualism.

10   Singular Anti-Individualism and Twin Situations

Let us start our discussion of singular anti-individualism by considering recognition-based thoughts about objects. Suppose that a subject has developed a recognitional capacity for a certain person, x, and thinks the recognition-based thought that that person (x) is F. According to the account of recognitional capacities outlined above, if S has a recognitional capacity for x, then there is no relevant duplicate she would mistake for x. This claim about recognitional capacities for objects grounds a distinct claim about recognition-based thoughts about objects. Suppose that the subject thinks a recognition-based thought about x. It is part of her having a recognitional capacity for that object that there is no relevant duplicate. Thus, there is no relevant twin situation in which she instead encounters a duplicate and thinks a recognition-based thought about the duplicate. Thus twin situations are not relevant for recognition-based thoughts about particular objects.

A second important category of thoughts taken to be externally individuated are perceptual demonstrative thoughts. Suppose that a subject sees an object x and thinks that that object (x) is F. Is there a relevant twin situation in which she instead sees and thinks about a duplicate? I will argue that the case of perceptual demonstrative thought is less clear-cut than the other kinds of thought examined so far. There are some circumstances in which a twin situation does seem relevant, but also a large number of circumstances in which it does not.

For instance, suppose that S is in an agricultural packing factory looking at an endless flow of similar red apples moving down a conveyor belt into boxes. Seeing apple a, she thinks that that apple (a) is red. In this case, it seems a relevant alternative that S might have been looking at a duplicate apple, say, if the apples had happened to come down the belt in a slightly different order. Or, perhaps, the subject is looking at one of a flock of seagulls as they wheel around above her, and she thinks that that bird (b) is agile. Given the number of similar birds in the flock, it may be a relevant alternative that she is instead looking at a duplicate bird and thinks a twin thought. But, although some kinds of objects, such as cans of beer, apples, and seagulls, often have duplicates, others, such as people, only rarely do: most of us don't have identical twins.

Further, even for kinds of objects that do have duplicates, a twin situation may not always be relevant. Suppose that I look out of my office at the huge beech tree opposite, t, and think that that tree (t) is beautiful. A twin situation would be one in which there is a distinct duplicate tree, say d, occupying the very position of the beech so that I instead see and think about the duplicate. We could imagine special circumstances in which an alternative situation in which a duplicate occupies the position of the beech is relevant: perhaps a millionaire tree-lover has left enough money in her will that if the beech were to die or be damaged, a full-grown duplicate tree would be transplanted to the very spot. But, outside such special circumstances, the twin scenario does not seem relevant. The same point holds even for some less stable and more transient objects. Suppose I see my colleague draw up in car, *c*, leading me to think that that car (*c*) is large. In special circumstances, a twin situation in which an identical car replaces *c* might be relevant—say, my colleague's partner works in the trade and they get a new car every six months. But such a twin situation is not normally relevant.

It seems, then, that an appeal to relevance provides us with a less satisfying solution in the case of perceptual demonstrative thoughts than it does for social and natural kind anti-individualism, as well as anti-individualism about recognition-based thoughts about objects. In the latter cases, we have seen that if a subject thinks the externally individuated thought that *p*, then there is normally no relevant twin situation. By contrast, in the case of perceptual demonstrative thoughts, whether there is a relevant twin situation depends on the details of the case. This result might raise doubts about the strategy of defending compatibilism by challenging the relevance of alternative situations. Before addressing this worry, I want to complete our discussion of the relevance strategy by examining the other main kind of alternative situation, namely, no-reference situations.

11   No-Reference Situations

In a no-reference situation, the subject is not suitably related to an object or kind to think about it. In one type of no-reference situation, the subject suffers a perceptual illusion. In a second type of no-reference situation, the subject does not suffer a perceptual illusion, but rather takes herself to have encountered a single object or kind when in fact she has confused several similar objects or kinds. Both types of no-reference situation could be developed for either a thought about an object or a thought about a natural kind.

At the moment, I will leave it open what thoughts a subject has in a no-reference situation and, in particular, whether or not she suffers an illusion of thought. Let us start by considering the first type of no-reference situation. Suppose that, in the actual situation, S perceives a wasp (w) and thinks the perceptual demonstrative thought that that wasp (w) is angry. There is an alternative situation in which S instead suffers an illusion of perceiving just such a wasp. Such an illusion situation may be relevant in certain special circumstances, for instance, in the case of Sally who frequently suffers illusions of hearing wasps. However, such an illusion situation is not normally relevant. In general, humans only rarely suffer illusions of seeing objects. That we only rarely suffer such illusions is central to the way we gain perceptual knowledge about the world. Ordinarily, we suppose that subjects can gain knowledge on the basis of their perceptual experiences. For instance, if S sees a wasp and is in good viewing conditions, she can gain knowledge of the world—say, that there is a wasp there. If subjects frequently suffered illusions of seeing objects, then it would be a relevant alternative that she is not seeing a wasp but instead is suffering an illusion. In these circumstances, she could use her perceptual experience to gain knowledge of the world only when combined with some further evidence that rules out the illusion possibility. Thus, if this kind of illusion were frequent and so normally relevant, then our perceptual knowledge would have a different basis than it currently has.

Further, if this kind of illusion were normally relevant, then this might undermine the very possibility of our gaining knowledge of the world from perception. We have seen that, if illusions were normally relevant, then S can gain perceptual knowledge of the world only by combining her perceptual experience with other evidence that she is not suffering an illusion. Such evidence is likely to consist in further experiences, say, the experience as of asking another person for confirmation, or experiences from other sensory modalities (say, touch). But, if illusion were pervasive, then the same worry arises for these further experiences as for the original one: it is a relevant possibility that these further experiences are illusory, and the subject needs to gain further evidence to rule this out. It is unclear how to stop this regress. It seems, then, that the fact that illusions are not normally relevant is central to our ability to gain knowledge of the world through perception. (Notice this is so regardless of whether knowledge merely requires reliability or also discrimination.)

If, as suggested, general epistemological considerations show that the possibility of illusion is not normally relevant for perceptual knowledge of the world, then it is not normally relevant for knowledge of one's thoughts. Consider the situation in which S sees wasp w and thinks the perceptual demonstrative thought that that wasp (w) is angry. If it is not normally a relevant alternative that S suffers an illusion of seeing a wasp then, a fortiori, it is not normally a relevant alternative that she suffers an illusion of seeing a wasp and thus fails to think a perceptual demonstrative thought about a wasp. Similar considerations apply to recognition-based thoughts, whether about objects or kinds. Suppose that S has experiences as of encountering lakes and rivers full of a watery liquid, and she takes it that there is dominant natural kind in the lakes and rivers to which she attempts to refer with 'water'. In fact, the lakes and rivers are mostly composed of H_2O, so she expresses the concept water by 'water'. Since illusions are not normally relevant, it is not a relevant alternative that she is on Dry Earth where there are no such lakes and rivers and she has illusory experiences.

Having argued that the first type of no-reference situation is not normally relevant, let us now consider the second type in which the subject confuses several different objects, or kinds, for one. This second type of no-reference situation is particularly relevant for recognition-based thoughts. Suppose that S encounters an object or kind, x, and thereby develops a recognitional capacity for x and thinks that that (x) is F. Is there a relevant alternative situation in which she instead confuses several objects or kinds for one and so fails to have a recognitional capacity for x or recognition-based thoughts about x? That such an alternative situation is not relevant can be seen by appealing again to the account of what it is to have a recognitional capacity. Earlier, I argued that if S has a recognitional capacity for an object or kind, then there is no relevant duplicate that she would mistake for that object or kind. Thus, if S has a recognition-based thought about x, there is no relevant alternative situation in which she instead encounters and thinks about a duplicate. It follows that there is no relevant alternative situation in which she instead encounters several duplicates and confuses them for a single object or kind.

The second kind of no-reference situation is also relevant for perceptual demonstrative thoughts. As noted in chapter 3, some hold that perceptual demonstrative thoughts are based on the ability to track objects perceptually over short periods of time. This view allows that, on occasion, a subject may base a perceptual demonstrative thought on a momentary perception, but argues that perceptual demonstrative thoughts are normally based on perceptual tracking. Suppose, then, that S perceptually tracks a person x for a few minutes as she walks down the street, and she thinks that that person (*x*) is *F*. A potentially knowledge-undermining alternative situation would be one in which she instead confuses several people for one. If perceptual demonstrative thoughts are connected to the ability to track objects perceptually then, in this alternative situation, she fails to think a perceptual demonstrative thought about *x*. We can construct scenarios in which such an alternative situation is relevant. Perhaps *x* is part of a large crowd of similarly dressed demonstrators so that it is easy to lose track of her within the crowd. However, despite such examples, it remains a central fact about us that we have the ability to track objects perceptually over short periods. This ability enables us to combine information from successive perceptions of a single object (e.g., that bird can sing high and low notes) and to act on objects perceived to have certain qualities (e.g., return the five-pound note to the man who just dropped it; or, choose the puppy that just nibbled the slipper).[13] Given that we have this ability, the alternative situation in which one fails to track a single object and so fails to have perceptual demonstrative thoughts about it is not normally relevant.

I have now argued that if a subject thinks the externally individuated thought that *p*, then an alternative no-reference situation is not normally relevant. Thus, such no-reference situations do not normally undermine a subject's a priori knowledge of her thought contents. This is so regardless of what view one takes of no-reference situations and, in particular, regardless of whether one accepts the illusion view, according to which she suffers an illusion of thought, or the descriptive view, according to which she has a descriptive thought.

12   The Relevance Strategy and Alternatives

Let us summarize our discussion of the relevance strategy. Suppose that S thinks the externally individuated thought that p. Two kinds of alternative situation may undermine S's ability to know a priori that she thinks that p: twin and no-reference situations. I have argued that for a wide range of anti-individualist views, including social, natural kind, and singular anti-individualism, neither twin situations nor no-reference situations are normally relevant.[14] There is one exception to this general conclusion: if a subject has a perceptual demonstrative thought about an object, x, then whether or not there is a relevant twin situation depends on the details of the case. In a great many cases, no twin situation is relevant. However, in some other cases, such as the apple-packing factory example, it is relevant. That the relevance strategy does not provide a full compatibilist solution in the particular case of perceptual demonstrative thoughts is disappointing. A further concern about the strategy is that it may seem to make a subject's ability to have a priori knowledge of her thought contents a mere accident of the kind of environment she is in. Let us consider each of these concerns.

Suppose that the relevance strategy were to make privileged access a mere accident of the kind of environment one is in. Nonetheless, the relevance strategy would still have established a substantive result, namely that, with one exception, the fact that a subject's thoughts are individuated partly in terms of her environment is compatible with the claim that the subject can have a priori knowledge of her thought contents. In particular, she can know her thought contents without investigating those features of the environment that partly individuate her thought, such as the chemical composition of substances or the particular linguistic practices of her community. Thus, the strategy fulfills the task set earlier for a successful compatibilist response (see chap. 2). In any case, the strategy does not make privileged access merely a matter of environmental accident. In the case of a recognition-based thought about an object or a kind, the fact that there is no relevant twin or motley situation is not an accident of the environment, but rather a consequence of the nature of recognitional capacities. It is a condition of having a recognitional capacity for an object or kind that there is no relevant duplicate. Thus, if a subject has a recognition-based thought about an object or a kind, then there is no relevant twin situation in which she instead encounters a duplicate. A fortiori, there is no relevant motley situation in which she instead encounters several duplicates and mistakes them for one. In the case of socially individuated thoughts, twin situations could not be normally relevant for the key features of slow switch cases would be undermined if slow switch cases became the norm. In particular, if, say, subjects were routinely switched between the U.K. and the United States, then this would undermine linguistic differences between the two variants of English and would undermine ignorance of remaining differences.

Last, consider no-reference situations in which one suffers an illusion of encountering an object or kind. I have not argued that there is any logical or conceptual incoherence in the idea that such illusions might be pervasive. However, it is a deep fact about us that perceptual illusions are not pervasive. That they are not is fundamental to our ability to gain knowledge of the world on the basis of perceptual experience. In conclusion, with the exception of perceptual demonstrative thoughts, the relevance strategy shows that a subject can have knowledge of externally individuated thoughts without basing that knowledge on investigation of the environment. Further, the view does not make privileged access wholly accidental.

How should we respond to the other concern, that the relevance strategy does not supply a full compatibilist response for perceptual demonstrative thoughts? While this is disappointing, it is worth stressing that the strategy works for a large range of anti-individualist views and types of thought. In addition, the strategy shows how, in many cases, a subject can have a priori knowledge of the contents of even perceptual demonstrative thoughts. The strategy shows that no-reference situations are not normally relevant for perceptual demonstrative thoughts and that, in many cases, twin situations are not relevant either. Thus, the relevance strategy provides a substantial, if not total, compatibilist solution.

Further, the relevant alternatives strategy could be used by a wide range of compatibilists with different views about the requirements for knowledge. The strategy may be used both by those who hold that knowledge requires discriminative abilities and those who hold that it requires only reliable belief. If the alternative situations are not normally relevant then they are not normally knowledge-undermining, even if knowledge requires discriminative abilities. Thus, the strategy offers a solution to the discrimination argument for those unsatisfied by a response that consists merely in pointing out the reliability of a subject's cogito thoughts. In addition, the strategy may be used by those who think that knowledge requires only reliability. In effect, when combined with reliabilism about knowledge, the relevant alternatives strategy provides a two-pronged response to the discrimination argument. This response consists in pointing out that, first, the supposedly knowledge-undermining alternative situations are not normally relevant; and, second, if they were relevant, they would not undermine reliability and so knowledge. In addition, the relevant alternatives strategy helps neutralize a problem for the reliabilist response to the illusion argument. The reliabilist can show that even if illusions of thought are relevant, they do not undermine local reliability. But knowledge plausibly requires global reliability as well as local reliability. It is harder for the reliabilist to show that a relevant possibility of suffering an illusion of thought does not undermine global reliability. However, if such illusion situations are not normally relevant, then they are not normally-knowledge undermining, whatever the precise requirements for global reliability turn out to be. It seems, then, that the relevant alternatives strategy is not a rival to the reliabilist strategy, but can be combined usefully with it.

13   Conclusion of Chapters 2 through 4

This chapter concludes my discussion of the problem of how a subject can have privileged access to the contents of thoughts that are externally individuated. I have defended and elaborated the strategy of responding to this problem by denying the relevance of potentially knowledge-undermining alternative situations. With the exception of perceptual demonstrative thoughts, this strategy applies to a wide range of anti-individualist views and types of thought.

In the rest of the book, I turn to consider other issues. In the next chapter I consider the objection that anti-individualism undermines a subject's reasoning ability. This leads to a discussion in chapter 6 of whether it is possible to combine anti-individualism and the Fregean notion of sense, as some prominent anti-individualists have tried to do. In the last two chapters, I examine what consequences would arise from a view that combines anti-individualism and privileged access and, in particular, whether this view would have the result that a subject can gain a priori knowledge of the existence and nature of her environment.

The arguments of the rest of the book are independent of the conclusions and arguments advanced so far. In particular, from now on I leave aside the controversial issue of whether knowledge requires discriminative abilities or only reliable belief. In the following chapters, where my arguments rest on a claim about knowledge, they rest only on the minimal and widely held view that knowledge requires reliability. This leaves it open whether knowledge also requires discriminative abilities.

5   Anti-Individualism and Reasoning

1   Introduction

In this chapter, I investigate the objection that anti-individualism undermines a subject's ability to reason. The objection is grounded in the claim that anti-individualism undermines subject's ability to grasp a priori whether two thoughts, or thought constituents, have the same or different content. According to anti-individualism, a subject's thought contents are individuated partly by the environment. Thus, whether two thoughts have the same or different content depends on environmental factors of which the subject may be ignorant. This suggests that a subject may need to investigate the environment in order to realize whether two thoughts have the same, or different, content; further, without such information, she may make mistakes about whether two thoughts have the same or different content.

Sameness and difference of content are crucial for reasoning. If a subject makes mistakes about sameness and difference of content, she may make mistakes about the logical properties of her thoughts. Suppose that a subject meets the anti-individualist's conditions for having the concepts expressed by two terms. It is part of anti-individualist theory that a subject can have the concept expressed by a term even if she is ignorant of some of the empirical factors that individuate it. This opens up the possibility of a mismatch between the subject's view about sameness and difference of content and the facts.

For instance, the subject might take it that she expresses different concepts by two terms even though her environmental relations determine that she expresses the same concept by them, say, because the terms express the same concept in her linguistic community or refer to the same natural kind. As a result, she may fail to realize that some of her beliefs can be combined in simple valid inferences. Further, she may fail to realize that certain of her beliefs are inconsistent. To correct her view she would need to gain empirical information about her environment. Alternatively, a subject might take it that she expresses the same concept by a pair of terms, but her environmental relations determine that she expresses different concepts by them, say, because the terms have different meanings in her linguistic community, or refer to different natural kinds. As a result, she may take certain inferences to be valid that are in fact invalid. To correct her view she would need to gain empirical information about her environment.

As a result of this sort of line of reasoning, some have argued that anti-individualism threatens a fundamental part of our conception of a rational agent. They admit that even a rational subject may make mistakes in her reasoning, and that she may fail to see logical relations the grasp of which requires complex and/or sophisticated reasoning. But, they claim, it is part of the concept of a rational subject that, in good conditions (e.g., when she is not distracted and when given adequate time to reflect), she can grasp the simple logical properties of her thoughts a priori and so would not make simple invalid inferences or form obviously contradictory beliefs. Further, she would make simple valid inferences from her thoughts, or at least those that are relevant to her current interests (I will leave this qualification implicit in the following discussion).

The slow switch argument considered in chapter 2 shows that anti-individualism may undermine a subject's ability to tell a priori whether two thoughts that she has at different times have the same or different content. A subject unwittingly switched between Earth and Twin Earth would be disposed to judge falsely that the thought she now expresses by 'Water is wet' has the same content as the thought she used to express in this way. However, it is a subject's ability to grasp sameness and difference of content between simultaneously held thoughts that seems relevant to rationality. It does not undermine a subject's rationality if she believes that p at an earlier time, then later loses this belief and comes to believe instead that not-p. Of course, we can ask whether the subject's change of belief was rational, but merely believing that p at one time and then believing that not-p at another is not in itself indicative of irrationality. Indeed, the subject may have changed her mind for good reason.

Thus, the relevant notion of a rational agent could be made more precise by saying that, with respect to simultaneously held thoughts, a rational subject should avoid simple contradictions in belief, make simple valid inferences, and avoid making simple invalid inferences. Correspondingly this chapter will focus on whether a subject can grasp a priori relations of sameness and difference of content between simultaneously held thoughts. More precisely, I consider whether anti-individualism is compatible with the following two principles:

Transparency of sameness of content: for any two thoughts, or thought constituents, that S entertains at time t, if they have the same content then, at t, S can realize a priori that they have the same content.

Transparency of difference of content: for any two thoughts, or thought constituents, that S entertains at time t, if they have different contents then, at t, S can realize a priori that they have different contents.

In the first part of the chapter, I consider the standard arguments that anti-individualism does undermine transparency. I extend these arguments by considering whether they apply to Fregean anti-individualism. In the second part of the chapter I consider whether it would be an objection to anti-individualism if it did undermine transparency.

Throughout this chapter, as in the rest of the book, I follow an established use of "a priori" according to which knowledge may be a priori even if based on conscious attitudes. In this sense, a subject's knowledge of her thought contents and the relations between them may be a priori. However, we may reformulate the issue and the ensuing discussion independently of this use as follows. According to anti-individualism, whether two of a subject's thoughts have the same or different content depends partly on their environmental relations. So, it seems that a subject needs to know about those environmental relations in order to realize whether two of her thoughts have the same or different content; without such information, she might be mistaken. Sameness and difference of content are crucial to the logical relations between thoughts. This suggests that anti-individualism has the consequence that in order for a subject to know the logical properties of her thoughts she needs environmental information and that, without such information, she might be mistaken. But, it is claimed, it is part of the concept of a rational agent that she can know the logical relations between her thoughts without investigation of her environment and that, at least in simple cases, she wouldn't make mistakes about their logical relations. Thus, anti-individualism seems to undermine the idea that we are rational agents.

2 Transparency of Sameness of Content

It has become commonplace to argue that anti-individualism is incompatible with transparency of sameness of content (see, e.g., Owens 1989; Boghossian 1992, 1994; Millikan 1993; Falvey and Owens 1994). According to anti-individualism, a subject's thought contents are individuated partly by environmental factors. But since the subject may be ignorant of these environmental factors, it is argued that she may be unable to realize that two thoughts have the same content without empirical information. In Falvey and Owens's example, Rudolf partially understands the terms 'coriander' and 'cilantro' and defers to experts for their correct explication. He knows that each term names a herb, although he is ignorant that they name the same herb. Rudolf knows cilantro as the fresh herb used in Mexican cooking and is familiar with its appearance and flavor. By contrast, he knows coriander as a dried herb and is again familiar with its appearance and flavor. In virtue of these facts, it seems that an anti-individualist would accept that Rudolf has the concepts expressed by 'cilantro' and 'coriander'. Suppose that he assents both to 'Cilantro should be used sparingly' and 'Coriander should be used sparingly'. Since 'cilantro' and 'coriander' have the same referent, Falvey and Owens argue that an anti-individualist should hold that Rudolf expresses the same concept by these terms, and that he expresses the same thought by the relevant utterances. However, since Rudolf is ignorant of the fact that the terms are coreferential, he is not in a position to discover that he expresses the same thought by these two utterances without using empirical information about how the terms are used. Thus, Falvey and Owens conclude, anti-individualism is incompatible with transparency of sameness of content (Falvey and Owens 1994, pp. 110–111).

If sameness of content is not transparent, a subject may fail to make a simple valid inference since she cannot realize a priori that it is valid. For example, suppose that Rudolf has two beliefs that he would express linguistically in the following way:

(1)   Coriander grows in Britain.

(2)   Cilantro grows in France.

If the thought constituents Rudolf expresses by 'coriander' and 'cilantro' have the same content, then there is a simple valid inference to the conclusion that something grows in both Britain and France.[1] However, since Rudolf is unable to realize a priori that the relevant thought constituents have the same content, he is unable to realize a priori that this inference is valid. To realize that it is valid, he needs to use the empirical information that the relevant constituents are coreferential.

Rudolf's inability to realize a priori that the relevant thought constituents have the same content may also undermine his ability to realize a priori that he has inconsistent thoughts. On the basis of two distinct articles, of which one uses only the term 'cilantro' and the other only the term 'coriander', Rudolf may come to have the beliefs he would express by saying 'Cilantro was known to the ancient Romans' and 'Coriander was not known to the ancient Romans'. However, he would not realize that these beliefs are inconsistent as he does not realize that the relevant thought constituents have the same content. To realize that these beliefs are inconsistent, he would need to acquire empirical information about his environment.[2]

Although the Rudolf case uses natural kind terms, it is applicable to singular anti-individualism. Further, since Rudolf understands the terms partially and defers to the experts for their correct explication, in principle, the case seems applicable to social anti-individualism and not just natural kind anti-individualism. However, care is needed in applying the argument to Burge's position, which combines social anti-individualism and the denial that synonymous terms express the same concept (Burge 1976, 1986b, pp. 115–117). Given this, one cannot show that Burge's position is incompatible with transparency of sameness of content by considering a subject who partially understands two synonymous terms. On Burge's view, the case cannot be developed into one in which a subject unwittingly expresses the same concept by two terms and can discover her mistake only empirically. However, we can demonstrate the incompatibility of Burge's position and transparency of sameness of content using an example of Segal's (Segal 2000, pp. 73–74). In Segal's case, a subject mistakenly thinks that a term that in fact has just one meaning has two meanings, a generic and a more specific meaning. (Segal uses the example to support the different conclusion that, whether or not there is a type of content that is socially individuated, there is also a type of content that is individualist.)

Suppose that Alf thinks that 'optician' has two meanings, denoting either any specialist in optics, or a specialist in optics who is commercially involved in the correction of people's sight. In fact, 'optician' has just one meaning, a specialist in optics who is commercially involved in the correction of people's sight. Further, suppose that, in all his uses of 'optician', Alf would defer to experts in his community for its correct explication. In some of his uses of 'optician', Alf, if asked, would give the correct explication of the term. Given this and the fact that he defers to the experts, the social anti-individualist should hold that, in these uses, Alf expresses the same concept by the term as the experts. In other uses, Alf would provide an incorrect explication of the term, for he mistakenly thinks that there is a second use of 'optician'. However, it seems that the social anti-individualist should hold that in these uses too, Alf expresses the same concept as the experts, for in these uses, he defers to the experts. In addition, his misunderstanding seems no more radical than, say, the misunderstanding of Burge's arthritis patient to whom social anti-individualists attribute the concept arthritis.

So, the social anti-individualist should accept that, in all Alf's uses of 'optician', Alf expresses the same concept as the experts. Now the experts express just one concept by their uses of 'optician', for 'optician' has only one meaning. As a result, all of Alf's uses express the same concept. However, Alf would suppose that his different uses of 'optician' express two different concepts. Further, he would need to gain empirical information about his language in order to realize that he associates the same concept with the two terms. Thus, it seems that social anti-individualism is inconsistent with transparency of sameness of content. This argument does not rest on the assumption that the experts associate the same concept with two synonymous terms: Alf's uses of 'optician' lead back to only one expert term and concept. So, it applies even to Burge's position, which combines social anti-individualism and the denial that synonymous terms express the same concept.

I have now outlined an argument for the claim that anti-individualism, whether natural kind, social, or singular, is incompatible with transparency of sameness of content. However, I will now show that the argument applies only to non-Fregean anti-individualism, and not to Fregean anti-individualism (these terms were introduced in chap. 1, sec. 6). Consider again the case of Rudolf, who is ignorant of the fact that 'cilantro' and 'coriander' name the same herb. Falvey and Owens argue that an anti-individualist should accept that Rudolf expresses the same thought by 'Cilantro should be used sparingly' and 'Coriander should be used sparingly', since 'cilantro' and 'coriander' are coreferential. However, they say, Rudolf cannot realize this a priori, since it is part of the case that he is ignorant that the terms name the same herb. Given Rudolf's ignorance, he could take different attitudes to thoughts expressed by sentences involving the terms. For example, he may dissent from 'Coriander is an herb characteristic of Mexican cuisine' while assenting to 'Cilantro is an herb characteristic of Mexican cuisine'. Recall that Fregeans individuate sense by potential difference of attitude: if it is possible rationally to believe that p and not believe that q, then the contents p and q are distinct (see, e.g. Frege 1892, 1980; Evans 1982, pp. 18–20; Peacocke 1983, p. 108; Campbell 1987, pp. 281–286.). Thus, Fregeans would hold that Rudolf associates different senses with the two terms although they have the same reference.

So, on this Fregean view, the case of Rudolf is not a counterexample to transparency of sameness of content, which states that, for any two thoughts, or thought constituents, that S entertains at time t, if they have the same content, then, at t, S can realize a priori that they have the same content. On the Fregean view, the relevant thoughts

have different contents. As a result, the Fregean anti-
individualist would deny that her position undermines a
subject's reasoning. Although Rudolf may assent to 'Coriander was known to the ancient Romans' and 'Cilantro was
not known to the ancient Romans', he does not thereby
express contradictory beliefs, for the concepts he expresses
with 'cilantro' and 'coriander' have different contents.
Further, although Rudolf fails to combine the beliefs he
would express by 'Coriander grows in Britain' and 'Cilantro
grows in France' to draw the conclusion he would express
by 'Something grows in both Britain and France', he does
not fail to draw a valid inference. On the Fregean view,
Rudolf associates different concepts with the relevant terms,
and the inference is not valid.

In conclusion, it is straightforward to show that non-
Fregean anti-individualism is incompatible with transparency of sameness of content. As a result, non-Fregean
anti-individualism has the consequence that a subject
cannot always grasp a priori that two thoughts are contradictory or that an inference is valid, even in simple cases.
By contrast, a Fregean anti-individualist would reject the
arguments for the incompatibility of her position and
transparency of sameness of content by appeal to the notion of sense. Before investigating the consequences of these
conclusions for rationality, let us consider whether anti-
individualism threatens transparency of difference of
content.

3   Transparency of Difference of Content

Slow switch cases have been used to argue that anti-
individualism is incompatible with transparency of difference of content (see, e.g., Boghossian 1992; Falvey and

Owens 1994; Goldberg 1999). Suppose that Sally is a member of the current Earth community and has the term 'aluminum' in her repertoire although she does not know the chemical composition of aluminum. Nevertheless, anti-individualists accept that in virtue of her interactions with aluminum and her membership of the Earth community, Sally has various beliefs involving the concept of aluminum, say, that aluminum is a metal, that it is gray, and that it is light. In addition, as a result of a school geography lesson, Sally has the belief she would express with

(1)   Aluminum is mined in Australia.

Even now, she can vividly recall the interesting lesson on Australia.

Now suppose that one night Sally is whisked off to Twin Earth unawares, where she starts interacting with twaluminum. Most anti-individualists accept that, after a period, Sally acquires a new concept. For simplicity I will assume that the new concept is the concept twaluminum. (There is disagreement among anti-individualists about whether she comes to have a twin or an amalgam concept. See Ludlow 1995b; Tye 1998; Heal 1998.) Along with other new beliefs, she acquires the belief that she would express with

(2)   Aluminum is mined in the Soviet Union.

This belief is based on Twin Earth newspaper reports about the Twin Soviet Union and involves the concept twaluminum. Since Sally is unaware of the switch, it seems that she is also unaware of the change in her thoughts. Although she has thoughts involving distinct concepts at different times, she would mistakenly suppose that they involve the same concept. Further, it seems that Sally could find out that the relevant thoughts involve different concepts only by using empirical information about the switch.

The case does not yet constitute a counterexample to transparency of difference of content, which states that, for any two thoughts, or thought constituents, that S entertains at time t, if they have different contents, then, at t, S can realize a priori that they have different contents. To provide such a counterexample we need to assume that, as a result of the switch, Sally not only acquires a new concept, but also retains her old concept. In fact, many anti-individualists would accept that, after the switch, Sally has two concepts that she expresses with the term 'aluminum', say, the concepts aluminum and twaluminum. In particular, they would argue that, after the switch, the belief Sally expresses by (1) involves the concept aluminum, whereas the belief she expresses by (2) involves the concept twaluminum. I will examine this two-concept view in more detail later (sec. 4). But, in outline, the view may be defended by arguing that the two beliefs differ in their causal and deferential connections (see, e.g., Boghossian 1992, pp. 19–20) and/or that it is part of the function of memory to preserve the contents of earlier thoughts so as to make them available at later times (see, e.g., Burge 1998). If the beliefs Sally expresses by (1) and (2) post-switch involve different concepts, then since Sally is ignorant of the switch, she would be ignorant of the fact that these beliefs involve different concepts. To find out that they involve different concepts, she would need to use empirical information. As a result of her ignorance, Sally would be mistakenly disposed to put these beliefs together in inference. For example, she might put the beliefs (1) and (2) together in inference to form the conclusion she would express by 'Something is mined in Australia and the Soviet Union'. In fact, this inference is a simple invalid one, but

Sally is unable to realize this without using empirical information and, in particular, the information that the relevant terms refer to different substances.[3] This argument for the incompatibility of anti-individualism and transparency of difference of content could be applied to anti-individualism about singular thoughts and natural kind thoughts, as well as social anti-individualism. Further, the argument applies to both Fregean and non-Fregean anti-individualism. We saw earlier that the Fregean would deny that her position leads to a failure of transparency of sameness of content. In particular, where a non-Fregean anti-individualist holds that a subject has two thoughts with the same content without realizing it, the Fregean invokes the notion of sense to argue for a difference of sense and thus thought content. However, the Fregean cannot use the notion of sense in a similar way to avoid the conclusion that her position undermines transparency of difference of content. If the concepts Sally expresses by 'aluminum' in (1) and (2) differ in extension then they differ in content, whether or not they differ in sense. The notion of sense might introduce further differences in their content, but it cannot be used to argue that the relevant thoughts have the same content. (In chap. 6, I apply the argument for the incompatibility of anti-individualism and transparency of difference of content to Fregean anti-individualism about perceptual demonstrative thoughts.)

It seems, then, that both Fregean and non-Fregean anti-individualism are incompatible with transparency of difference of content and may lead a subject to make a simple invalid inference that she can know to be invalid only by using empirical information. Thus, both views undermine the conception of a rational agent as one who would not make simple invalid inferences and can know the logical properties of her thoughts a priori. Given its implications for rationality, it is important to see if the anti-individualist can respond to the argument that her position is incompatible with transparency of difference of content. There are two main ways in which an anti-individualist might try to do so. First, she might reject the claim that, as a result of a slow switch, a subject acquires two distinct concepts that she expresses by a single word. On this view, the case would fail to show either that an anti-individualist should reject transparency of difference of content, or that she should accept that a subject may make a simple invalid inference owing to an equivocation of concepts. Second, the anti-individualist might accept that a subject may acquire two concepts as a result of a slow switch and thus that anti-individualism undermines transparency of difference of content, but deny that this would lead her to make a simple invalid inference. I discuss each of these possible responses in the next two sections.

4   Slow Switch and Conceptual Change

Some anti-individualists reject the view that, as a result of a slow switch, a subject may come to have two distinct concepts that she expresses by a single word. Instead, they argue that, at any point in the switch, the subject has just one concept, though a different one before and after the switch. Applying this view to the case of Sally, she may argue that, before the switch, Sally has the concept aluminum; after the switch, she gains a new concept, say twaluminum, and loses the old concept. I will consider several arguments against the two-concept view. We will see that whether an anti-individualist accepts the two-concept view in part depends on her account of thought content.

Tye (1998) argues against the two-concept view by claiming that the content of a memory is not determined by the environment in which the memory is formed, but rather by the environment at the time of recollection. He considers a case in which a subject, MT, spends his youth on Earth where he acquires the concept of water before being switched to Twin Earth. After he has spent many years on Twin Earth, MT attempts to reminisce about his youth, expressing his reminiscences thus (the numerals are added merely for convenience of reference):

(1)   Water is the only thing I now drink before 5 P.M.

(2)   Many years ago, however, I drank water fortified with gin in the afternoons.

(3)   I enjoyed those afternoons.

(4)   Water is improved by mixing it with gin.

Tye argues that MT uses a single concept, twater, throughout this inference, including (2), which is based on memories of MT's youth on Earth. If that is right, then MT misremembers his doings in his youth, misremembering events involving water as instead involving twater. If all of MT's memories have their contents determined in this way by the environment at the time of recollection, then, as a result of the switch, MT would lose the concept water and would acquire only the concept twater.

Tye takes it as granted that (1) and (4) involve the concept twater, for by stipulation, (1) expresses a belief about the current environment formed in the Twin Earth setting, and (4) is a tenseless belief. Tye then exploits the rationalizing links between (1)–(4) to argue that (2) also involves the concept twater. Tye says that (2) intuitively involves the very same concept as (1): (1) and (2) involve MT's comparing his drinking of the very same stuff in his youth and later life (1998, p. 81). Further, since (4) involves the concept twater, so does (2), for (4) is offered as an explanation of (3), but "[t]his would hardly make sense if what [he] really believed is that [he] drank water with gin during those afternoons" (ibid.). Again, Tye says, "it seems obvious that [he] cannot rationally offer such an explanation, unless [he] believes that [he] drank twater with gin on those occasions" (p. 84). Tye's example focuses on a water thought, but the argument could be applied to any version of anti-individualism.

However, Tye's argument against the two-concept view cannot be used to defend the compatibility of anti-individualism and transparency of difference of content, for it implicitly relies on the assumption of transparency of difference of content, namely that for any two thoughts, or thought constituents, that S entertains at time t, if they have different contents then, at t, S can realize a priori that they have different contents. Suppose, instead, that a subject could mistakenly suppose that two thought constituents have the same content. If that were possible, then Tye could not infer that (1) and (2) involve the same concept from the fact that the subject takes it that they do. Further, the subject could rationally offer (4) as an explanation of (3) even if (2) and (4) involve different concepts. Given that Tye's argument rests on the unargued assumption of transparency of difference of content, it provides no independent grounds for the claim that anti-individualism is compatible with transparency of difference of content.

Heal (1998) argues against the two-concept view in the case of natural kind thoughts by arguing that the concept a subject expresses by her use of a natural kind term at a time is fixed by what exemplars she would then regard as standard-setting; the term applies to x if and only if x is of the same underlying nature as the standard-setting exemplars. Consider a standard switch scenario in which a subject is initially on Earth and applies 'water' to samples of water. At this stage, the subject would select examples of water as standard-setting, and thus she expresses the concept water by 'water'. However, after she is switched to Twin Earth, Heal plausibly claims that the subject's standard-setting exemplars would include not only specimens from Twin Earth, but also some from Earth, which she might pick out using such descriptions as 'the stuff I swam in as a child', or 'the stuff the chemistry teacher poured out of the bottle labeled "distilled water" when I was at school'. Heal concludes that, after the switch, the subject would lose the concept water and gain an amalgam concept whose extension includes both H_2O and XYZ.

One could develop an analogous view for Burge's anti-individualism. On this analogous view, the concept a subject expresses by her use of a term at a time depends on which individuals she would then defer to for the correct explication of that term. Consider a subject switched between two linguistic communities, say the U.K. and the United States, whose linguistic practices diverge, although she is unaware of this. While initially in the U.K. and before the switch, it seems likely that she would defer to various U.K. experts for the correct explication of her thoughts. However, after the switch to the United States, she would start to cite U.S. experts as well as U.K. ones to explain the content of her thoughts. If that is right, then, the slow switch would not result in the subject acquiring two distinct concepts that she expresses by a single term. Rather, where U.K. and U.S. practice differs, say, in the meaning of 'chicory', she would lose the concept expressed in the U.K. with 'chicory' and instead associate with the term an amalgam concept that applies to the extensions of both the U.K. and U.S. terms.

Heal's argument against the two-concept view is based on a particular anti-individualist view about content individuation: the content of a subject's thoughts at a time, t, is determined by the samples (and possibly experts) that the subject herself would regard as standard-setting at t. However, many anti-individualists (for instance, teleofunctionalists and causal theorists of content) reject this view and instead hold that the content of a thought is determined by certain past factors, not by the subject's current dispositions. So, this argument against the two-concept view would not be accepted by many anti-individualists.

The idea that content is determined by historical factors stands in an interesting relation to the debate about the conceptual impact of a slow switch: it may be used to argue for or against the two-concept view. Consider the thoughts that the subject would express with the term 'water' after being switched to Twin Earth. Some of these thoughts are caused and sustained only by events on Earth, such as those based on memories of events on Earth. By contrast, others are mainly caused and sustained by events involving twater, such as thoughts formed on Twin Earth as a result of interaction with twater. If the anti-individualist treats all the thoughts the subject expresses with 'water' as of a single type whose content is determined by their causal relations then, after the switch, the subject does not express two distinct concepts with 'water'. Instead, the anti-individualist may argue that with 'water', the subject expresses an amalgam concept that applies to both water and twater. Alternatively, in virtue of the fact that water and twater do not form a single natural kind, she may argue that the subject fails to express any concept with 'water'. However, the causal view of content could instead be used to argue for the two-concept view. Suppose that the causal theorist holds that content is more locally determined, by the causal relations of particular thoughts considered individually, or by the causal relations of subgroups of thoughts. In that case, the causal theorist could use the different causal relations of the switch subject's thoughts to argue that some of the relevant thoughts involve the concept water, whereas others involve the concept twater.

A different way to defend the two-concept view is suggested by Burge, who argues that one of the functions of memory is to fix the content of a memory-induced thought to that of the remembered one. Thus, on his view, even after a slow switch, a subject retains her Earth concepts, and they figure in the content of certain thoughts based on memory. Burge's view may be motivated at least in part by the idea discussed above that content depends on causal relations (see Burge 1998, p. 359). However, Burge also motivates the two-concept view with his account of the function of preservative memory, which he defends independently of anti-individualism. Burge (1993) rejects the view that long demonstrations must include premises about what the subject remembers (e.g., I remember earlier proving that p; I remember reading the symbols carefully). He allows that substantive memory of particular events may be part of a demonstration in specific circumstances in which memory is called into question. However, he says, normally, memory functions merely to preserve past thought contents and make them available later, rather than to contribute premises about remembered events (1993, pp. 462–465). Burge justifies this view by appeal to the intuition that a demonstration, even a long one, can be purely logical or mathematical and need not involve possibly empirical claims about what the subject contingently recalls.

In this section, I have been considering whether an anti-individualist can deny that her position is inconsistent with the transparency of difference of content by rejecting the two-concept view of slow switch cases. Heal rejects the two-concept view on the basis of her account of content. However, this account would be rejected by many anti-individualists. The more popular view, that content is determined by historical relations, could be used to argue either for or against the two-concept view. In addition, the two-concept view may be supported by Burge's view of preservative memory. In conclusion, it seems that many anti-individualists would indeed accept that, as a result of a slow switch, a subject may have two concepts that she expresses by a single term.

5   Two Concepts and Inference

An anti-individualist who accepts the two-concept view may nevertheless argue that this does not lead subjects to make simple invalid inferences. There are two ways in which she could do so. First, she could argue that even if a subject unwittingly has two distinct concepts, only one may figure in a single piece of reasoning. Second, she could argue that, even if a single piece of reasoning may involve two different concepts, the relevant inference implicitly contains an identity premise, so that the inference is valid although the identity premise is false.

Burge argues that although a slow switch may result in a subject acquiring two distinct concepts, only one concept may figure in a single inference. Burge defends this view by appeal to his notion of preservative memory. As we have seen, one of the functions of preservative memory is to preserve the contents of earlier thoughts so as to make them available later. However, Burge also holds that preservative memory functions to tie together the concepts used in the steps of a single piece of reasoning. He says that a subject "holds constant, through preservative memory within the argument, the concept used in the first premise in her thinking the second premise" (1998, p. 367). He argues that this rules out the possibility that, as a result of a slow switch, a subject may make an invalid inference that she can know to be invalid only empirically.

To see how the function of preservative memory rules out this possibility, return to our earlier example of Sally who is switched from Earth to Twin Earth, which differ in the substance called 'aluminum'. While on Earth, and before the switch, she has the belief she would express with (1) 'Aluminum is mined in Australia', which involves the concept aluminum. After the switch she forms the belief she would express with (2) 'Aluminum is mined in the Soviet Union', which involves the concept twaluminum. From the thoughts she expresses with (1) and (2), she then infers the thought she would express with (3) 'So, something is mined in both Australia and the Soviet Union'. Although Burge accepts that, after the switch, Sally has both the concepts aluminum and twaluminum, he denies that both concepts can figure in a single piece of reasoning. He holds that since the first premise of Sally's inference involves the concept of aluminum, so does the second. If Sally's inference involves only the concept of aluminum, then the inference is valid.

However, I will now argue that the combination of views that Burge holds—that a slow switch subject may unwittingly have two distinct concepts that she expresses by a single term but that cannot both figure in a single piece of reasoning—is counterintuitive and poorly motivated. Burge's position has the counterintuitive consequence that the order in which a subject reasons may affect the content of the thoughts reasoned about. To see this, reconsider the inference that Sally would express with (1)–(3) above. The belief Sally expresses with (1) was formed pre-switch and involves the concept of aluminum. So, if Sally starts her inference with this belief, Burge holds that the second premise also involves that same concept. However, suppose that Sally had instead started with the belief she would express with (2). This belief was formed post-switch and involves the concept of twaluminum. So, Burge would hold that if Sally had started the inference with this belief, then the second premise would also have involved this concept. Thus, Burge is forced to deny the intuitively plausible view that what thoughts a subject entertains is independent of the order of her reasoning. This is not merely an ad hominem argument against Burge's particular position, but would apply to any position that combines the two-concept view with the denial that both the relevant concepts can figure in a single inference.

One of the standard motivations for the two-concept view is that it enables subjects to recall their earlier thoughts even after a slow switch (see Ludlow 1995b, p. 315; Gibbons 1996, p. 305; Burge 1998, p. 357). However, this motivation is undermined if the two-concept view is combined with the view that the relevant concepts cannot both figure in a single inference. On the combined view, even if a slow switch subject can recall her earlier thoughts "neat," she may not be able to do so in the context of an inference. In particular, if she starts an inference with a thought whose content is determined by the current post-switch environment, then this may lead her to misremember thoughts formed in the pre-switch environment. In addition, even when a subject can recall her earlier thoughts "neat," this is of dubious value: surely the point of memory is not to enable us to bring our past thoughts to mind merely to contemplate them, but rather to use them in reasoning in combination with other thoughts, past and present. We ordinarily assume that, if a subject can remember a past thought, then she can freely use that thought in inference; but the combined view denies this. Thus, one of the main motivations for the two-concept view—that it enables slow switch subjects to recall their earlier thoughts—is undermined when that view is combined with the claim that the relevant concepts cannot both figure in a single inference.

An alternative way of arguing that although the slow switch subject unwittingly has two distinct concepts, this does not lead her to make invalid inferences, is to claim that the relevant inferences contain an implicit identity premise. Suppose that Sally's inference contained a judgment identifying the two concepts that she would express with the term 'aluminum'. Then, even though the first and second premises involve different concepts, this does not lead her to make an invalid inference. Rather, the inference she makes is valid though unsound, since the identity premise is false.

The identity view contrasts with the alternative view that Sally merely relies on the putative identity of the concepts she would express with 'aluminum' through the inference, rather than making an identity judgment. If Sally merely relies on the putative identity, then her inference is invalid after all. So, we need to ask: what might motivate the identity view as opposed to the view that Sally merely relies on the putative identity?

It would surely be ad hoc to argue that it is only when a subject unwittingly has two distinct concepts that inferences that turn on the putative identity of concepts contain an identity premise. Certainly we cannot justify this restricted claim by using the subject's first-person perspective. It is part of the case that Sally is unaware that she expresses two distinct concepts with 'aluminum'. The inference she would express using 'aluminum' seems to her just like one in which the relevant premises genuinely involve just one concept. It seems, then, that the identity-premise view must be part of a more general view that a subject cannot just rely on the identity of concepts in inference; rather, the relevant inference must involve an identity premise. However, we will see that the idea that one can never rely on the identity of concepts through an inference leads to an infinite regress. (The argument is based on Campbell's argument for the related view that a subject must sometimes be able to rely on the coreference of singular terms in inference: see Campbell 1987, p. 276.)

Let us set aside Sally's inference concerning aluminum and consider instead an inference made by an ordinary non-switch subject. Suppose that Susan is an ordinary Earth subject who has never been switched and who expresses just one concept by 'water'. Further, she has never heard of anti-individualism and does not realize that changes in the environment can affect thought content. She makes the inference she would express thus:

(1) Water is clear.

(2) Water is good to drink.

(3) So something is clear and good to drink.

Since Susan expresses just one concept by 'water', the inference is valid as it stands. However, on the view that one can never rely on the identity of concepts through an inference, the inference implicitly contains an identity premise that Susan would express with

(4)   Water is water.

But, even with the addition of this identity premise, the argument still relies on the identity of concepts. In particular, it relies on the fact that the concept expressed by the first use of 'water' in (4) is identical with the concept expressed by the use of 'water' in (1); and, that the concept expressed by the second use of 'water' in (4) is identical with the concept expressed by the use of 'water' in (2). If one can never rely on the identity of concepts through an inference, the argument needs supplementing with further identity premises. But we have now started a regress. Any additional identity premise of the form 'Water is water' relies on an identity between the concept expressed by the first use of 'water' in this premise and that expressed by the use of 'water' in some other premise. If one is never allowed to rely on the identity of concepts, the inference must involve a further identity premise. But the same issue arises with any such further premise.

Someone might hope to break the regress by adding a different kind of additional premise, say, the premise that there is no conceptual equivocation between the first two premises, or that the concept expressed with 'water' in the first premise is identical with the concept expressed with 'water' in the second. However, it seems implausible that Susan's inference must contain any premise that involves the concept of a concept. Surely Susan could make a ground-floor inference about water without invoking a premise that involves the concept of a concept. It seems, then, that to block the regress without making implausible assumptions, we need to accept that a subject can sometimes rely on the identity of concepts used in an inference. But, this opens up the possibility that a subject may make an invalid inference through equivocation of concepts. This happens, as in the case of Sally's aluminum inference when, owing to environmental factors of which she is ignorant, she equivocates between two different concepts.

In conclusion, once an anti-individualist has accepted that a subject can unwittingly express two distinct concepts by a single term, it is hard for her to deny that this may lead the subject to make simple invalid inferences. The view that although a subject may have two distinct concepts, they cannot figure in a single inference, has counterintuitive consequences and undermines one of the main motivations for the two-concept view. In addition, it seems hard to motivate the view that an inference containing the two concepts must involve an identity premise, given that, in any case, we should accept that a subject can sometimes rely on the identity of concepts through an inference.

6   Rationality and A Priority

In the last two sections, I have argued that a great variety of anti-individualist views are incompatible with either transparency of sameness of content or transparency of difference of content and, as a result, undermine a subject's ability to grasp the logical properties of her thoughts a priori. In more detail, non-Fregean anti-individualism is incompatible with the transparency of sameness of content and has the consequence that a subject cannot always realize a priori that two of her beliefs are contradictory or that a certain simple valid inference is valid. A variety of anti-individualist views, including both those that reject Fregean sense and those that accept it, are incompatible with the transparency of difference of content and have the consequence that a subject may make an invalid inference that she can realize is invalid only empirically.

Some have taken it to be a serious objection to anti-individualism that it undermines a subject's a priori grasp of the logical properties of her thoughts, for, they say, this is incompatible with our conception of a rational agent. Boghossian (1992) claims that it is a key part of our intuitive conception of ourselves as rational agents that "the logical properties of the inferences we engage in must be judgeable purely a priori" (p. 17). Boghossian (1994) expands his account of what our intuitive conception of a rational agent involves:

What does a person have to do in order to count as a good reasoner? Clearly, it is not at all a question of knowing empirical facts, of having lots of justified true beliefs about the external world. Rather, it is a matter of being able, and of being disposed, to make one's thoughts conform to the principles of logic on an a priori basis. A surreptitiously envatted brain—transplanted from its normal adult body into a vat and attached to a computer that seamlessly duplicated and continued its previous course of experience—could be as good a reasoner as it ever was, despite the sharp escalation in the number of its false beliefs about the external world. . . . Since rationality is taken to consist in the ability and disposition to conform to the principles of logic on an a priori basis, any rational subject, regardless of his external conditions, may be expected to obey certain laws (or counterfactual-supporting generalisations): namely, those generalisations that mirror the introspectively obvious consequences of a person's propositional attitudes. (p. 42)

On Boghossian's conception, "rationality is taken to consist in the ability and disposition to conform [one's thoughts] to the principles of logic on an a priori basis." Anti-individualism undermines this conception of rationality by undermining the transparency of content. We have seen that if content is not transparent, then, even in simple cases, a subject may fail to make valid inferences, may have contradictory beliefs, and may make invalid inferences. If a subject needs empirical information in order to grasp sameness and difference of content, then she needs empirical information in order to grasp the logical properties of her thoughts. Boghossian concludes that anti-individualism undermines the notion that ordinary subjects are rational.

However, it is not clear that it is an objection to anti-individualism that it has the consequence that ordinary subjects are not rational in the sense Boghossian outlines (henceforth, *B-rational*), for anti-individualism gives us reason to reject the idea that ordinary subjects are B-rational by undermining transparency. No matter how sophisticated a subject's grasp of logic, if sameness and difference of content is not transparent to her, she will be unable to make her thoughts conform to the principles of logic a priori. Even the world's best logician would be unable to do so if content is not transparent. Thus, by undermining transparency, anti-individualism gives us reason to reject the idea that ordinary subjects are B-rational. Instead, anti-individualism suggests that we should distinguish two abilities—the ability to grasp a priori that thoughts specified as having a certain form have certain logical properties, and the ability to grasp a priori of what form one's thoughts are (Campbell 1987). Given failure of transparency, the anti-individualist argues that a subject could have the first of these abilities while lacking the second. For example, a subject may grasp a priori that an inference of the form "p, if p then q, q" is valid. But, if sameness of content is not transparent, then she may need to use empirical information to grasp that certain of her thoughts instantiate this form and thus constitute a valid inference.

The rejection of the idea that ordinary subjects are B-rational is also motivated by considerations that are independent of the truth of anti-individualism. There is much evidence that subjects do not always conform their thoughts to the laws of logic a priori. Subjects sometimes make mistakes in their reasoning, or have inconsistent beliefs, when only a little logical acumen is required to reveal the mistake. For example, recalling an earlier conversation with my partner, I may be disposed to assent to both 'Rupert is in London today' and (recalling reading the relevant page in his diary) 'Rupert is meeting Helen in her office today'. I may also believe that Helen's office is in Edinburgh, and that if Rupert is in Edinburgh today, then he's not in London. However, I may fail to put these beliefs together or notice the inconsistency. Psychologists have shown that even subjects of above average intelligence and education are systematically prone to certain kinds of mistakes in both probabilistic and nonprobabilistic reasoning (Wason and Johnson-Laird 1972; Kahneman 1982; Tversky and Kahneman 1983).

For example, Wason's famous selection task involves a deck of cards each of which has a number on one side and a letter on the other. Subjects are presented with four cards, each with only one side visible; they show 'A', 'K', '4', and '7' respectively. Subjects are asked which cards they need to turn over in order to test the truth of the rule: 'If a card has a vowel on one side, then it has an even number on the other'. Most subjects answered either that they needed to see both sides of the 'A' and '4' cards, or just both sides of the 'A' card. In fact they need to look at the 'A' and '7' cards. But very few subjects said they needed to see the '7' card. Further, a large number of these subjects found it hard to recover from their mistake. Even once it had been explained to them, they continued to make it in repeat trials, and some insisted that their original choice was still correct. Given this study, it does not seem that such subjects are able and disposed to conform their thoughts to the laws of logic a priori.

Owens has argued that transparency fails regardless of the truth of anti-individualism. It that were the case, it could hardly be an objection to anti-individualism in particular that it undermines transparency and so the idea that ordinary subjects are B-rational. Owens's most persuasive argument[4] starts from the fact that philosophers have disagreed over whether the following sentences express the same proposition:

(i) No one doubts that whoever believes that Mary is a physician believes that Mary is a physician.

(ii) No one doubts that whoever believes that Mary is a physician believes that Mary is a doctor.

Kripke and Church hold that (i) and (ii) express the same proposition, one that is true (Kripke 1979, n. 23, 45; Church 1954). However, Burge and Mates argue that although (i) is true, (ii) is false, and so they conclude that (i) and (ii) differ in content (Burge 1976; Mates 1952). This disagreement about whether the sentences (i) and (ii) express the same proposition can be used to argue that there is a pair of thoughts that each philosopher thinks although they disagree about whether these thoughts have the same or different content. Each philosopher believes that the thought he expresses when he utters either of these sentences is the thought expressed by the sentence in the public language (Falvey and Owens 1994, p. 113). This seems prima facie plausible, for we may suppose that each philosopher would correctly explicate each of the terms in (i) and (ii) and correctly understands how the meaning of each sentence is built up out of the meaning of its parts. If, by (i) and (ii), each philosopher expresses the thought expressed by the sentence in the public language, then there is a pair of thought contents that, say, both Kripke and Burge entertain, although they disagree about whether these contents are of the same or different type. Of course, one of these philosophers must be wrong. Further, Owens argues that introspection is not enough to determine which is wrong; empirical investigation is required (Owens 1989, pp. 305–311; Falvey and Owens 1994, pp. 112–113). Thus, either transparency of sameness or difference of content fails: either the pair of thoughts have the same content and one philosopher falsely believes that they have different contents, where this mistake can be corrected only empirically; or, the thoughts have different contents and one philosopher falsely believes that they have the same content, where this mistake can be corrected only empirically.

Let us now assess whether this argument shows that, regardless of the truth of anti-individualism, transparency is false. To do so, we must consider whether it is compatible with individualism to hold that all of Burge, Mates, Church, and Kripke have the thoughts expressed by (i) and (ii) while disagreeing about whether those thoughts have the same or different content. It might be said that this description of the case is incompatible with individualism, since a motivation for the Burge/Mates view that (i) and (ii) express different thoughts is Burge's anti-individualist position. This position combines social anti-individualism and the view that synonymous terms do not express the same concept. Social anti-individualism allows that a subject may have a concept without fully understanding it. For example, it allows that a subject could have the concepts doctor and physician although, because she misunderstands the concept physician, she sincerely asserts 'Mary is a doctor', but denies 'Mary is a physician'. Further, if 'physician' and 'doctor' express different concepts, then a subject might believe that Mary is a doctor but fail to believe that Mary is a physician. (If the two terms express the same concept, then it is impossible for a single subject to believe simultaneously that Mary is a doctor but not believe that Mary is a physician.) Thus anyone who accepts Burge's position should hold that (i) is true while (ii) is false and, thus, that (i) and (ii) express different thoughts.

However, although the view that (i) and (ii) express different thoughts is motivated by Burge's position, that view does not require that Burge's position is correct. Rather, a subject persuaded by Burge's views would hold that (i) and (ii) express different thoughts even if, unknown to her, Burge's position were in fact false. Holding that (i) and (ii) have different contents does not require that 'doctor' and 'physician' express different concepts, or that any subject actually has a concept while incompletely understanding it, but only that one accepts these claims. In particular, it is part of the case that Burge and Mates do fully understand the terms 'doctor' and 'physician'. They are motivated to suppose that (i) and (ii) express different contents not by incomplete understanding of any of the relevant terms, but rather by their theoretical commitments regarding synonymous terms and anti-individualism. Thus, individualism is compatible with all of Burge et al. having the thoughts expressed by (i) and (ii).[5]

It seems, then, that whether or not anti-individualism is true, psychological experiments on reasoning and the Mates argument show that subjects ordinarily judged rational may make mistakes about content and the simple logical properties of their thoughts, where these mistakes are persistent and not easily correctable. As a result, it seems that ordinary subjects are not B-rational: they are not disposed to conform their thoughts to the laws of logic. Thus, it can hardly be an objection to anti-individualism in particular that it has the consequence that ordinary subjects are not B-rational.

However, even if subjects are not B-rational, we still need a conception of rationality if we are to continue to assess reasoning as rational, or irrational, and to predict and explain action. In explaining and predicting action, we seem implicitly to use general psychological principles that mirror the laws of logic, for example:

If S occurrently believes p and occurrently intends to F if p, and if S has no independent reason for not F-ing, then S will intend to F or, at the very least, will be disposed to intend to F; and,

If a subject wants q and believes that if she Fs then q, believes that she can F, has no conflicting desires, and does not believe that there is a better way to obtain q, then S will be disposed to F.

(See Churchland 1970; Boghossian 1992; Fodor 1987; Millikan 1993.) Boghossian (1994) thinks that it will be difficult for an anti-individualist to reconfigure a notion of rationality to use in predicting and explaining action. He says that any adequate refashioning of the notion of rationality needs to reflect our intuitive distinction between cases of contradiction in belief and invalid inference where a subject is absolved from fault, and cases where she is not. Boghossian rejects two suggestions about when a subject is absolved from believing a contradiction: (1) when she doesn't or can't see the contradiction and (2) when the contradictory character of the proposition she believes is inaccessible to mere a priori reflection (pp. 42–46). He rejects (1) since, he says, irrationality often consists in not being able to see a contradiction. He rejects (2) since, he claims, if anti-individualism is true, any contradictory proposition will be such that its contradictory character cannot be accessed merely by a priori reflection.[6]

However, anti-individualism is in a better position than Boghossian thinks. Even if there are counterexamples to transparency, we may still be able to use the psychological principles outlined above as a guide to prediction and explanation.[7] As long as cases in which a subject unwittingly has synonymous terms, or unwittingly expresses two different concepts by a single term, are infrequent, then the psychological generalizations will still be generally true. Thus, we can continue to use these principles as a basis for prediction and explanation tempered by evidence about whether the subject realizes the relations of sameness and difference between her thought contents. The anti-individualist may also suggest a way of drawing the distinction between those logical failings for which we blame agents, and those for which we do not. It does indeed seem intuitive to say that Rudolf is blameless for holding contradictory beliefs and that Sally is blameless for making an invalid inference. By contrast, someone who believed that there is a single herb, cilantro, that both was and was not known to the ancient

Romans would indeed be rationally at fault; such a belief would indicate something wrong with her reasoning. One way to draw this distinction would be to say that a subject is blameless for having a pair of contradictory beliefs of the form a is F and a is not F if, were the question to arise, she would doubt or deny that the beliefs concern the same object. Similarly, we may say that a subject is blameless for making an inference that is invalid through a fallacy of equivocation if she would mistakenly affirm the relevant identity, were the question to be raised. These principles seem to separate clearly the cases Boghossian plausibly takes to be cases of blameless logical failing from those for which we would properly blame the agent: on being asked whether cilantro is coriander, Rudolf would either say he's unsure or deny it. And, were Sally to be asked whether the relevant beliefs she expresses by 'aluminum' concern the same stuff, she would respond affirmatively.

7 Conclusion

I have been examining the objection that anti-individualism is incompatible with the transparency of content and thus undermines a subject's reasoning. I have argued that anti-individualism of a variety of kinds is incompatible with transparency of difference of content, and/or transparency of sameness of content. More precisely, non-Fregean anti-individualism is incompatible with transparency of sameness of content and a variety of anti-individualist views, both Fregean and non-Fregean, are incompatible with transparency of difference of content. As a result, anti-individualism undermines a subject's ability to grasp a priori the logical properties of her thoughts. Thus, if anti-individualism is true then, even in simple cases, a subject may have contradictory beliefs, make invalid inferences, or fail to make valid inferences.

However, I have argued that it is no objection to anti-individualism that it has these consequences. Anti-individualism provides reason to reject the concept of a rational subject as one who is able and disposed to conform her thoughts to the laws of logic a priori. Further, regardless of whether anti-individualism is true, there is reason to reject the idea that subjects ordinarily judged rational are disposed to conform their thoughts to the laws of logic a priori. Despite this, I have argued that an anti-individualist can still regard psychological principles that mirror the laws of logic as providing useful generalizations for the purposes of prediction and explanation. I have also suggested that the anti-individualist can make sense of the distinction between those logical failings for which we blame agents and those for which we do not.

6   Anti-Individualism and Fregean Sense

1 Introduction

So far I have been assuming that it is possible to combine anti-individualism and the Fregean notion of sense, and thus that one can distinguish Fregean from non-Fregean versions of anti-individualism. Indeed, a number of prominent anti-individualists have accepted the notion of sense, for example, Evans, Campbell, McDowell, and Peacocke. Fregeans argue that we need the notion of sense to provide an adequate psychological understanding of agents. In particular, they argue that the notion of sense is needed to explain informative identity judgments, inferences, and belief ascriptions, and to avoid attributing contradictory beliefs to subjects. Fregean anti-individualists hope to take advantage of the Fregean explanations of these phenomena while also endorsing anti-individualism. Thus, the question of whether anti-individualism is compatible with Fregean sense is crucial for our psychological understanding of agents.

Some have argued that anti-individualism and Fregean sense are incompatible because they assume that whenever a subject thinks of something via a sense, or mode of presentation, she thinks of it via some description (see, e.g., Kripke 1980; Salmon 1986). For example, suppose that a subject is looking at a vase and thinks the perceptual demonstrative thought that that vase is pretty. A Fregean would argue that she thinks of the vase via a certain sense or mode of presentation. Suppose that this amounted to her thinking of the vase via a description, such as the vase that I am now looking at. In that case, the content of her thought is independent of the particular vase she is looking at. She would have the same thought in a counterfactual situation in which she sees a different vase, or merely suffers an illusion of seeing such a vase. Thus, on the descriptive understanding of sense, the claim that a subject thinks of x via a certain sense is incompatible with the anti-individualist claim that her thought is individuated partly by x.[1]

Those who have attempted to combine anti-individualism and the notion of sense have rejected the descriptive model of sense. They have developed instead the notion of an object-dependent sense, a way of thinking about an object that would not be available to be thought in the absence of that object (see, e.g., Evans 1982; Peacocke 1983; McDowell 1986; Campbell 1994). If the subject in our example were to think of the vase via such an object-dependent sense, then she would not have the same thought in a counterfactual situation in which she sees a different vase, or merely suffers an illusion of seeing such a vase: in such a counterfactual situation, the object-dependent sense that she uses in the actual situation would not be available. Thus, this different understanding of sense avoids the problems faced by the attempt to combine the descriptive understanding of the notion of sense with anti-individualism. However, in this chapter, I present a new reason for thinking that even the object-dependent notion of sense may be in tension with anti-individualism.

The argument turns on issues raised in the last chapter concerning transparency of content. Let me briefly summarize the conclusions established there. We saw that many varieties of anti-individualism undermine transparency, although Fregean and non-Fregean versions of anti-individualism affect transparency differently. The following two principles were central to the argument:

Transparency of sameness of content: For any two thoughts, or thought constituents, that S entertains at time t, if they have the same content then, at t, S can realize a priori that they have the same content.

Transparency of difference of content: For any two thoughts, or thought constituents, that S entertains at time t, if they have different contents then, at t, S can realize a priori that they have different contents.

We saw that non-Fregean anti-individualism is incompatible with transparency of sameness of content, and that Fregean anti-individualism is compatible with transparency of sameness of content. By contrast, it turned out that many varieties of anti-individualism, whether Fregean or non-Fregean, are incompatible with transparency of difference of content. If sameness and/or difference of content is not transparent, then a subject may make mistakes about the logical properties of her thoughts, mistakes that she cannot correct without empirical information. In the last chapter, I rejected the suggestion that since anti-individualism undermines transparency, it undermines the idea that we are rational subjects. I rejected the claim that it is part of the concept of a rational subject that, at least in simple cases, she can always grasp the logical relations between her thoughts a priori and so would not have simple contradictory beliefs, would not make simple invalid inferences, or would not fail to make simple valid inferences. In this chapter, I will leave aside the controversial issue of the nature of rationality, which, as we will see, is in dispute between Fregeans and non-Fregeans. However, the argument does use the results of the last chapter concerning transparency.

Here, I argue that the classic Fregean arguments for sense rely on the assumption of the transparency of sameness of content and a certain conception of rationality. That the Fregean arguments rely on transparency of sameness of content does not directly make it difficult to combine anti-individualism and Fregean sense. As we saw in the last chapter, although non-Fregean anti-individualism is incompatible with transparency of sameness of content, Fregean anti-individualism is compatible with transparency of sameness of content. However, I argue via a more indirect route that the Fregean argument's reliance on the assumptions of transparency of sameness of content and on a related conception of rationality makes it hard to combine Fregean sense and anti-individualism. The indirect route uses the notion of the transparency of difference of content. In the last chapter, we saw that many varieties of both Fregean and non-Fregean anti-individualism are incompatible with transparency of difference of content. I argue that it is hard to motivate the key assumptions of the Fregean argument for sense—transparency of sameness of content and the relevant conception of rationality—if one rejects transparency of difference of content. Thus, I conclude that there is a tension between anti-individualism and Fregean sense.

Section 2 begins the discussion by showing how the classic Fregean arguments for sense rely on the assumptions of transparency of sameness of content and a certain conception of rationality.

2   The Contrast between Fregean and Non-Fregean Anti-Individualism

Given that non-Fregean anti-individualists reject Fregean sense, they hold that the semantic value of the singular component of a thought is exhausted by its referent, if any. By contrast, Fregeans argue that there is a component of thought content not accounted for by non-Fregean anti-individualism, namely, sense. Recall that sense is individuated by potential difference of attitude:

If it is possible rationally to believe that p and not believe that q, then the contents p and q are distinct.

Consider the standard example of a subject, call her Celeste, who unwittingly has two terms for the planet Venus—'Phosphorus' and 'Hesperus'. She applies the term 'Phosphorus' to a bright star visible in the morning; she applies 'Hesperus' to a bright star visible in the evening. Fregeans argue that non-Fregean anti-individualism cannot accommodate various features of Celeste's cognitive life. As we will see, the Fregean argument depends partly on a conception of rationality that we rejected in the last chapter. However, I won't rely on that rejection here. Rather I will argue that, whether or not the Fregean conception of rationality is correct, it cannot be well motivated for someone who also accepts anti-individualism.

Consider the identity judgments Celeste would express by:

(1)   Phosphorus is Phosphorus.

(2)   Phosphorus is Hesperus.

The Fregean argues that, given that Celeste thinks that 'Hesperus' and 'Phosphorus' refer to distinct stars, Celeste would find the identity judgment expressed by (2) informative and that expressed by (1) uninformative. Certainly, if Celeste came to accept (2), this would be an important empirical discovery that would enable her to bring together a host of information about Phosphorus and Hesperus, which she previously kept separate. On the non-Fregean view, the thought constituents corresponding to 'Phosphorus' and 'Hesperus' have the same content and thus so do the thoughts corresponding to (1) and (2), for 'Hesperus' and 'Phosphorus' have the same referent. But, the Fregean asks, how can (1) and (2) differ in informativeness if they have precisely the same content? (Frege 1892, 1980; p. 80).

Second, the Fregean points out that, before discovering that Hesperus is Phosphorus, Celeste would fail to put Hesperus and Phosphorus thoughts together in inference. For example, suppose that Celeste has the attitudes she would express by:

(3)   Hesperus is clearly visible in the evening.

(4)   It is crucially important to make as many observations as possible of Phosphorus.

Celeste would fail to draw the conclusion she would express by:

(5)   It is crucially important to make as many observations as possible of Hesperus in the evening.

and she might fail to make any observations of Hesperus in the evening. On the non-Fregean view, the thought constituents corresponding to 'Hesperus' and 'Phosphorus' have the same content, and the inference is a simple valid one. But, given that Celeste is a rational subject, how could she fail to make such a simple inference? Third, Celeste would sincerely assent to the following sentences, providing strong evidence that she believes the corresponding thought contents:

(6)   Phosphorus rises in the morning.

(7)   It is not the case that Hesperus rises in the morning.

This suggests that the non-Fregean is committed to saying that Celeste believes a proposition and believes its negation. But, the Fregean argues that this is deeply implausible, given that Celeste is supposedly rational and a rational person would not have simple contradictory beliefs.

A last problem for the non-Fregean anti-individualist is that Celeste's behavior may appear to provide evidence for the view that she believes the proposition she would express by 'Phosphorus rises in the morning' and that she does not believe the proposition she would express by 'Hesperus rises in the morning'. Indeed, this is intuitively how we would describe her psychological state. On the non-Fregean view, these sentences express the same proposition so how can Celeste, being rational, believe the proposition expressed by the one sentence but not the proposition expressed by the other?

The Fregean concludes that non-Fregean anti-individualism cannot accommodate the facts about Celeste. Instead, she argues that the thought constituents Celeste expresses with 'Hesperus' and 'Phosphorus' differ in sense and thus content. The Fregean uses this difference in content to explain how Celeste can find the identity judgment 'Hesperus is Phosphorus' informative, and why she fails to put Hesperus and Phosphorus thoughts together in inference. Further, she can avoid the conclusion that Celeste has beliefs with contradictory contents, for on her view, the beliefs Celeste expresses with (6) and (7) do not contradict each other since they involve different ways of thinking of Venus. Last, the Fregean can accommodate the intuition that Celeste believes that Phosphorus rises in the morning but does not believe that Hesperus rises in the morning. Since the Fregean holds that different senses are associated with 'Hesperus' and 'Phosphorus', on her view, Celeste, while remaining rational, may believe that Phosphorus rises in the morning but not believe the different proposition that Hesperus rises in the morning.

The Fregean arguments for sense rely on two key assumptions: a certain conception of rationality and the transparency of sameness of content. We can see this by seeing how the non-Fregean can counter the Fregean arguments by rejecting both assumptions. Consider the argument that the non-Fregean cannot explain why Celeste, a rational person, fails to inferentially combine 'Hesperus' and 'Phosphorus' thoughts. Suppose that sameness of content is not transparent and thus that a subject may have two thoughts, or thought constituents, with the same content at a single time, yet believe mistakenly that they have different contents and be unable to correct her view without using empirical information. This would provide an alternative explanation of Celeste's failure of inference that is compatible with the non-Fregean view that the thought constituents corresponding to 'Hesperus' and 'Phosphorus' have the same content. On this rival explanation, Celeste fails to make the simple valid inference (3)–(5) since she does not realize that the relevant thought constituents have the same content and thus that the inference is valid. Further, she can come to the correct view only by using empirical information. On this view, her failure to make the simple valid inference (3)–(5) does not impugn her rationality, for even a rational subject would fail to make a valid inference that she does not realize is valid.[2]

Next, consider the argument that non-Fregean anti-individualism has the implausible result that Celeste, a rational subject, has beliefs with contradictory contents. The non-Fregean would respond by saying that this result would not be implausible if sameness of content were not transparent. In that case, a subject could have two thoughts, or thought constituents, with the same content at a single time, yet believe mistakenly that they have different contents and be unable to correct her view without using empirical information. As a result, she may easily end up with contradictory beliefs that she cannot see are contradictory without empirical information. Such contradictory beliefs would not impugn her rationality.

The idea that subjects may mistakenly suppose that two thought constituents have different contents also undermines the Fregean argument from informative identity judgments.[3] On the non-Fregean view that the thought constituents associated with 'Hesperus' and 'Phosphorus' have the same content, the relevant identity judgments cannot differ in their semantic information. However, the non-Fregean anti-individualist may attempt to explain away our intuition of a difference in informativeness. She may argue that, given the set up, Celeste would suppose mistakenly that 'Hesperus' and 'Phosphorus' express thought constituents that have different referents and contents. Further, Celeste could come to realize that the thought constituents have the same referent and content only by gaining empirical information. So, the judgment Celeste expresses with

'Hesperus is Phosphorus' has an important cognitive effect for Celeste—it leads her to bring together the information she previously associated separately with 'Hesperus' and 'Phosphorus'. These are the facts, the non-Fregean anti-individualist alleges, that the Fregean mistakenly takes as evidence that the thought constituents associated with 'Hesperus' and 'Phosphorus' differ in semantic informativeness and thus content (see, e.g., Millikan 1993, p. 335).

The claim that sameness of content cannot always be grasped a priori does not enable the non-Fregean anti-individualist to answer the last of the Fregean arguments, from opacity of attitude ascriptions. Recall that Celeste's behavior provides evidence that she believes the proposition she would express by 'Phosphorus rises in the morning', and that she does not believe the proposition which she would express by 'Hesperus rises in the morning'. On the non-Fregean view, the same thought is expressed by the two sentences. But, it is surely inconsistent to claim that a subject believes and does not believe one and the same proposition. One cannot overcome this problem by arguing that sameness of content cannot always be grasped a priori. Instead, non-Fregean anti-individualists have employed a number of other strategies, arguing that belief ascriptions claim implicitly or suggest pragmatically that a subject believes a certain proposition under a certain guise (Salmon 1986; Crimmins and Perry 1989); or that they implicitly involve reference to a sentence in the language (Carnap 1946; Davidson 1969). I will not examine the details of these responses here. My aim is not to determine which of the Fregean and non-Fregean explanations of the phenomena is preferable, but rather to examine whether the Fregean explanation is compatible with anti-individualism.

We can summarize the contrast between the Fregean and non-Fregean approaches as follows. The Fregean explains the facts about informativeness, inferential transitions, and apparently contradictory belief by arguing that the thought constituents corresponding to 'Hesperus' and 'Phosphorus' have different contents. Further, the Fregean's argument that non-Fregeans cannot account for these phenomena relies on two key assumptions: the transparency of sameness of content and a connected conception of rationality. According to transparency of sameness of content, for any two thoughts, or thought constituents, that S entertains at time t, if they have the same content then, at t, S can realize a priori that they have the same content. As a result, at least in simple cases, a rational subject can grasp those relations that turn on sameness of content, such as contradiction and validity, without using empirical information. Thus, a rational subject would not hold simple contradictory beliefs, or fail to make simple valid inferences.

As we have seen, the non-Fregean may counter the Fregean arguments by rejecting transparency of sameness of content. Instead of explaining facts about informativeness, inferential transitions, and putative contradictory beliefs by appeal to differences of content, she explains them by arguing that subjects cannot always realize a priori that two thoughts or thoughts constituents have the same content. Thus, on this view, a rational subject may have simple contradictory beliefs and fail to make simple valid inferences, for she is not always able to grasp simple instances of contradiction and validity without using empirical information.

It seems, then, that the debate between the Fregean and the non-Fregean turns on whether sameness of content is transparent and on the correct conception of rationality. The Fregean position is well motivated only if the assumptions of transparency of sameness of content and the related Fregean conception of rationality are well motivated. In the rest of the chapter, I examine whether these assumptions can be well motivated for someone who also accepts anti-individualism.

3   Fregean Anti-Individualism and Transparency of Sameness

In the last chapter, we saw that it is commonplace to argue that anti-individualism is incompatible with transparency of sameness of content. If these positions were incompatible, then anti-individualism would be directly in tension with Fregean sense, given that transparency of sameness of content is a key assumption behind the classic arguments for sense. However, in the last chapter, we also saw that the standard incompatibilist argument applies only to non-Fregean anti-individualism. Let us briefly remind ourselves of why this is so.

According to the standard argument, since a subject may be ignorant of the environmental facts that, according to anti-individualism, partly individuate her thoughts, she may be unable to know that two thoughts have the same content without empirical information. In Falvey and Owens (1994), Rudolf is acquainted with the terms 'coriander' and 'cilantro', although he is ignorant of the fact that they name the same herb. He assents to both 'Cilantro should be used sparingly' and 'Coriander should be used sparingly'. Falvey and Owens argue that an anti-individualist should accept that these two thoughts have the same content, for 'coriander' and 'cilantro' have the same extension. However,

Rudolf cannot realize a priori that these thoughts have the same content, for he thinks that the terms name different herbs. They conclude that anti-individualism is incompatible with the transparency of sameness of content (pp. 110–111).

A Fregean anti-individualist would agree that content depends on contextual matters of which the subject may be ignorant. However, in any case in which a subject unwittingly has two terms that in fact refer to the same object or kind, the subject could take different attitudes to sentences involving the terms. In the cilantro/coriander case, Rudolf may dissent from 'Coriander is a herb characteristic of Mexican cuisine' while assenting to 'Cilantro is a herb characteristic of Mexican cuisine'. Now the notion of sense is partly individuated by potential difference of attitude: if it is possible rationally to believe that p and not believe that q, then p and q have different contents. Thus, the Fregean anti-individualist would argue that although the concepts the subject associates with the two terms have the same extension, they differ in sense and hence content. Thus, the Fregean anti-individualist would deny that the example shows that sameness of content is not transparent, that is, that a subject may have two thoughts with the same content at the same time and yet be unable to realize a priori that they have the same content; on her view, Rudolf associates different thoughts with the sentences 'Cilantro should be used sparingly' and 'Coriander should be used sparingly'. It seems, then, that the standard argument for the incompatibility of anti-individualism and transparency of sameness of content does not apply to Fregean anti-individualism.

Nevertheless, it is useful to consider the views of a prominent Fregean anti-individualist, John Campbell, who seems to provide a different argument for the incompatibility of Fregean anti-individualism and transparency of sameness of content. Campbell (1987) argues that Fregean anti-individualism is incompatible with what he calls "transparency of sense." Since, for the Fregean anti-individualist, sense is one component of thought content, Campbell's conclusion might be taken to suggest that Fregean anti-individualism is incompatible with transparency of sameness of content.

Campbell combines anti-individualism and the notion of object-dependent sense, a way of thinking of an object that would not be available if one lacks a suitable relation to the relevant object. Campbell argues that sometimes a particular sense is made available to a subject in virtue of the fact that she perceptually tracks the object across time or across different sensory modalities. Such a sense enables the subject to think of the object in the same way across different times and sensory modalities. However, since a subject may think mistakenly that she has successfully tracked an object when she has not, she may suppose mistakenly that she is thinking of one object via a single sense although she is not. Thus Campbell concludes that his Fregean anti-individualist view is incompatible with transparency of sense.

Consider a subject who attempts to think the inference she would express with

(1)   That glass is F.

(2)   That glass is G.

(3)   So, there is something that is both F and G.

Suppose that the subject takes herself to be looking at a single glass over a period of time and thinking about it via a single sense. Campbell argues that if it is the same glass that is being thought about in the two premises, then they involve the same sense and the subject is correct. Now suppose instead that a clever switch takes place during the inference so that, unbeknownst to the subject, she is looking at different glasses when she attempts to think the relevant premises. In that case, Campbell argues, the premises do not involve the same sense and the subject is mistaken in thinking that they do involve the same sense. To realize her mistake she would need to use empirical information about the switch. Campbell concludes that the case shows that sense is not transparent (1987, pp. 281–290).

However, contrary to first appearances, the case is no counterexample to the principle of the transparency of sameness of content: for any two thoughts, or thought constituents, that *S* entertains at time *t*, if they have the same content then, at *t*, *S* can realize a priori that they have the same content.[4] Campbell's case is not one in which a subject in fact has two thought constituents with the same content, yet mistakenly thinks that they have different contents. Rather, the case shows that whether a subject is having two thought constituents with the same sense and content depends on matters outside the subject, and so a subject may think that she is having two thought constituents with the same sense and content, when she is not. As a result, a subject is reliable, but not infallible, about whether she is having two thoughts involving the same sense and content (Campbell 1987, p. 279).

There are two possible views about a case where a subject mistakenly thinks she is having two thought constituents with the same sense and content. On one view, apparently favored by Campbell, the subject suffers an illusion of thought: although it seems to her as if she is thinking the premises of an inference, she is not (ibid. p. 285). On a second view, the subject thinks two thoughts, but each concerns a different object. On this view, the case would constitute a counterexample to the distinct principle of the transparency of difference of content: for any two thoughts, or thought constituents, that S entertains at time t, if they have different contents then, at t, S can realize a priori that they have different contents.

Rather than objecting to transparency of sameness of content, Campbell argues that if two thoughts involve the same sense, then the subject knows that they are the same immediately: "[I]f, for example, one does succeed in keeping track of a particular wasp over time, or from sensory modality to sensory modality, and makes the judgements, 'that wasp is F', and 'that wasp is G', then one must know immediately that it is the same thing that is in question" (p. 285). Further, Campbell seems to endorse the idea that the validity of an inference should be obvious to a subject, not something that the subject can discover only by gaining empirical information about her environment: "[T]he form of a valid argument must do more than merely secure that if the premises are true, so too is the conclusion. The form of a formally valid argument . . . must furthermore make it possible for one who grasps it to move from premises to conclusion in a series of steps, each of whose correctness is individually obvious" (p. 277). Admittedly, Campbell accepts that a subject can suppose mistakenly that she is thinking a valid inference when she is not, such as in the switching example. However, he seems to hold that when a subject is in fact thinking a valid inference, this must be obvious to her.

Given the dependence of sameness of sense on environmental factors, a subject who is in fact thinking about just one object through an inference may wonder whether the premises concern the same object and thus whether the inference is valid. However, once the subject has raised this question, the subject could rationally take conflicting attitudes to the objects of the two premises. Thus, standard Fregean criteria for the individuation of sense show that she is thinking of the object by different senses in the two premises (Campbell 1987, pp. 284–285). Thus, Campbell argues, such a case would not be one in which a subject has two thought constituents with the same content but cannot realize a priori that they have the same content, nor one in which she makes a valid inference but cannot realize a priori that it is valid. Rather, it is a case in which she has two thought constituents with different contents, but wonders whether they have the same referent. Thus, such a doubt does not directly threaten transparency of sameness of content. (These comments reflect the Fregean rejection of the view that the inference "Fa, Gb, so something is F and G" is valid iff a and b are coreferential. Instead, Fregeans hold that the inference is valid iff a and b have the same sense as well as reference [see, e.g., Campbell 1987, p. 277]. For instance, Fregeans deny that there is a valid inference from the beliefs that Phosphorus rises in the morning and Hesperus rises in the evening to the conclusion that something rises in the morning and the evening. This Fregean understanding of validity is required if the validity of an inference is to be obvious to one who grasps it.)

In conclusion, one potential threat to the coherence of Fregean anti-individualism has been removed—the claim that, qua Fregean, it must endorse transparency of sameness of content but that, qua anti-individualist, it must reject it. The standard argument that non-Fregean anti-individualism is incompatible with transparency of sameness of content does not apply to Fregean anti-individualism. And, Campbell's argument that his Fregean anti-individualist view is incompatible with transparency of sense does not undermine transparency of sameness of content. However, I will argue that the coherence of Fregean anti-individualism is threatened in a different way: Fregean anti-individualism is incompatible with transparency of difference of content (sec. 4), but this makes it hard to motivate the key assumptions behind the Fregean argument for sense, namely, transparency of sameness of content and the related conception of rationality (sec. 5).

4   Fregean Anti-Individualism and Transparency of Difference

The last chapter established the conclusion that anti-individualist positions that accept the two-concept view of slow switch cases are incompatible with transparency of difference of content. Since I aim to use this result to show that there is a tension in Fregean anti-individualism, it is important to show in detail how the conclusion of the last chapter applies to Fregean anti-individualism and to attempt to broaden the range of anti-individualist views to which this conclusion applies. After summarizing the slow switch argument from the last chapter, I show how it applies to the kind of position characteristic of modern Fregean anti-individualism, Fregean anti-individualism about singular thought. I then use an argument due to Bryan Frances to show that transparency of difference of content is threatened not only by the two-concept version of anti-individualism but by any version. (Frances's argument that anti-individualism is incompatible with transparency of difference of content does not show that anti-individualism leads the subject to make mistakes in reasoning and so was not mentioned in the discussion of anti-individualism and reasoning in chapter 5.)

In the last chapter, I argued that the two-concept version of anti-individualism undermines transparency of difference of content. The argument concerned a subject Sally, who, as a result of a slow switch, acquires two different concepts—aluminum and twaluminum—which she expresses with the single term 'aluminum'. The concept aluminum figures in beliefs based on memories of events on Earth, such as the belief she expresses with 'Aluminum is mined in Australia'. By contrast, the concept twaluminum figures in beliefs acquired on Twin Earth, through interactions with Twin Earth speakers and twaluminum itself, such as the belief she would express with 'Aluminum is mined in the Soviet Union'. Since Sally is ignorant of the switch, she is ignorant of the fact that she expresses two distinct concepts with the term 'aluminum'. She could come to realize that she does so only by gaining empirical information about the switch. Thus, on the two-concept reading, the case is a counterexample to the transparency of difference of content: for any two thoughts, or thought constituents, that S entertains at time t, if they have different contents then, at t, S can realize a priori that they have different contents. Further, I argued that since Sally is ignorant of the fact that she expresses two distinct concepts with 'aluminum' she might make simple invalid inferences, say, from the beliefs she expresses with 'Aluminum is mined in Australia' and 'Aluminum is mined in the Soviet Union' to the conclusion that a single substance is mined in both Australia and the Soviet Union. To know that the inference is invalid, she needs empirical information about the switch.

Not all anti-individualists accept the two-concept view. However, the two-concept view may be defended on the widely held anti-individualist view that a subject's thought contents depend on historical relations, and by appeal to the function of memory (Burge 1998). Further, I rejected two ways of arguing that even if Sally expresses two distinct concepts with 'aluminum', this does not lead her to make invalid inferences: (1) Burge's view that even if she has distinct concepts, they cannot both figure in a single inference; and (2) the view that the relevant inference involves a (false) identity premise (Aluminum is aluminum) so that it is unsound rather than invalid. It seems, then, that any anti-individualist who accepts the two-concept view should reject transparency of difference of content and accept that a subject may make simple invalid inferences.

For the purposes of this chapter, it is important to note that the Fregean cannot use the notion of sense to avoid this conclusion. In particular, a Fregean cannot reply to the slow switch argument concerning transparency of difference of content in a way analogous to the way she replied to the argument concerning transparency of sameness. Faced with a putative example of a subject who has two thought constituents with the same referent and content but who fails to realize that they have the same content, the Fregean argues that the two constituents differ in sense and thus content. Thus, according to the Fregean, the example is not a counterexample to transparency of sameness of content. However, the Fregean cannot respond in an analogous way to a putative example in which a subject has two thought constituents with different referents and contents although the subject fails to realize this. The notion of sense may introduce further differences between the contents of the two thought constituents but cannot be used to argue that those constituents have the same content.

Given our concern in this chapter with the viability of Fregean anti-individualism, it is important to apply the slow switch argument to the type of view characteristic of modern Fregean anti-individualism, namely, Fregean anti-individualism about singular thoughts. Someone might wonder whether the slow switch argument applies to thoughts about individuals rather than thoughts about kinds, as in the aluminum example. In particular, she might wonder if the argument applies to those modern Fregean anti-individualist views, e.g., the views of Evans and Campbell, which endorse tougher requirements on thought than non-Fregean anti-individualist views. So, I will spend some time applying the slow switch argument to the Fregean anti-individualist view that when a subject thinks demonstratively about an object, the content of the demonstrative component of her thought is individuated by the object thought about and an object-dependent sense.

Suppose that a subject, Eve, takes herself to be looking at a particular apple and attempts to think the inference she would express with:

(1)   That apple is green.

(2)   That apple is from New Zealand.

(3)   Something is green and from New Zealand.

Consider a possible situation in which, between Eve's thinking of the first and second premises, someone substitutes a different but indistinguishable apple. Thus, when she attempts to think the thought she would express with (1), she is looking at apple *a*, whereas when she attempts to think the thought she would express with (2), she is looking at a different apple, *b*. The case would constitute a counterexample to the transparency of difference of content if, by (1) and (2), Eve expresses thoughts whose demonstrative components have different referents and contents. Since Eve is unaware of the switch, she would not realize that the demonstrative components differ in content, and she could realize this only by using empirical information about the switch. Further, on the two-concept view of the case, it is hard to deny that Eve would be disposed to make simple invalid inferences, say from (1) and (2) to (3). Recall, in the last chapter, our rejection of the two main ways of arguing that the two-concept view need not lead a subject to make simple invalid inferences. So, the key question is whether one should accept the two-concept view of the Eve case.

It may seem easy to support the two-concept view merely by pointing out that Eve is looking at different apples when she attempts to think the thoughts she would express with (1) and (2). However, the issue is less straightforward on some developed Fregean accounts that connect perceptual demonstrative thought with the ability to track objects over time and across sensory modalities. For instance, Evans and Campbell hold that if a subject perceptually tracks an object over a time period then she may think of it via the same sense over this period. However, they argue that, if she loses track of the object, then she fails to have a perceptual demonstrative thought and instead suffers an illusion of thought. On this view, it may be argued that since Eve loses track of the apples during the switch, she fails to think a thought corresponding to either (1) or (2). If that is right, then the case is not a counterexample to the transparency of difference of content: for any two thoughts, or thought constituents, that S entertains at time t, if they have different contents, then, at t, S can realize a priori that they have different contents. On the view suggested instead of having two thoughts with different contents, she suffers an illusion of thought. Further, on this view, Eve does not make a simple invalid inference, but rather suffers an illusion of making an inference. We could overcome this first problem for the two-concept view by modifying the Eve case. Even if the ability to think demonstrative thoughts is connected to the ability to keep track of objects, this surely cannot amount to the requirement that for a subject to think demonstratively about an object at a time, she must not lose track of it at any later time. This seems far too demanding. Instead, Fregeans should and do allow that a subject can think about an object if she keeps track of it over a substantial period of time, even if she later loses track of it (see, e.g., Evans 1982, pp. 195–196). So, we could overcome the tracking objection by modifying the case so that Eve tracks apple *a* for a sufficient period to have thoughts about it before the switch, after which she tracks apple *b* for a sufficient length of time to have thoughts about it. With this view in place, we could appeal to memory links to argue that, after the switch, Eve has the ability to think about both apple *a* and apple *b*. For example, Eve's thought that that apple is green is based on her memory of seeing apple *a* and is about *a*; by contrast, her thought that that apple is from New Zealand is based on her current perception of apple *b* and is about apple *b*. So, the view that demonstratives are connected with our abilities to track objects over time is compatible with the two-concept view.

There is another strand to Evans's thought, which would lead him to deny that even in the modified case Eve can think demonstratively both about apple *a* and apple *b*. As we saw in chapter 3, Evans argues that a subject can think about an object only if she can distinguish it from every other object. In the case of a spatiotemporal object, this requires that to think of an object, a subject must know

where the object is located, or know what it is for an object
so located to be the relevant object: "[A]n adequate Idea of
an object involves either the conception of it as the occupant
of such-and-such a position (at such-and-such a time), or
knowledge of what it is for an object so identified to be the
relevant object . . ." (1982, p. 149). Consider Eve in the modified case after the apples have been switched. It seems that
she can meet Evans's discrimination requirement for thinking about apple b, since she can, for instance, pick out apple
b. However, she no longer knows where apple a is located.
In addition, it seems that she does not know what it is for
an apple located at a certain place and time to be a. After all,
she is ignorant of the switch and falsely supposes that she
has been seeing just one apple over the entire period.[5] So,
Evans would deny that she can think demonstratively about
apple a and apple b. Thus, he would deny that the case is a
counterexample to the transparency of difference of content.

However, Evans's discrimination requirement has not
been widely accepted by anti-individualists. It is rejected by
those, such as causal theorists and teleofunctionalists, who
argue that the content of a thought is fixed by past historical factors, not the subject's current state and dispositions.
Evans's requirement has also been rejected by many of those
who hope to combine anti-individualism and the Fregean
tradition (e.g., Peacocke 1983, p. 171; Brewer 1999,
pp. 251–252). Thus, at best, Evans's argument shows only
that transparency of difference of content is compatible with
a narrow class of anti-individualist views, namely, those
that endorse Evans's discrimination requirement.

In conclusion, the slow switch case can be applied to both
non-Fregean and Fregean versions of anti-individualism
that accept the two-concept view. Fregeans cannot reject
the slow switch argument for the incompatibility of

anti-individualism and transparency of difference of content in the same way they responded to the argument for the incompatibility of anti-individualism and transparency of sameness of content. Further, we have applied the slow switch argument to the paradigm case to which Fregean anti-individualists apply their view, the case of perceptual demonstrative thoughts. We have seen how one can defend the two-concept view even if perceptual demonstrative thoughts are connected to perceptual tracking. Admittedly Evans would reject the two-concept view because of his discrimination requirement for thought. But this restrictive requirement would be rejected by many anti-individualists, including Fregean anti-individualists. Thus, it seems that many Fregean anti-individualists should reject transparency of difference of content and accept that a subject may make simple invalid inferences.

In section 5 I argue that there is a tension between the rejection of the transparency of difference of content and the key assumptions of the argument for Fregean sense, namely, transparency of sameness of content and the related conception of rationality. This tension is more problematic the wider the class of anti-individualist views that are incompatible with transparency of difference of content. So, it is worthwhile examining Frances's argument for the incompatibility of anti-individualism and transparency of difference of content, which is intended to apply to any anti-individualist view and not just to the two-concept version.

4.1   Frances's Einsteinium/Fermium Case

In Frances's example, a subject, say, Clara, is acquainted with the terms 'Einsteinium' and 'Fermium' and knows that each names an element. She is ignorant that they name distinct elements and ignorant of their chemical composition. However, she has such causal and/or deferential relations that an anti-individualist would accept that she has beliefs involving the concepts of these elements.[6] For example, Clara believes that Einsteinium is an element and that Fermium is an element. However, she wonders whether her two beliefs have the same content, since she is unsure whether 'Einsteinium' and 'Fermium' name the same element. After all, many elements high in the periodic table have had several names. Given that Clara's beliefs refer to different elements, they in fact have different contents. But, Clara can know that they have different referents only empirically by gaining knowledge either about the relevant natural kinds, or about linguistic practice. Thus, Clara can realize that the two beliefs have different contents only empirically, and transparency of difference of content is false. As Frances puts it:

[T]he beliefs are distinct according to any plausible view of belief, at least in part since the elements are distinct, but there is nothing in [her] experiential history that provides [her] with the conceptual resources necessary to discriminate between the Einsteinium and Fermium thoughts; introspective reflection is inadequate here. Thus, it is false that if thought A is not identical with thought B, then I can know by reflection alone that thought A is not identical with thought B. (1999, pp. 216–217)

Frances's argument has wider application than the slow switch argument for the incompatibility of anti-individualism and transparency of difference of content. As we have seen, the slow switch argument applies only to anti-individualist positions that accept the two-concept view of slow switch cases. Frances's argument has no such limitation. Given the way it is set up, Frances's case ensures that the concepts Clara expresses by 'Einsteinium' and 'Fermium' have separate causal and deferential connections. Given Clara's uncertainty about whether 'Einsteinium' and 'Fermium' refer to the same element, she would regard her Einsteinium beliefs as being correctly explicated by how the experts explain 'Einsteinium', and her Fermium beliefs as being correctly explicated by how the experts explain 'Fermium'. Since these terms refer to different elements, the experts would explicate them differently. Further, her uncertainty about whether the elements are identical prevents her from putting Einsteinium and Fermium beliefs together in inference and thus helps preserve their distinct causal histories. The distinct causal and deferential relations of her Einsteinium and Fermium beliefs undermines the suggestion, which may be made in the slow switch case, that the subject has only one concept, not two.

For instance, consider Heal's view, which may be used to argue against the two-concept interpretation of the slow switch case. On Heal's view, the concept expressed by a term in the mouth of a speaker at a time is determined by the samples and/or experts she would then regard as authoritative. We have seen that Frances's subject would regard her Einsteinium beliefs as being correctly explicated by how the experts explain 'Einsteinium', and her Fermium beliefs as being correctly explicated by how the experts explain 'Fermium'. Since the experts would explicate 'Einsteinium' and 'Fermium' differently, even Heal should agree that the subject expresses different concepts with 'Einsteinium' and 'Fermium'. It seems, then, that unlike the slow-switch argument, Frances's argument applies to any version of anti-individualism according to which content is individuated partly by the natural kinds present in the environment and/or by linguistic practices.

Given the broader scope of Frances's argument, if it could be applied to Fregean anti-individualism it would show that all versions of this view are incompatible with transparency of difference of content, not just the two-concept version. However, someone might think that Frances's case depends implicitly on a non-Fregean view. We need to rule out this worry to show that Frances's argument applies to Fregean anti-individualism.

At the core of Frances's argument is the claim that Clara may think that the concepts she expresses with 'Einsteinium' and 'Fermium' have the same referent and therefore the same content. This chain of thought is coherent only if Clara implicitly takes a non-Fregean approach to content. Clara need not have heard of the Fregean and non-Fregean positions or the philosophical arguments for them. Nevertheless, the relevant train of thought would not be coherently available if she took the Fregean position according to which two concepts may have different contents even if they have the same referent. On this Fregean view, one cannot justify the claim that two concepts have the same content merely by noting that they have the same referent. As a result, one might wonder whether Frances's argument can be non-question-beggingly applied to Fregean anti-individualism. Clearly, Frances's argument would beg the question against the Fregean view if it relied on the truth of the non-Fregean view. However, it relies only on a subject's accepting the non-Fregean view, whether or not it is true. Suppose that the Fregean view were correct and that the concepts Clara expresses with 'Einsteinium' and 'Fermium' differ in both sense and reference. This is compatible with Clara's accepting the non-Fregean view and thinking that the concepts may have the same content since they may have the same referent.

The Fregean may challenge Frances's argument in a different way by arguing that, on the Fregean view, Clara may realize that the concepts she expresses with 'Einsteinium' and 'Fermium' have different contents without using empirical information. On the Fregean view, the concepts Clara expresses by 'Einsteinium' and 'Fermium' differ in both sense and reference. Clara can find out that the terms differ in reference only empirically. But, perhaps, she can realize a priori that they differ in sense. If the Fregean is right in supposing that content is determined by reference and sense, then this view is presumably established by philosophical arguments. Clara could use those arguments to gain a priori knowledge of the existence of sense and that it is partly individuated by potential difference of attitude. Since it is part of the case that Clara is unsure about whether 'Einsteinium' and 'Fermium' name the same element, she could potentially take different attitudes to thoughts she would express with these terms. For example, she might assent to 'Einsteinium is rare' but fail to assent to 'Fermium is rare'. Clara can know a priori that she is unsure whether the relevant thoughts are about the same element and thus that she may rationally take different attitudes to thoughts about Einsteinium and Fermium. She may put these facts together with Fregean theory to gain a priori knowledge that the relevant concepts differ in content since they differ in sense.

The core idea of this Fregean response is that Clara can know a priori that the concepts differ in content by acquiring a priori knowledge of Fregean theory via philosophical argument. However, this response fails to take proper account of the fact that many subjects are ignorant of Fregean theory and even some of those who know Fregean arguments remain unconvinced by them. It is implausible to claim that if Frances's subject is ignorant of, or unconvinced by, Fregean arguments, then she can realize a priori that the relevant concepts have different content, since if she were to acquire Fregean theory she could do so. Let us consider some different examples. Suppose that I am faced with a problem that can be solved only by using trigonometry but I am ignorant of that theory. It is surely counterintuitive to say that I can now solve the problem in virtue of the fact that if I were to learn trigonometry I could do so. Rather, before I learn the theory, I cannot solve the problem. Or, consider a mathematician considering a problem that can be solved only by using differential calculus at a time before its discovery. It is counterintuitive to say that she can solve the problem since if she were to develop the theory of differential calculus she could do so. Rather, before she learns of differential calculus, she cannot solve the problem. I conclude that one cannot defend the claim that Clara can realize a priori that the concepts she expresses with 'Einsteinium' and 'Fermium' have different contents in virtue of the fact that if she acquired Fregean theory she could do so.[7]

It seems, then, that Frances's argument is applicable to both Fregean and non-Fregean anti-individualism. The argument does not depend on the truth of the non-Fregean view, but only on the possibility that a subject implicitly accepts this view. Further, the Fregean cannot adequately reply to the argument by claiming that, if the subject were to acquire Fregean theory by philosophical argument, she could use it to gain a priori knowledge of the difference in content. To strengthen the case that Frances's argument applies to Fregean anti-individualism, it is useful to apply it to the view typically defended by modern Fregean anti-individualists, namely, Fregean anti-individualism about perceptual demonstrative thoughts (earlier, we applied the slow switch argument to Fregean auti-individualism about perceptual demonstrative thoughts). To see just how wide an application the argument has, consider Evans's Fregean anti-individualist position. Evans places tougher requirements on having a thought than nearly any other anti-individualist, including Fregean anti-individualists. Thus, if Frances's example can be applied to Evans's position, it should be applicable to most, if not all, versions of singular anti-individualism.

Evans argues that a subject can think about an object only if she can distinguish that object from all other objects. In the case of a spatiotemporal object, this requires that to think of an object, a subject must know where the object is located, or know what is for an object so located to be the relevant object (1982, p. 149). Perceiving an object normally allows a subject to think about it, since it usually allows a subject to discover what type of thing it is and to locate it.

Suppose that Sally is in a concert hall listening to a live performance. The large symphony orchestra on stage includes four clarinetists. As Sally watches one of the clarinetists, she thinks the thought she would express with 'That clarinetist is beautiful'. While still watching the player, Sally hears a lovely clarinet solo, and judges on the basis of the sound the thought she would express with 'That clarinetist is musical'. Sally then wonders whether the two demonstrative thought constituents have the same content, since she wonders whether the clarinetist she hears is identical with the clarinetist she is watching. In fact, the two clarinetists are distinct. As in Frances's original example, the fact that Sally is unsure about whether the two thought constituents have the same referent prevents her from putting the relevant beliefs together in inference and thus helps to preserve their distinct causal histories. Thus, a causal theorist about content should accept that the two thought constituents differ in content.

Further, the example meets even Evans's tough conditions for thought. Each of the perceptual relations in which the subject stands suffices for her to identify the type of object in question (a clarinetist) and where the object is. For it to be a live issue for Sally whether the heard and seen clarinetists are one and the same, we must suppose that she has not yet located both of them. However, on Evans's view, that is compatible with her having demonstrative thoughts about each one; having a perceptual demonstrative thought about an object requires only that one is able to locate it, not that one already has (1982, p. 172). Thus, Sally has two thoughts, which differ in content. However, she may wonder whether they have the same content since she thinks they may have the same referent. She could come to know that they differ in content only by acquiring empirical information that they differ in reference. For example, she might watch the seen clarinetist to see whether her hands move in the appropriate way for the sounds she is hearing. (We saw above that the Fregean cannot argue that a subject can realize a priori that the thoughts differ in content by using knowledge of philosophical arguments for the existence and nature of sense.) Thus, Evans's anti-individualist account of singular thought is incompatible with the transparency of difference of content.

This discussion of Frances's argument shows that any version of anti-individualism, whether Fregean or not, is incompatible with transparency of difference of content. As a result, any version of anti-individualism should accept that even a rational subject may be unable to grasp certain simple logical relations between her thoughts without using empirical information. In the slow switch example, Sally cannot realize a priori that she has two distinct concepts that she expresses with the term 'aluminum'. As a result, she would be disposed to make simple invalid inferences. For example, she might combine the beliefs she would express with 'Aluminum is mined in Australia' and 'Aluminum is mined in the Soviet Union' to conclude invalidly that some substance is mined in both Australia and the Soviet Union. Since she cannot realize a priori that she expresses two distinct concepts with 'aluminum', she cannot realize a priori that the inference is invalid.

Frances's example establishes a similar conclusion.[8] Consider the beliefs Sally would express with 'That clarinetist is beautiful' and 'That clarinetist is musical'. Since the two demonstrative thought constituents refer to different clarinetists, they have different contents. However, Sally is unsure about whether the thought constituents have different referents and contents, and cannot realize a priori that they have different contents. As a result, she would be unsure whether these two beliefs can be combined together in a valid inference, say, to the conclusion that some clarinetist is beautiful and musical. To realize that the inference is invalid she needs to realize that the demonstratives have different contents. But, she cannot realize a priori that they have different contents. It seems, then, that any version of anti-individualism must reject transparency of difference of content and hold that a subject cannot always grasp a priori that a simple invalid inference is invalid.

5   Fregean Anti-Individualism

We are now in a position to consider whether the notion of sense is compatible with anti-individualism. In the last section, I argued in detail that any version of anti-individualism, whether Fregean or not, is incompatible with transparency of difference of content, the claim that for any two thoughts, or thought constituents, that S entertains at time t, if they have different contents, then, at t, S can realize a priori that they have different contents. As a result, any version of anti-individualism should accept that a rational subject cannot always realize a priori that a simple invalid inference is invalid. In addition, the slow switch case involves a subject making a simple invalid inference.

Earlier in the chapter (sec. 2), we examined the classic arguments for Fregean sense and saw that they depend on two key assumptions: transparency of sameness of content and a certain connected view of a rational subject. According to the transparency of sameness of content, for any two thoughts, or thought constituents, that S entertains at time t, if they have the same content, then, at t, S can realize a priori that they have the same content. According to the accompanying conception of rationality, at least in simple cases, a rational subject can always realize a priori that an inference is valid, or that a pair of beliefs is contradictory, and would not hold contradictory beliefs or fail to make simple valid inferences.

These results may make us wonder if it is coherent to combine Fregean sense and anti-individualism as the Fregean anti-individualist tries to do. *Qua* Fregean, the Fregean anti-individualist assumes transparency of sameness of content; *qua* anti-individualist, she denies transparency of difference of content. It seems curiously asymmetric for a single position to affirm transparency of sameness of content but deny transparency of difference of content. Furthermore, *qua* Fregean, the Fregean anti-individualist insists that a rational subject can always grasp a priori simple instances of validity and contradiction, but *qua* anti-individualist she accepts that a rational subject cannot always grasp a priori simple instances of invalidity. What could motivate the view that a rational subject can grasp a priori simple instances of some logical properties but not others? Last, *qua* Fregean, the Fregean anti-individualist insists that a rational subject would make simple valid inferences and would not have contradictory beliefs but, *qua* anti-individualist, allows that a rational subject may make simple invalid inferences. What could motivate the view that a rational subject could make only one of these sorts of simple logical mistake?

Someone might wonder whether the claims made by Fregean anti-individualism are logically compatible. If they were incompatible, then this would provide a quick route to the conclusion I am defending, that there is a tension in combining anti-individualism and Fregean sense. Consider the combination of affirming transparency of sameness of content but denying transparency of difference of content. Transparency of sameness of content and transparency of difference of content make claims about different kinds of case: transparency of sameness of content makes a claim about cases where a subject has two thoughts with the same content; transparency of difference of content makes a claim about cases where a subject has two thoughts with different contents. Given this distinction, it is not straightforwardly incompatible to hold transparency of sameness of content but deny transparency of difference of content.[9] Assume transparency of difference of content is false, and thus that a subject may have two thoughts with different contents at a single time, although she cannot realize this a priori. It does not follow that transparency of sameness of content is false, and that a subject may have two thoughts with the same content at a single time, while being unable to realize this a priori. An analogy may help. Suppose that S is red/green color-blind and cannot distinguish red and green, although she is ignorant of her condition. It follows that, in some cases where S looks at two samples, each of a different color, she falsely believes that they are the same. It does not follow that there are any cases where she looks at two samples of the same color and judges falsely that they are different colors.

Similarly, it is not inconsistent to hold that a rational subject can always grasp a priori simple cases of validity and contradiction, but cannot always grasp a priori simple instances of invalidity. Since these claims concern different types of case they are not directly incompatible. Suppose that a subject supposes that a simple inference is valid when it is invalid, and that she cannot correct this mistake except empirically. It does not follow that there is a simple valid inference that she mistakenly supposes to be invalid where she can correct her mistake only empirically. Even if a subject sometimes thinks mistakenly that an invalid inference is valid, it does not follow that she ever thinks that a valid inference is invalid.

However, even if the commitments of the Fregean notion of sense and anti-individualism are not logically incompatible, they seem to be in tension. Since transparency of sameness of content and the accompanying notion of rationality are key assumptions of the classic Fregean arguments for sense, those arguments are well motivated only to the extent that these assumptions are. But it is hard to see how these assumptions could be well motivated for an anti-individualist. How could one motivate transparency of sameness of content if one denies transparency of difference of content? Why should someone suppose that sameness of content is always graspable a priori even if difference of content is not?

The Fregean anti-individualist insists that a rational subject can always grasp a priori simple instances of validity and contradiction. In the last chapter, I rejected this conception of a rational subject on grounds independent of the debate between individualism and anti-individualism. I am setting aside that objection here. Rather, I suggest that whether or not the Fregean conception of rationality is correct, it is hard to motivate if one also accepts anti-individualism: *qua* Fregean, the Fregean anti-individualist insists that a rational subject can always grasp a priori simple instances of validity and contradiction, but *qua* anti-individualist she accepts that a rational subject cannot always grasp a priori simple instances of invalidity. But what could motivate the view that it is part of the concept of a rational subject that she can grasp a priori simple instances of some logical properties if one accepts that she cannot grasp a priori equally simple instances of other logical properties? What could motivate the idea that a rational agent can always grasp simple instances of, say, validity, but not equally simple instances of invalidity? To put it slightly differently: *qua* Fregean, the Fregean anti-individualist insists that a rational subject would make simple valid inferences and would not have contradictory beliefs but, *qua* anti-individualist, she allows that a rational subject may make simple invalid inferences. But what could motivate the claim that it is part of the concept of a rational agent that she cannot make certain kinds of simple logical mistake, if one already allows that she can make other equally simple logical mistakes? What could motivate the view that a rational subject cannot have simple contradictory beliefs, if one already accepts that she may make equally simple invalid inferences?[10]

It seems, then, that Fregean sense and anti-individualism are in tension. The standard arguments for Fregean sense rely on assumptions about transparency and rationality that are hard to motivate if one also accepts anti-individualism. Notice that these problems do not arise for non-Fregean anti-individualism. As we have seen, the non-Fregean takes a symmetric attitude to transparency, denying both transparency of sameness and transparency of difference of content. As a result, the non-Fregean holds that a rational subject may be unable to grasp a priori simple instances of contradiction, validity, and invalidity. Further, non-Fregeans accept that a rational subject may make simple logical mistakes of a variety of kinds including making invalid inferences, forming contradictory beliefs, and failing to make valid inferences.

This completes the discussion in this chapter and the last chapter of how anti-individualism affects a subject's ability to reason. We have seen that all varieties of anti-individualism undermine transparency, although Fregean and non-Fregean versions of anti-individualism affect transparency differently. Fregean anti-individualism is compatible with transparency of sameness of content, whereas non-Fregean anti-individualism is not. Both Fregean and non-Fregean anti-individualism are incompatible with transparency of difference of content. Thus, anti-individualism of any sort has the result that a subject cannot always grasp a priori some of the simple logical relations between her thoughts. Some have taken this to show that anti-individualism undermines the idea that we are rational subjects. In the last chapter, I defended anti-individualism against this objection by arguing against the conception of a rational subject as one who can always grasp a priori simple instances of logical relations between her thoughts. In this chapter, I have set aside this conclusion about rationality and argued on independent grounds that there is a tension between Fregean sense and anti-individualism. If we cannot combine anti-individualism with the Fregean approach to psychological explanation, then we face a stark choice between anti-individualism and the Fregean explanation of key psychological data; those who are persuaded by the Fregean arguments for sense should reject anti-individualism.

7 The Reductio Argument: Transmission of Warrant

1 Introduction

Here, we return to the question of whether anti-individualism is compatible with privileged access, the view that a subject can have a priori knowledge of her thought contents. Unlike her knowledge of others' thoughts, a subject's knowledge of her own thoughts is typically not based on behavioral evidence. Further, although empirical investigation is used to form beliefs about the world, for example, whether Edinburgh is north of Glasgow, once a belief is formed one can know that one has a certain belief without further empirical investigation. Certainly, knowledge of one's thoughts does not depend on empirical investigation into those aspects of one's environment that anti-individualists claim partly individuate one's thoughts, such as the chemical composition of substances, and the practices of one's linguistic community. (Of course, a subject's knowledge of her own conscious thoughts is based on those thoughts. However, throughout the book I have been following a well-established use of "a priori" on which knowledge may be a priori even though based on conscious thoughts. By contrast, knowledge based on perceptual experience of the external world is empirical [see chap. 1, sec. 7.])

In the first part of the book we examined but rejected one problem for compatibility, the problem of how one can have privileged access to thought contents that are externally individuated. To put it in more detail, how can one have privileged access to one's thoughts if what thoughts one has, and indeed whether one has a thought at all, depends on environmental facts of which one may be ignorant? Following Davies (1998), we may call this the *achievement problem*. By contrast, this chapter and the next focus on what Davies calls the *consequence problem*, the problem of what consequences follow from the joint assumptions of anti-individualism and privileged access. The achievement and consequence problems are distinct. Even if, as suggested in chapter 4, the achievement problem can be solved, the consequence problem might raise a further problem for compatibility. Conversely, even if the consequence problem presents no objection to compatibilism, the achievement problem might do so. Here I examine only the consequence problem and leave the achievement problem aside.

To illustrate the consequence problem, consider natural kind anti-individualism. Suppose that Sally is an adult Earth subject who has interacted with water but is ignorant of its chemical composition. Natural kind anti-individualists claim that despite her ignorance Sally has the concept of water and has various beliefs involving that concept, such as that water is wet, that her environment contains water, and so on. Further, in virtue of their empirical grounding, many of these beliefs are also cases of empirical knowledge; for instance, she knows empirically that her environment contains water. According to the assumption of privileged access, a subject can have a priori knowledge of her thought contents. Thus, Sally can have a priori knowledge that she thinks that water is wet. According to anti-individualism, whether a subject has certain concepts depends partly on her environment. Some have argued that it follows from anti-individualism that a subject who is ignorant of the chemical composition of water can have the concept of water only if she is in a certain kind of environment. As we will see in the next chapter, there has been some debate about precisely what entailments from thought to the environment anti-individualism is committed to. But, for simplicity, assume that Sally can have the concept of water only if water exists in her environment (or has existed; I will leave this qualification implicit in what follows).

It has been further argued that, since anti-individualism is a philosophical theory established using philosophical arguments, a subject could use those arguments to gain a priori knowledge of anti-individualism and its consequences. If that is right, then Sally can know a priori that if she thinks that water is wet, then her environment contains water. But, then, Sally could combine this knowledge with her a priori knowledge of her thought content to gain a priori knowledge that her environment contains water. Thus, the assumptions of privileged access and anti-individualism seem to show that Sally can have a priori knowledge of the nature of her environment, that it contains water.

We have already seen that Sally has empirical knowledge that her environment contains water. But it seems strange indeed that she could also have an a priori route to knowledge of this fact. Surely, a subject can know that her environment contains a particular natural kind only by empirical investigation. For example, surely one could know whether a certain country contains reserves of natural gas only by empirical investigation. If it is indeed absurd that Sally could have a priori knowledge that her environment contains water, then the above line of reasoning constitutes a reductio of the joint assumptions of anti-individualism and privileged access (McKinsey 1991; Brown 1995; Boghossian 1997; Davies 1998, 2000; Wright 2000). We can formulate the main steps of the argument as follows:

(R1)   Sally can know a priori that she thinks that water is wet. *(From the assumption of privileged access.)*

(R2)   Sally can know a priori that if she thinks that water is wet, then her environment contains water. *(From the assumption of anti-individualism.)*

(R3)   Sally can know a priori that her environment contains water. *(From (R1) and (R2).)*

(R4)   But (R3) is absurd.

(R5)   So, anti-individualism and privileged access are incompatible. *(From (R1)–(R4).)*

Although I have stated the argument using the notion of a priori knowledge, it could be formulated independently of this notion: if it is both the case that anti-individualism is true and a subject can have introspective knowledge of her thought contents, then a subject could gain knowledge of substantive facts about the world merely by reflection on her thought contents and thinking through the philosophical arguments for anti-individualism. But, surely, it's implausible that a subject could have knowledge, say, that her environment contains a certain natural kind just by reflection on her thoughts and a bit of philosophy or, as Davies puts it, merely by "armchair reflection" (Davies 2000, p. 386). Those who prefer not to term a subject's knowledge of her own thoughts "a priori" should rephrase the following discussion as suggested. Someone might challenge (R1) arguing that it is undermined by the anti-individualism underlying (R2). In particular, they may say, how can Sally know a priori that she thinks that water is wet when, by (R2), her having this thought requires the empirical fact that her environment contains water? This worry is misguided in two ways. First, (R1) follows from one of the assumptions of the argument, the assumption of privileged access. Second, the worry seems to be merely a restatement of the achievement problem: how can a subject have privileged access to the contents of thoughts that are externally individuated? But, we have already seen that the achievement problem is irrelevant to the consequence problem, which merely considers what consequences would follow if anti-individualism and privileged access were both true. It is silent about whether the achievement problem has been solved: it merely asks us to assume both privileged access and anti-individualism for the purposes of reductio. In any case, note that doubt about the cotenability of (R1) and (R2) cannot be used as a way of defending the compatibility of anti-individualism and privileged access.

Someone might question whether (R2) follows from the assumption of anti-individualism. First, she might question whether anti-individualism supports any entailment between thought and the environment that is suitable for the argument. I will examine this response in the next chapter. Second, even if anti-individualism does support such an entailment, she might question whether it's knowable a priori. After all, not all subjects have heard of anti-individualism, let alone know the philosophical arguments for this position. However, some subjects do have such knowledge, and let us suppose that Sally is one of them. It would be problematic if a subject with knowledge of the philosophical arguments for anti-individualism could use them to gain a priori knowledge of her environment even if a subject ignorant of those arguments could not do so. Another main line of response has been to deny (R4) and argue that it is not absurd to suppose that Sally can have a priori knowledge that her environment contains water. This line of thought is often supported by pointing out that Sally already has empirical knowledge that her environment contains water (see, e.g., Sawyer 1998, p. 532; Brewer 1999, p. 267; DeRose 2000). If it is not absurd that Sally could come to have a priori knowledge of her environment, then it is not an objection to compatibilism that it has this consequence. Rather, it might be an advantage. If Sally can know a priori that her environment contains water, it seems that she can also know a priori that there is an external world. Thus, on this alternative view, compatibilism would provide an answer to skeptics who claim that we cannot have knowledge of the nature and existence of the external world (Warfield, 1994 1998; Sawyer 1998).

However, the suggestion that it is not absurd to suppose that subjects can have a priori knowledge of substantive facts about the environment is unconvincing. Consider the point that compatibilism would enable a subject to gain a priori knowledge only of propositions of which she already has empirical knowledge. As Davies points out, it was part of the set up of the argument that Sally already knows that her environment contains water on empirical grounds. Despite this, it seems problematic to suppose that, in addition, Sally has an a priori route to this same claim. Compare the case of natural gas: even if someone has empirical knowledge that a certain country has reserves of natural gas, it seems problematic to suppose that she also has an a priori route to knowledge of this fact. Thus, in what follows, I take it that it is indeed absurd to suppose that Sally can have a priori knowledge that her environment contains water. The discussion in this chapter concentrates on a fourth line of response offered by Davies and Wright. They agree that it is absurd to suppose that Sally can have a priori knowledge of her environment, but, they argue, the joint assumptions of anti-individualism and privileged access do not have this result. They claim that (R3) does not follow from (R1) and (R2), arguing that even if a subject has a priori knowledge of her thought contents and that her having those thought contents requires certain facts about her environment, this does not enable her to gain a priori knowledge of her environment.

In the following sections, I situate Davies's and Wright's view by contrasting it with the denial of the closure of knowledge. I then present and criticize several reasons for claiming that warrant and so knowledge fail to transmit across the inference relevant to the reductio. Although my discussion of Wright and Davies treats the Sally argument as a threat to compatibilism, it is also relevant to the rival view that the argument shows that anti-individualism and privileged access can together provide a response to skepticism: both ways of taking the argument assume that Sally can gain a priori knowledge of the world by combining her a priori knowledge of her thought contents and her a priori knowledge that her having those thought contents entails certain facts about her environment.

2   Closure and Transmission

As we have seen, Davies and Wright challenge the reductio by arguing that even if a subject has a priori knowledge that she thinks that water is wet and that her thinking that water is wet entails that her environment contains water, this does not enable her to gain a priori knowledge that her environment contains water. It is useful to present Davies's and Wright's view by focusing on the following simpler argument, which I will call the *water argument*:

(W1)   I think that water is wet.

(W2)   If I think that water is wet, then my environment contains water.

(W3)   My environment contains water.

In effect, Davies and Wright argue that even if Sally has a priori knowledge of (W1) and (W2) she cannot thereby gain a priori knowledge of (W3). Davies's and Wright's view may seem counterintuitive. The inference from (W1) to (W3) is a simple valid inference of the form: p, if p then q, q. But surely one can gain knowledge by thinking through a valid argument. Davies and Wright accept that one can often gain knowledge by thinking through a valid argument. However, they claim that this is not always the case.

Nozick and Dretske famously argued that one cannot always use a valid argument to gain knowledge of its conclusion. Consider the following inference:

(BIV1)   I see a table in front of me.

(BIV2)   If I see a table in front of me, then it's not the case that I have just become a BIV.[1]

(BIV3)   It's not the case that I have just become a BIV.

Suppose that a subject is in ordinary circumstances and seems to see a table in front of her. We would ordinarily suppose that her experience gives her warrant and knowledge of (BIV1). Further, it seems that she can know (BIV2) merely by some minimal conceptual analysis. However, Nozick (1981) argues that even if a subject knows (BIV1) and (BIV2) she does not know (BIV3). On his account of knowledge, S knows that p only if, were p false, she would not believe that p. However, if the subject had just become a BIV, then she would still believe that she has not just become a BIV. Thus, Nozick denies the closure of knowledge, the claim that whenever a subject knows the premises of a valid argument and believes in its conclusion on the basis of her recognition of its validity, her belief in the conclusion constitutes knowledge.[2] Dretske (1970) similarly argues that the following inference is a counterexample to the closure of knowledge:

(Z1)   The animal in the pen is a zebra.

(Z2)   If the animal in the pen is a zebra, then it is not a disguised mule.

(Z3)   The animal in the pen is not a disguised mule.

However, the denial of closure cannot be used to support the Davies/Wright response to the reductio argument. It is implausible to claim that even if Sally has knowledge of (W1) and (W2), she lacks knowledge of (W3). According to the anti-individualist view that is the target of the reductio, Sally has the concept of water in virtue of her past interactions with water; she has drunk it, showered in it, swum in it, and so on. These seem just the right kind of interactions to give her empirical knowledge that water exists. Thus, if Sally has had the kind of empirical interactions required for her to have the concept water and thus entertain the premises (W1) and (W2), she has empirical knowledge of (W3), that her environment contains water. Relatedly, Sally's belief that her environment contains water does meet Nozick's necessary condition for knowledge. Given the anti-individualist view that is the target of the reductio, if Sally's environment did not contain water, then she would lack the concept of water and thus would not believe that her environment contains water.

Davies and Wright defend a more limited claim than Nozick and Dretske. Roughly, instead of arguing that there are cases in which someone knows the premises of an argument but fails to know its conclusion, they argue that there are cases in which someone knows the premises but fails to know the conclusion in one particular way—by inference from the premises. More precisely, they argue that the water argument is a counterexample to the transmission of knowledge, the claim that whenever a subject knows the premises of a valid argument and believes its conclusion on the basis of her recognition of its validity, her belief in the conclusion thereby constitutes knowledge.[3] The main difference between closure and transmission is that the closure principle makes no claim about what makes the subject's belief in the conclusion knowledge, whereas the transmission principle claims that her belief in the conclusion constitutes knowledge in virtue of the fact that it is inferred from the known premises of an inference that is known to be valid. If knowledge fails to transmit across the water argument, then one cannot gain a priori knowledge that one's environment contains water by inference from one's a priori knowledge of one's thoughts and one's a priori knowledge of entailments from one's thoughts to the environment. Thus, even if anti-individualism and privileged access were both true, they would not have the absurd result that one can gain a priori knowledge of one's environment merely by reflection on one's thoughts and philosophy.

Given the difference between closure and transmission, failure of transmission of knowledge does not entail failure of closure of knowledge. Even if knowledge fails to transmit from the premises of a valid argument to its conclusion, it may be that anyone who has knowledge of the premises would independently have knowledge of the conclusion. For example, even if the water argument is a counterexample to the transmission of knowledge, it is not a counterexample to closure. However, if there are counterexamples to the closure of knowledge, they are also counterexamples to transmission: if a subject fails to know the conclusion of a valid argument on any basis, then she fails to know it on the basis of inference from its premises.

Davies and Wright argue that the water argument is one example of a wider class of arguments in which knowledge fails to transmit, including the zebra and BIV arguments, as well as Moore's "proof" of the external world. They argue that knowledge fails to transmit across these arguments since warrant is a necessary condition for knowledge, and these arguments are counterexamples to the transmission of warrant, the claim that whenever a subject has warrant for the premises of a valid argument and believes its conclusion on the basis of her recognition of its validity, she thereby acquires warrant for its conclusion.

From now on, I will focus on whether the relevant arguments are counterexamples to the transmission of warrant. From Davies's and Wright's work, we can distinguish three reasons for a failure of transmission of warrant: that the arguments are circular, that anyone sane who doubts the conclusion would have background beliefs relative to which the alleged evidence for the premises would be no evidence, and that warrant for the premises fails to rule out the relevant alternatives to the conclusion. Davies and Wright place different emphasis on these ideas: Wright stresses the first idea whereas Davies stresses the latter two ideas. My presentation reflects this difference of emphasis. However, it should not be taken to suggest that there is no commonality between their views; indeed one can find each of these three ideas in both Davies's and Wright's work.

3   Wright and Conditional Warrant

Wright argues that warrant fails to transmit across the water, BIV, and zebra arguments since these arguments are implicitly circular.[4] One simple example of a circular argument is one whose premises contain its conclusion. Such an argument could not move one to rational conviction of its conclusion. Rather, only someone who is already rationally persuaded of the conclusion would be rationally persuaded of the premises. Thus, warrant fails to transmit across such arguments: warrant for the premises cannot provide one with a warrant to accept the conclusion (Wright 2000, pp. 140–141).

The water argument is not explicitly circular. However, Wright argues that it fits a certain template and that any argument fitting this template is implicitly circular. More specifically, he claims that, for any argument meeting his template, having warrant for its first premise is conditional on having prior and independent warrant for its conclusion. Thus, one cannot acquire warrant for the conclusion from one's warrant for the premises. Rather, one must already have independent warrant for the conclusion in order to have warrant for the premises, and the inference is a counterexample to the transmission of warrant. An argument fits the template if it is of form [A, (if A then B), B] and meets the following conditions:

(i) A entails B.

(ii) There is a proposition C incompatible with A.

(iii) My warrant for A consists in my being in a state that is subjectively indistinguishable from a state in which C would be true.

(iv) C would be true if B were false. (Wright 2000, p. 155)[5]

Suppose that (iii) holds, that is, my warrant for the premise A consists in my being in a state subjectively indistinguishable from a state in which the incompatible C would be true. Given this, Wright argues that my warrant for A entitles me to move beyond the disjunction (A or C) only if I have prior and independent entitlement to discount C. Further, he holds that since (iv) C would be true if B were false, it follows that I have warrant for A only if I have prior and independent entitlement to B (ibid.). Thus, warrant for premise A is conditional on prior and independent entitlement for the conclusion B. Wright concludes that, for any argument that meets his template, warrant for the premise A is conditional on prior and independent warrant for the conclusion, B. Thus, any such argument is characterized by a failure of transmission of warrant.

We may illustrate Wright's view with the zebra argument:

(Z1) The animal in the pen is a zebra.

(Z2) If the animal in the pen is a zebra, then it is not a cleverly disguised mule.

(Z3) The animal in the pen is not a cleverly disguised mule.

This fits Wright's template with A = 'The animal in the pen is a zebra'; B = 'The animal in the pen is not a cleverly disguised mule'; and C = 'The animal in the pen is a mule cleverly disguised to look like a zebra'. In particular, my warrant for A, 'The animal in the pen is a zebra', consists in my perception as of a striped horselike animal. This warrant is not only compatible with A but also with C, 'The animal in the pen is a mule cleverly disguised to look like a zebra'. How, then, does my evidence entitle me to the claim that the animal in the pen is a zebra, rather than the more tentative disjunction (the animal in the pen is a zebra or a mule cleverly disguised to look like a zebra)? Wright argues that I am entitled to the claim that the animal is a zebra only if I am already entitled to discount the possibility that the animal is a cleverly disguised mule. But, the claim that the animal is a cleverly disguised mule is just the negation of the conclusion, B, 'The animal in the pen is not a cleverly disguised mule'. So, my having warrant for A depends on my having prior and independent warrant for the conclusion, B (Wright 2000, pp. 155–156).

I will now argue that Wright's defense of a failure of transmission of warrant across the zebra, BIV, and water arguments faces several serious objections. As we have seen, at the heart of Wright's case is his claim that, for any argument meeting his template, warrant for the first premise is conditional on prior and independent warrant for the conclusion. From now on, for brevity, I will use the expression *conditional analysis* to refer to this claim of Wright's. In the following sections, I argue that (1) many would reject Wright's conditional analysis; (2) his analysis invites skepticism about whether we have warrant for ordinary claims; and (3) his solution to the reductio is no less problematic than the original puzzle it was designed to solve.[6]

3.1 Challenging the Conditional Analysis

To investigate Wright's conditional analysis, let us focus on the zebra argument. According to Wright, one's evidence as of seeing a striped horselike animal warrants the claim that the animal in the pen is a zebra (Z1) only if one has prior and independent warrant that the animal in the pen is not a disguised mule (Z3). We may start to examine Wright's claim by first exploring our ordinary commonsense view of the warranting power of the experience as of seeing a striped horselike animal. Ordinarily, such experience would be taken as warranting (Z1) even though it does not rule out the possibility that the animal is instead a disguised mule and even if one lacks any positive evidence against that skeptical possibility.

Of course, things would be different if one had positive reason to believe that the animal is a disguised mule, for example, if the local press had reported that the cash-starved zoo has been passing off fakes to an unsuspecting public. In that case, one's perceptual experience as of a striped horse-like animal would no longer warrant the claim that it is a zebra. It would regain its warranting power only if one acquired evidence against the skeptical possibility. But in the ordinary case, in which one has no reason to believe that the animal is a disguised mule, one's perceptual evidence is taken to warrant the claim that the animal is a zebra even though one lacks any positive evidence against the skeptical possibility. That this is so is crucial to defending our epistemic situation against the skeptic. After all, one's perceptual experience, say, of seeing a table, does not rule out the skeptical alternative that one has just become a BIV being stimulated to have nonveridical experiences. And the BIV hypothesis is designed so that one has no evidence against it. So, if having warrant for claims about the external world required having evidence against the BIV hypothesis, then our experience would not warrant any claims about the external world.

It seems, then, that according to our ordinary, common-sense view of the zebra case, unless there is positive reason for the disguised mule possibility, one's evidence warrants (Z1) even if one has no positive evidence against the disguised mule possibility. That one has no evidence against the disguised mule possibility does not amount to the claim that one has positive warrant for the claim that what one is seeing is not a disguised mule. In general, one's lacking evidence that not-q does not entail that one has positive warrant that not-q.[7] It seems, then, that our ordinary understanding of the zebra case provides a more minimal rival view to Wright's. On this minimal view, one's perceptual experience warrants the claim that the animal is a zebra even though one has no positive warrant against the possibility that it is a disguised mule. By contrast, on Wright's view, one's warrant for (Z1), the animal is a zebra, is conditional on one's having prior and independent warrant for (Z3), the animal is not a disguised mule. If the more minimal view were correct, then Wright would not have shown that warrant fails to transmit across the zebra argument, for this more minimal view does not support the conditional analysis central to Wright's argument for a failure of transmission of warrant.

Can Wright rule out the more minimal analysis? Recall that Wright supported the conditional analysis of the zebra, BIV, and water arguments by claiming that they fit a certain template: they are arguments of the form "A, (if A then B), B," where (i) A entails B; (ii) there is a proposition C incompatible with A; (iii) the subject's warrant for A consists in a state subjectively indistinguishable from one in which the incompatible proposition C would be the case; and (iv) C would be true if B were false. Given condition (iii), Wright argues that one has warrant for A only if one has prior and independent warrant against C:

> The key question is what, in the circumstances, can justify me in accepting A? Why not just reserve judgement and stay with the more tentative disjunction, "A or C"—for it is all the same which disjunct is true as far as what is subjectively apparent to me is concerned. The answer has to be, it would seem: because I am somehow additionally entitled to discount the other disjunct, C. . . . (Wright 2000, p. 155)

Wright's argument here seems to reflect an internalist epistemology that many would reject. Wright draws no distinction between possible substitutes for C in terms of how remote they are from the actual situation. For Wright, if the subject's warrant for A consists in a state subjectively indistinguishable from one in which an incompatible proposition C would be true, then, no matter how bizarre C is, it raises the question of how one is entitled to move past the disjunction (A or C) to A. Wright argues that one is entitled to do so only if one has prior and independent entitlement to discount C. However, externalists argue that a subject's epistemic position with respect to a proposition p is undermined by only some of the alternatives to p, those that are "relevant" or "nearby" (Goldman 1976, 1986; Nozick 1981). In addition, externalists reject the idea that a subject's epistemological position with respect to a proposition depends exclusively on how things are subjectively for the subject. Instead, they insist that a subject may have warrant for, and knowledge of, one of two disjuncts in virtue of her external relations to that disjunct, even when the difference between the two disjuncts makes no subjective difference to her.

Thus, the concern that drives Wright to his conditional analysis need not be shared by externalists for whom epistemic entitlement is partly a matter of the subject's relations to her environment.

We can illustrate this by reference to Goldman's reliabilist account of warrant, according to which a subject's belief that p is warranted only if produced by a reliable process, that is, one that tends to produce true beliefs and to inhibit false ones.[8] Consider the BIV argument. Wright's analysis has the result that one has warrant for (BIV1), I am seeing a table, only if one has prior and independent warrant for (BIV3), It's not the case that I have just become a BIV. This is because one's warrant for (BIV1) consists in an experiential state that is subjectively indistinguishable from a state in which one has instead just become a BIV. However, Goldman would reject this conditional analysis. First, he would hold that whether I have warrant for (BIV1) depends on whether that belief was produced by a reliable process, independently of whether other beliefs such as (BIV3) are produced by such processes. Second, although Goldman holds that I have warrant for beliefs about what I see, he should reject the claim that I have prior and independent warrant for the belief that I have not just become a BIV. Perception provides one with a reliable process for producing beliefs about what one is seeing and thus, for Goldman, warrant for such beliefs. The most obvious reliable process for producing the belief that I have not just become a BIV is by inference from other beliefs, for example, by the inference from (BIV1) to (BIV3). However, this process cannot provide prior and independent warrant for the belief that I have not just become a BIV. Further, it seems that I have no evidence that I have not just become a BIV for, by hypothesis, everything would seem the same to me had that happened.

It seems, then, that I lack a reliable process for producing the belief that I have not just become a BIV that could provide prior and independent warrant for that belief. Thus, Goldman should reject the conditional analysis of the BIV arguments and similar arguments. (Goldman would accept the different claim that warrant for the first premise of the BIV argument depends on the truth of the conclusion, (BIV3). If (BIV3) were false, and I had just become a BIV, then forming beliefs about the external world on the basis of apparent perceptual experiences would no longer be a reliable belief-forming process. However, the view that warrant for the premises of an argument is conditional on the truth of the conclusion does not support a limitation on the transmission of warrant (see sec. 3.3)).

In conclusion, it seems that many would reject Wright's conditional analysis of arguments fitting his template. An alternative more minimal view is that one's evidence warrants the premises of these arguments although it fails to rule out the possibility that the conclusion is false and one has no other positive warrant for the conclusion. Wright's own argument for the conditional analysis seems to rest on an internalist epistemology that would be rejected by epistemological externalism.[9] This is particularly relevant to the reductio since it seems likely that many anti-individualists who hold that thought partly depends on the world would also adopt externalist epistemologies according to which one's epistemic state depends partly on the world.

3.2   The Conditional Analysis and Skepticism

In this section I argue that Wright's conditional analysis raises a certain skeptical threat. According to Wright's analysis, one's warrant for the first premise of the zebra and BIV arguments is conditional on one's having prior and independent warrant for the conclusion. For example, one has warrant for (Z1), The animal in the pen is a zebra, only if one has prior and independent warrant for (Z3), The animal in the pen is not a disguised mule. Similarly, one has warrant for (BIV1), I am seeing a table, only if one has prior and independent warrant for (BIV3), I have not just become a BIV. Thus, the conditional analysis makes warrant for ordinary claims, such as that's a zebra, depend on whether one has warrant against skeptical hypotheses, such as that's not a disguised mule. But it may be doubted whether one has prior and independent warrant against such skeptical possibilities. If one lacks such warrant, then, on the conditional analysis, one also lacks warrant for the relevant ordinary claims.

There are two ways in which one could have warrant against a skeptical hypothesis. First, one could have evidence against it. But we often take it that we have warrant for some ordinary claim even though we lack evidence against the relevant skeptical hypothesis. For example, experience as of a striped horselike animal is normally taken to warrant the claim that the animal in the pen is a zebra even if one has no evidence that it is not a disguised mule, e.g., one has not closely examined its hide, or taken evidence from an expert zoologist. Similarly, we ordinarily take ourselves to have warrant for such claims as that one is seeing a table even though one has no evidence against the skeptical hypothesis that one has just become a BIV. Indeed, if it were a requirement for having warrant for such claims that one has evidence against the BIV hypothesis, then we would lack warrant for any claims about the external world, for the BIV hypothesis is carefully designed to be consistent with any possible evidence. So, one cannot have evidence that one is not a BIV.

Second, it might be suggested that one could have warrant against a skeptical hypothesis without having evidence against it. For example, although there can be no empirical evidence against the BIV hypothesis, one might have a "standing" entitlement against it. However, it is not clear how one can have an entitlement against some hypothesis despite lacking any evidence against it. The situation does not seem obviously altered if, as in the BIV case, there could not possibly be any evidence against the hypothesis. Why not conclude that the nonavailability of such evidence shows that one cannot have warrant against the hypothesis, rather than suppose that this gives one a special kind of positive warrant against it—a standing entitlement? Even if we were to grant that one can have a standing entitlement against the BIV hypothesis, it seems implausible that one can have a standing entitlement against skeptical hypotheses for which empirical evidence is potentially available, for example, the hypothesis that the animals in the cage are disguised mules. Where empirical evidence is potentially available against some hypothesis, surely we can have warrant to discount the hypothesis only by gaining suitable evidence.

It seems, then, that Wright's analysis threatens warrant for, and knowledge of, ordinary claims. Take a proposition, O, that we ordinarily take to be warranted on the basis of certain experiences. Skeptics attempt to undermine one's warrant for, and knowledge of, O by constructing a skeptical hypothesis, SK, incompatible with O, such that if SK were true, one would be in a state subjectively indistinguishable from the state one is actually in. Wright argues that in such a case one's experience warrants O only if one has a prior and independent reason to discount SK. But it's hard to see how one could have a warrant against SK on the basis of no evidence. Some skeptical hypotheses are designed so that there is no possible evidence against them. Further, even if evidence against SK is potentially available, we typically suppose that a subject can have warrant for O without conducting the empirical investigations that might yield evidence against SK. Thus, the conditional analysis threatens our warrant for, and knowledge of, ordinary propositions.

3.3   A Priori Entitlement

So far I have argued that Wright's conditional analysis of a failure of transmission of warrant would be rejected by many and raises skeptical worries. A third concern is whether the analysis provides a satisfactory solution to the reductio. Wright attempts to defend compatibilism by showing that the joint assumptions of privileged access and anti-individualism do not have the absurd result that a subject can have a priori knowledge of substantive facts about the world. On Wright's view, even if a subject has a priori knowledge of the premises (W1), I think that water is wet, and (W2), If I think that water is wet, then my environment contains water, she cannot thereby gain a priori knowledge of the conclusion (W3), My environment contains water. As we have seen, Wright argues that warrant fails to transmit across an argument where warrant for one of the premises depends on prior and independent warrant for the conclusion. Applied to the water argument, his view is that warrant for the premise (W1), I think that water is wet, is conditional on prior and independent warrant for the conclusion (W3), My environment contains water. Thus, at the heart of Wright's response to the reductio are two claims: (1) a subject can have a priori knowledge of (W1); but (2) her warrant for (W1) is conditional on having prior and independent warrant for (W3). This raises the question of what kind of warrant the reductio subject has for (W3) on which her a priori warrant for (W1) is conditional.

Suppose that the only prior warrant the reductio subject has for the conclusion (W3) were empirical. This might raise the worry that her warrant for the premise (W1) would also be empirical, for, on Wright's view, her warrant for (W1) is conditional on her prior and independent warrant for (W3). But if this is correct, then the conditional analysis can be used to defend compatibilism only if the reductio subject has prior and independent a priori warrant for (W3), My environment contains water. This line of thinking is apparently endorsed by Wright himself, who says "[I]f one has a priori warrant for both premises of the McKinsey [i.e., the water] argument, it is courtesy of an a priori entitlement to discount the possibility of illusions of content, and hence to discount any scenario that would generate such an illusion" (2000, p. 217). Note that according to the kind of anti-individualism to which Wright thinks the reductio is suitably targeted, if one's environment does not contain water, then one would suffer an illusion of thought.[10] So, in this quote, Wright is claiming that one has an a priori entitlement to discount the possibility that one's environment does not contain water, or, alternatively, one has a positive entitlement for the claim that one's environment does contain water.[11] But if Wright's own analysis has the consequence that a subject has a priori warrant for the claim that her environment contains water, then it is not clear how it can be a satisfactory solution to the reductio. The reductio was originally problematic precisely because it seemed to show that the combination of privileged access and anti-individualism has the consequence that subjects can have a priori knowledge of substantive facts about the world, say, that one's environment contains water.

Someone might try to show that Wright's analysis is not committed to the view that subjects can have a priori warrant for substantive claims about the world by pointing out that a priori warrant and knowledge may be conditional on propositions that can be known only empirically. For example, a subject S may derive a priori warrant for and knowledge of a mathematical proposition p by deducing it validly from a priori known premises. However, her having this a priori warrant may depend on certain conditions that can be known to obtain only empirically, say, that it is not the case that, through some brain deterioration, she has lost her mathematical ability.

However, this line of thought cannot be used to defend Wright's view. Wright does not claim that one's a priori warrant for the premise (W1), I think that water is wet, depends on the truth of the conclusion (W3), My environment contains water. Rather, he claims that one's a priori warrant for the premise (W1) depends on one's having prior and independent warrant for the conclusion (W3). Further, this seems to be an essential part of his view. It seems plausible that warrant fails to transmit across an argument where warrant for one of the premises is conditional on having prior and independent warrant for the conclusion. By contrast, on the view that warrant for one of the premises is conditional merely on the truth of the conclusion, having warrant for the premises requires neither that one believe the conclusion, nor that one have warrant for it. So, there seems no reason to suppose that warrant would fail to transmit across an argument in which warrant for the premises is conditional on merely the truth of the conclusion. Suppose, then, that Wright is committed to the claim that the reductio subject has a priori warrant for (W3), My environment contains water. Wright might point out that, on his view, a subject cannot have this a priori warrant for (W3) by inference from (W1) and (W2), for he argues that this inference is a counterexample to the transmission of warrant. But, this seems no defense. What initially seemed problematic was the idea that the reductio subject can have a priori knowledge of substantive facts about the world, not merely that she can acquire this knowledge in one particular way. Similarly, it seems problematic to suppose that the reductio subject can have a priori warrant for substantive claims about the world, not merely that she can acquire this warrant in one particular way. If that is right, then the "solution" Wright offers to the reductio is just as problematic as the original problem the reductio posed.

This section ends my discussion of Wright's view that warrant fails to transmit across the relevant arguments. I have argued that his conditional analysis of these arguments would be rejected by many, especially externalist epistemologists; that it raises a skeptical threat; and that it fails to produce a satisfactory solution to the reductio.

Davies's papers on the reductio suggest several distinguishable reasons for thinking that warrant fails to transmit across the water, zebra, and BIV arguments (though the reasons are not distinguished by him). At times Davies suggests that warrant fails to transmit since the conclusion is already assumed in the premises. For example, Davies (1998) suggests that warrant fails to transmit from the premises of the relevant arguments to their conclusions since warrant cannot be transmitted from within an epistemic project to its presuppositions or assumptions (see, e.g., p. 154). This idea is similar to Wright's circular analysis. Since I have examined Wright's view in detail, I won't discuss it further. Davies suggests two other reasons why warrant may fail to transmit across the relevant arguments: that they beg the question and that warrant for the premises fails to rule out relevant alternatives to the conclusion. I discuss these ideas in the next two sections.

4   Begging the Question

Davies (1998, 2000) argues that warrant fails to transmit across the zebra, BIV, and water arguments because they beg the question in Jackson's sense, that is, "anyone—or anyone sane—who doubted the conclusion would have background beliefs relative to which the evidence for the premises would be no evidence" (Jackson 1987, p. 111).[12] Consider the BIV argument. Suppose someone doubts (BIV3), It's not the case that I have just become a BIV, and she thinks that she may have just become a BIV. In that case, she would not take her perceptual experience as of seeing a table as warranting (BIV1), I am seeing a table. So, even if she has the perceptual experience as of seeing a table and she has evidence for (BIV2), If I am seeing a table, then it's not the case that I have just become a BIV, this would not give her warrant for the conclusion, (BIV3). Thus, it may be suggested that warrant fails to transmit across the BIV argument.

However, this line of thought fails to show that question-begging arguments instantiate a failure of transmission of warrant. Someone who doubts (BIV3) and thinks she may have just become a BIV might have perceptual experiences as of seeing a table. But, for such a subject, these experiences would not warrant the claim that she is seeing a table, although they would normally be taken to do so. Thus, in virtue of her doubt about the conclusion, (BIV3), she no longer has warrant for the premise, (BIV1). Thus, this subject is not someone who has a warrant for the premises of the BIV argument that fails to transmit to the conclusion; rather, she lacks warrant for the premises. This is compatible with saying that if someone were to have warrant for the premises, she could thereby acquire warrant for the conclusion, that is, that warrant transmits across the argument (Beebee 2001, pp. 358–359).

5 Warrant and Ruling Out Alternatives

Davies (2000) emphasizes a different reason for a failure of transmission of warrant, namely, that one's warrant for the premises of these arguments fails to rule out the salient or relevant alternatives to the conclusion. Consider the zebra argument. Davies says that it is a relevant alternative to the conclusion (Z3), The animal in the cage is not a disguised mule, that it is a disguised mule. But one's evidence for the premises, namely one's experience as of seeing a striped horselike animal and one's warrant for the conditional claim, does not rule out the possibility that it is a disguised mule.[13]

Notice that this relevant alternatives analysis is distinct from either of the two other analyses considered so far. The idea that warrant for the premises fails to rule out relevant alternatives to the conclusion is different from the idea that the arguments beg the question, that is, someone who doubts the conclusion of the argument would have background beliefs relative to which the apparent evidence for the premises would be no evidence. Further, the relevant alternatives analysis is different from Wright's circular analysis according to which warrant for one of the premises is conditional on prior and independent warrant for the conclusion. It may be that the premises of an argument fail to rule out the salient alternatives to its conclusion, even though it is not circular.

For instance, consider the zebra argument. In section 3, I rejected Wright's suggestion that one's warrant for (Z1), The animal is a zebra, is conditional on one's having prior and independent warrant for (Z3), The animal is a disguised mule. Even if this is right, one's evidence for (Z1) and (Z2) fails to rule out the relevant alternative to the conclusion (that the animal is a disguised mule). Further, an argument could be circular even though it is not the case that the evidence for the premises fails to rule out the relevant alternatives to the conclusion. For example, suppose that one has a warrant for p that rules out the relevant alternatives to p. Despite this, the argument p therefore p is still circular. Given the distinctness of Davies's analysis of the relevant arguments, it is unaffected by the previous discussion and requires separate examination.

Davies's argument for a limitation on the transmission of warrant is offered in his discussion of the goal argument:

(G1)   A goal has been scored.

(G2)   If a goal has been scored, then a football match is in progress and this is not just a movie scene.

(G3)   This is not just a movie scene.

Suppose that walking into a stadium, it seems to S that a football match is in progress. As she watches, a player kicks the ball between the posts, the crowd roars, and the referee makes signals appropriate to a goal being scored. Thus, S has warrant for (G1). Further, reflection on the relevant concepts provides S with warrant for (G2). And suppose that S knows that the inference from (G1) and (G2) to (G3) is valid. Despite this, Davies argues that S cannot gain warrant for the conclusion (G3) by inference from the premises for, he says, the evidence for the premises fails to rule out the most salient alternative to the conclusion:

The evidence, even taken together with the considerations that support the conditional premise, does nothing to rule out the most obviously salient alternative hypothesis, namely that it is a movie scene which I am watching. That evidence would be of no help in resolving doubt and it does not confer knowledge. My epistemic warrants for the premises do not add up to an epistemic warrant for the conclusion. (2000, p. 400. See also Wright 2000, p. 154)

Having argued that warrant fails to transmit across the goal argument, Davies applies the same idea to the zebra and BIV arguments and Moore's proof of the external world. He then formulates two general principles limiting the transmission of warrant. The first of these is designed to limit the transmission of warrant across the goal, zebra, BIV, and Moore arguments. The second one is designed to apply specifically to the water argument. I won't discuss these limitation principles here since Davies's discussion of them provides no further argument for the idea that warrant fails to transmit across the arguments in question (2000, pp. 394–395 and secs. 6.1, 8.1, 8.2). Rather, the first limitation principle is designed to reflect the already argued for conclusion that warrant fails to transmit across the goal, zebra, BIV, and Moore arguments. The second limitation principle transposes the first limitation principle into a form that can be applied to the water argument. Further, Davies himself accepts that the limitation principles are likely to be open to counterexamples and need further refinement (ibid., p. 601).[14]

As we have seen, Davies claims that warrant fails to transmit from the premises to the conclusion of the goal argument since the warrant for the premises fails to rule out the salient alternatives to the conclusion. Thus, Davies seems to be committed implicitly to a general principle about warrant, namely that evidence warrants a proposition p by ruling out alternatives to it. Indeed, he endorses this view explicitly: "[I]n short, the evidence rules out various ways in which the hypothesis that a goal has been scored could have been false, and it is for this reason that the evidence provides a resource for resolving doubt. It is also by ruling out alternatives that the evidence confers knowledge. This is how evidence constitutes an epistemic warrant" (2000, pp. 399–400). But, on pain of skepticism, we should not accept that evidence warrants a proposition p only if it rules out all the possible alternatives to it. On that view, perceptual experience would fail to warrant beliefs about the world, such as there is a table in front of me, since it fails to rule out the possibility that one has just become a BIV. However, one could avoid this skeptical consequence by holding that a putative warrant warrants a proposition p only if it rules out a subset of the alternatives to it, those that are relevant, for the BIV possibility is not normally relevant (see Dretske 1970, 1981 and Nozick 1981). This relevant alternatives conception of warrant would block the transmission of warrant in the relevant arguments. Consider the conclusion of the goal argument again: (G3) This is not just a movie scene. A relevant alternative to (G3) is that this is a movie scene. But, the evidence for (G1), namely the behavior of players, referee, ball, and crowd, does not rule out the possibility that this is a movie scene. Similarly, this conception of warrant would show that warrant fails to transmit across the BIV and zebra arguments. (The idea that a putative warrant warrants a proposition only if it rules out the relevant alternatives to that proposition is consistent with Davies's remarks about why warrant fails to transmit across the goal argument—see the quoted passage on p. 261.)

We have seen that central to Davies's defense of a limitation on the transmission of warrant is the idea that a putative warrant warrants a proposition p by ruling out the relevant alternatives to it. However, I will argue that this conception of warrant has controversial consequences that would be rejected by a number of accounts of warrant or justification, both internalist and externalist (Davies treats the terms "warrant" and "justification" interchangeably throughout his paper).

Consider the following Gettier case (Dancy 1985, p. 25). Julie is watching television at the time advertised for the Wimbledon men's finals and sees McEnroe beat Connors. She forms the belief that

(McE1)   I have just seen McEnroe win this year's Wimbledon final.

Further, Julie knows that

(McE2)   If I have just seen McEnroe win this year's Wimbledon final, then McEnroe is this year's Wimbledon champion.

And so she infers

(McE3)   McEnroe is this year's Wimbledon champion.

In fact, owing to technical difficulties, the BBC is unable to transmit the current final and is showing last year's final in which McEnroe beat Connors. Thus Julie's belief (McE1) is false. As it happens, though, in the real final McEnroe *has*

just beaten Connors, so Julie's belief (McE3) is true. Intuitively, her belief (McE3) is also justified or warranted,
though not a case of knowledge. However, this would not
be so on the view that evidence warrants or justifies a proposition by ruling out relevant alternatives. To see this, consider existing relevant alternative accounts of knowledge.
Such accounts deal with Gettier cases by arguing that the
subject's accidentally true belief is not a case of knowledge
since it fails to meet the relevant alternative condition for
knowledge (see, e.g., Goldman 1986, pp. 54–55; Lewis 1996,
pp. 228–229).

For example, on Goldman's account, "a true belief that p
fails to be knowledge if there are any relevant alternative situations in which the proposition p would be false, but the
process used would cause S to believe p anyway" (1986, p.
46). Goldman would argue that Julie's belief (McE3) is not
knowledge since it is a relevant alternative that McEnroe is
not this year's Wimbledon champion and the broadcast is a
repeat. But, in this relevant alternative situation, use of the
same process of belief-formation would lead Julie to falsely
believe (McE3), McEnroe is this year's Wimbledon champion. Davies uses the established epistemological notion of
a relevant alternative in his account of warrant. So, on his
account, too, it is a relevant alternative to (McE3) that
McEnroe is not this year's Wimbledon champion and that
the broadcast is a repeat.[15] But, of course, Julie's evidence
for (McE1) and (McE2) fails to rule out this alternative to
(McE3). So, on Davies's view that evidence warrants a
proposition by ruling out relevant alternatives, Julie lacks
warrant for (McE3).

A second problem for the view that evidence warrants a
proposition by ruling out relevant alternatives is that it is

incompatible with the intuitive view that a false belief may be warranted or justified. Indeed, the possibility of a false but warranted or justified belief is used to generate many Gettier cases. In the Wimbledon example, Julie intuitively has a warranted but false belief in (McE1), I have just seen McEnroe win this year's Wimbledon final, from which she justifiably infers the true belief (McE3). However, given the set up, it seems a relevant alternative to (McE1) that Julie has not just seen McEnroe win this year's Wimbledon because the broadcast is a repeat. Surely, the nature of the actual situation should be included among the relevant alternatives to a believed proposition (see, e.g., Lewis's rule of actuality [1996, p. 225]). But, clearly, Julie's evidence for (McE1) does not rule out the possibility that she has not seen McEnroe win this year's Wimbledon and that the broadcast is a repeat.

More generally, suppose that S believes that p where actually not-p. Given that not-p is part of the way the world actually is, it is a relevant alternative to the believed proposition p. But S's evidence does not rule out not-p, but is rather compatible with it. So, on the view that evidence warrants or justifies p only if it rules out the relevant alternatives to p, a false belief cannot be warranted or justified.[16] (Notice that I am using the Gettier case not as a direct objection to Davies's limitation on the transmission of warrant, but rather as an objection to the account of warrant on which that limitation is based. I have argued that it is plausible that Julie has warrant for (McE1) and (McE3), but that Davies's account cannot allow this. I have not argued that the case constitutes a counterexample to his limitation on the transmission of warrant. Indeed, it would be hard to do so. If I am right, then Davies must reject the claim that Julie has warrant for

(McE1), and so, on his view, the question of transmission of warrant across the inference to (McE3) cannot arise.)

The notions of justification and warrant are currently the subject of much controversy. However, it is interesting that a variety of accounts of justification or warrant, both internalist and externalist, would allow that a false belief can be warranted/justified, and that Gettier cases involve true and warranted/justified beliefs. In broad terms, on an internalist account, whether a subject's belief is warranted/justified depends on the obtaining of certain conditions that are internally accessible to the subject. Consider Julie's belief (McE1), that she has just seen McEnroe win this year's Wimbledon. Although Julie's belief is false, this isn't a matter of her belief failing to meet certain conditions that are accessible to Julie. From the inside, her epistemic position seems just as good as it would be if, counterfactually, the broadcast were live, rather than a repeat. The problem is not with those conditions internally accessible to Julie, but with facts external to her. It seems, then, that an internalist account should treat Julie's belief in (McE1) as having the same degree of warrant/justification as it would have if, in fact, the broadcast were live, and her belief true. But, to avoid the skeptical conclusion that Julie's belief is not warranted/justified even in the counterfactual situation in which the broadcast is live and her belief true, the internalist should accept that Julie's belief in (McE1) is warranted/justified even though it is false.

A similar analysis suggests that internalists would accept that Julie has a warranted or justified belief in (McE3), that McEnroe is this year's Wimbledon champion. When considered solely internally, Julie's epistemic position with respect to (McE3) is good: she forms her belief in (McE3) on the basis of a known entailment from another belief that, from an internal perspective, is justified. Again, the problem is not that her belief fails to meet some internally accessible condition, but rather the way it links up with the world. Thus, the internalist should treat Julie's belief in (McE3) as having the same degree of warrant/justification as it would have in the more congenial situation in which her belief in (McE3) is arrived at by a justified inference from a belief that is both justified and true. To avoid saying that Julie's belief in (McE3) is not warranted/justified in this more congenial counterfactual situation, the internalist should accept that it is warranted/justified in the Gettier case.

As we saw earlier, it may be argued that compatibilist anti-individualists are likely to endorse an externalist approach to epistemology rather than an internalist one (sec. 3.1). However, as I will now argue, Davies's claims about warrant would be rejected even by some externalist accounts of warrant. For example, according to Goldman's externalist account, a belief is warranted/justified if it was caused by a reliable process, that is, one that tends to produce true beliefs rather than false beliefs (Goldman 1979, 1986). (By "reliability" here, I mean what I earlier called "global reliability" [chap. 4].) This basic idea can be applied directly to beliefs that are produced by processes whose inputs are not beliefs, such as perception. However, a slight reformulation is needed to deal with processes, like inference, whose inputs and outputs are beliefs. Goldman argues that a belief that is produced by such a "belief-dependent" process is justified if and only if the process is conditionally reliable, that is, tends to produce true rather than false beliefs, when its input beliefs are true. Clearly, a false belief could be caused by a process that is either reliable or conditionally reliable. So, on this view, a belief may be warranted/justified and false. Further, it seems that Goldman would agree that Gettier cases involve a subject's having a true and warranted/justified belief. Consider Julie's belief (McE3), that McEnroe is the champion. This belief is produced by a conditionally reliable process, that of inferring one belief by known entailment from another.[17]

So far, I have argued that Davies's account of warrant has controversial consequences that would be rejected by many accounts of warrant, both internalist and externalist.[18] It is not surprising that Davies's account has these controversial consequences, for, as we will see, his account effectively imports into warrant what are normally regarded as conditions for knowledge. It is plausible that knowledge that p requires what Goldman calls local reliability, reliability with respect to the specific proposition p. For example, Nozick (1981) argues that the true belief that p is knowledge if and only if (1) if it were false that p, then the subject would not believe that p; and (2) if it were true that p, then the subject would still believe that p. On Goldman's account, "a true belief that p fails to be knowledge if there are any relevant alternative situations in which the proposition p would be false, but the process used would cause S to believe p anyway" (1986, p. 46). As we have seen, Davies argues that a putative warrant w justifies or warrants p only if w rules out the relevant alternatives to p. In effect, this amounts to a local reliability condition for justification/warrant: the claim that w warrants the belief that p only if it rules out relevant alternative situations in which p is false. Thus, it is not surprising that Davies's account has counterintuitive consequences.

For example, the local reliability condition for knowledge is standardly used to obtain the intuitively desirable result that Gettier cases are not cases of knowledge. Consider Julie's belief (McE3), that McEnroe is the champion. Given the set up, it is a relevant alternative to (McE3) that McEnroe is not the champion and the broadcast is a repeat. But, if that alternative were actual, then Julie would still believe (McE3) on the basis of the repeat. Thus, an account of knowledge incorporating the local reliability condition has the result that Julie's belief in (McE3) is not knowledge. However, if one also builds the local reliability condition into one's account of warrant, this delivers the counterintuitive result that Julie's belief in (McE3) is not warranted either.

6 Conclusion

In this chapter we've considered one of the main responses to the reductio argument. The reductio threatens compatibilism since it seems to show that if anti-individualism and privileged access were both true, then a subject could gain a priori knowledge of substantive claims about the nature of her environment. Davies and Wright respond by arguing that warrant fails to transmit from the premises to the conclusion of the relevant inference, and thus, even if anti-individualism and privileged access were both true, a subject couldn't use her a priori knowledge of her thoughts and of philosophy to gain by inference a priori knowledge of her environment.

We have examined and rejected several reasons for supposing that warrant fails to transmit across the relevant inference and related arguments: that the arguments are circular, that they beg the question in Jackson's sense, and that the warrant for the premises fails to rule out relevant alternatives to the conclusion. I conclude that the threat posed to compatibilism by the reductio cannot be answered by limiting the transmission of warrant. Nevertheless, there may be other ways to counter this threat. In the next chapter, I consider whether any version of anti-individualism supports the claim, crucial to the success of the reductio, that a subject can have a priori knowledge of entailments between thought and the world.

8   The Reductio Argument: Entailments between Thought and the World

1   Introduction

In this chapter, we continue our examination of the reductio argument for the incompatibility of anti-individualism and privileged access. In the last chapter, we examined and rejected Davies's and Wright's responses to the reductio, that warrant and knowledge fail to transmit across the relevant inference. In this chapter, I want to examine a different response. To situate this response, it is useful to recall the steps of the reductio argument.

According to the reductio argument, the joint assumptions of anti-individualism and privileged access have the absurd consequence that a subject can have a priori knowledge of substantive facts about the world. We may illustrate the argument using natural kind anti-individualism. Suppose that Sally is an Earth subject who is ignorant of the chemical composition of water. Despite this, natural kind anti-individualists accept that in virtue of Sally's interactions with samples of water she has the concept of water and thinks, for example, that water is wet. The main steps of the argument proceed as follows:

(R1)   Sally can know a priori that she thinks that water is wet. *(From the assumption of privileged access.)*

(R2)   Sally can know a priori that if she thinks that water is wet, then her environment contains water. *(From the assumption of anti-individualism.)*

(R3)   Sally can know a priori that her environment contains water. *(From (R1) and (R2).)*

(R4)   But (R3) is absurd.

(R5)   So, anti-individualism and privileged access are incompatible. *(From (R1)–(4).)*

Notice that the reductio can be formulated independently of the notion of the a priori: it seems absurd to suppose that a subject can have knowledge of substantive facts about the world on the basis of her thoughts and philosophy (see chap. 7, sec. 1).

In the last chapter, I rejected a number of objections to the argument: that (R1) does not follow from the assumption of privileged access, that (R3) does not follow from (R1) and (R2), and that (R4) is false. If my rejection is correct, then the reductio can be challenged only by arguing that (R2) does not follow from the assumption of anti-individualism. In the rest of the chapter I will pursue this strategy (cf. Gallois and O'Leary-Hawthorne 1996; McLaughlin and Tye 1998). Proponents of the reductio argue that (R2) and analogous principles for other types of anti-individualism follow from the fact that anti-individualism is established by philosophical arguments. However, I will argue that even if we grant that anti-individualism is established by philosophical arguments, knowledge of those arguments would not allow Sally to know a priori that if she thinks that water is wet then her environment contains water. More generally, I argue that where the thought that p is partly individuated by some environmental condition E, knowledge of the arguments for anti-individualism does not enable a subject who thinks that p to know a priori that if she thinks that p then E.

As a first step in the discussion, notice that knowledge of the Twin Earth arguments alone is unlikely to yield a priori knowledge that if one thinks that p then E. First, the Twin Earth arguments concern a subject stipulated to be in certain environmental conditions, say, that she has interacted with samples of water (Putnam), or that she is part of a linguistic community (Burge). But, a subject could have only empirical knowledge that she is in such conditions and thus that the Twin Earth arguments apply to her. Second, these arguments most obviously establish a counterfactual dependence of thought on environment. They ask us to consider a subject in certain conditions and argue that, if she had been in different conditions, then she would have had a different thought. For instance, if instead of being brought up on Earth interacting with water, the subject had been brought up on Twin Earth interacting with twater, then she would have had the concept twater rather than the concept water. But this does not show that having a certain kind of thought, say, one involving the concept water, entails some particular environmental condition, say, that one's environment contains water. For instance, Burge accepts that if an Earth subject who actually has the concept of water but who is ignorant of the chemical composition of water, had instead been brought up on Twin Earth, she would have lacked the concept of water. But he denies that this shows that having the concept water entails that one's environment contains water, and indeed he rejects this claim. Instead, he says, one could have the concept water in a waterless world in which there are other speakers or in which one knows that water is H_2O. (See Burge 1982, p. 116. See also Brueckner 1992b; Gallois and O'Leary-Hawthorne 1996, pp. 11–12.)

Nevertheless, perhaps a subject could use anti-individualism to gain a priori knowledge of conditional principles of the form: if a subject is in a certain psychological condition and certain other conditions hold, then her environment must be some particular way. If a subject could know a priori that she meets the antecedent of one of these conditionals, then perhaps she could use it to gain a priori knowledge of some specific connection between her thoughts and the environment. I will investigate this idea in the rest of the chapter. Although I argue that each type of anti-individualism establishes conditional principles of the relevant form, I argue that a subject cannot know priori that she meets the antecedent of these conditionals. Thus, it turns out that a subject cannot use these conditional principles to gain a priori knowledge of some specific connection between her thoughts and the environment. I conclude that the reductio fails.

Combined with my earlier discussion of the achievement problem (chaps. 2–4), this concludes my defense of the compatibility of anti-individualism and privileged access. The argument below draws on some earlier work (Brown 1995 and 2001) but represents a change of mind: in those earlier papers, I argued that the reductio does indeed show that anti-individualism is incompatible with privileged access.

2   Natural Kind Anti-Individualism

In this section, we focus on natural kind anti-individualism, setting aside other anti-individualist theses. (Combinations of anti-individualist theses are considered in sec. 5.) According to natural kind anti-individualism, a subject's thought contents are individuated partly by the natural kinds that are in her environment. We have already seen that the Twin Earth arguments do not obviously support the idea that a subject could know a priori that, say, having the concept water entails that one's environment contains water. Rather, our question is whether a subject could use natural kind anti-individualism to gain a priori knowledge of a conditional principle of the form: if a subject is in certain psychological and other conditions, then her environment contains a certain natural kind. If the subject could know a priori that she meets the antecedent of such a conditional, she might be able to gain a priori knowledge that, say, if she thinks that water is wet then her environment contains water.

Let us start our investigation of this strategy by considering a subject who has a concept of a natural kind, that is, a concept that names, or refers to, a natural kind. In what circumstances could a subject have such a concept? She could have such a concept even if there are no instances of the relevant kind in her environment as long as she knows the fundamental nature of that kind, say, its chemical composition. For example, a subject who has the concepts of hydrogen and oxygen could put them together to yield the concept H_2O even if there are no samples of H_2O in her environment. So, let us restrict our attention to a subject who is ignorant of the fundamental nature of the relevant natural kind and has an atomic concept of that kind, that is, a concept that is not built up out of component concepts in the manner of H_2O.[1] (From now on, I will use the expression "chemically indifferent" to describe a subject ignorant of the fundamental properties of the relevant natural kind.) Suppose she has the concept gold. Natural kind anti-individualism allows that a subject who has interacted with samples of gold could have the concept gold even if she is ignorant of its fundamental nature. Now consider a counterfactual situation in which this same subject while being chemically ignorant is instead brought up in an environment in which there is no gold. It is hard to see how she could have the concept gold in this counterfactual situation. She is ignorant of the chemical composition of gold; and in this counterfactual situation, there is no gold in her environment. At the moment, we are considering only natural kind anti-individualism and setting aside other anti-individualist theses, such as social anti-individualism. So, even if there are other speakers, they cannot help her to have the concept gold. Thus, whatever concept, if any, she expresses with 'gold', it cannot be the concept gold. It seems, then, that natural kind anti-individualism establishes the following conditional principle:

(A)   If S has a concept that names a natural kind k_i, and she is chemically indifferent, then her environment contains instances of k_i.

(Here, and in the following principles, I abbreviate the claim that her environment now, or used to, contain instances of k_i by the claim that her environment contains instances of k_i.) Suppose that a subject could have a priori knowledge of this principle (for a full defense of this claim and (A) itself, see Brown 1995, 2001). If she could also have a priori knowledge that she meets the antecedent of the principle, then she could use it to gain a priori knowledge of connections between her thoughts and the world.

For instance, consider Sally, the subject of the Twin Earth thought experiment. She has the concept water in virtue of interacting with water despite the fact that she is chemically indifferent. If she could know a priori that she has the concept water, that it names a natural kind and that she is chemically indifferent, she could know a priori that if she thinks that water is wet then her environment contains water. But, unfortunately for the defender of the reductio, Sally cannot know a priori that she meets the antecedent of this principle, in particular, that she has a concept that names a natural kind. To show this, we need only rely on the widely held view that S's true belief that p is knowledge only if, were p false, she would not believe that p.[2] Consider a possible situation in which, although Sally intends 'water' to name a natural kind, it fails to do so. This could occur if she is on Motley Earth, where the stuff in rivers and lakes forms a motley of various natural kinds. Alternatively, it could occur if she is on Dry Earth, where, although it seems as if there are rivers and lakes full of a watery liquid, in fact there are no such rivers and lakes; rather, Sally and her community are just under the illusion that there are. In either scenario she would still believe that 'water' names a natural kind. She could correct her view only empirically. Thus, in the actual situation, she does not know a priori that 'water' names a natural kind. In general, it is an empirical matter whether a term intended to name a natural kind in fact does so. There are numerous examples of terms that were intended to name natural kinds but in fact fail to do so, such as 'phlogiston' and 'jade'. (E.g., see Brown 1995; Gallois and O'Leary-Hawthorne 1996, pp. 6–7; Boghossian 1997, p. 168.)

It seems, then, that our first attempt to defend (R2) has failed. A subject cannot have a priori knowledge that she meets the antecedent of principle (A), in particular, that she has a concept that names a natural kind. Two main ways of circumventing this problem have been suggested. In my (1995), I recommend broadening the target of the reductio from natural kind anti-individualism to a position that combines natural kind and social anti-individualism. The idea is that a reductio formulated against this broader position would not require a priori knowledge that a concept names a natural kind since the broader position applies to all concepts, not just a particular type of concept. I will discuss this strategy in section 5 below.

By contrast, Boghossian (1997) retains the target of the reductio as natural kind anti-individualism alone, but reformulates the reductio using the notion of a term that is intended to name a natural kind. It seems much more plausible that Sally could know a priori that she intends a certain term to name a natural kind, than that the term actually names a natural kind. The idea, then, is to show that someone who knows the arguments for anti-individualism could thereby gain a priori knowledge of an entailment from thought to world of the form: If S has a term t that she intends to name a natural kind and . . . , then t refers to a natural kind and her environment contains instances of that kind. If Sally could have a priori knowledge of such an entailment, she might be able to use it to gain a priori knowledge of connections between her thoughts and the world. For instance, if she can know a priori that she intends 'water' to name a natural kind and that she meets the other conditions in the antecedent, then she may be able to know a priori that if she thinks that water is wet then her environment contains water. I examine this general strategy here.

Let us consider, then, what natural kind anti-individualism would say about a term that is intended to name a natural kind. Suppose that Sally has a term t that she intends to name a natural kind, although she is ignorant of the fundamental properties of that supposed kind. If her use of the term is suitably connected to a natural kind, then natural kind anti-individualists would hold that she uses the term to express a concept of that kind. Now suppose that she is brought up in a situation in which, although she has the same history of individualistic states and intends that *t* name a natural kind, it fails to do so. This might be either because the stuff to which *t* is applied is a motley collection of natural kinds, or because (more radically) there is no stuff to which it is applied and Sally suffers illusory perceptual experiences. As we know, there are two possible views for a defender of natural kind anti-individualism to take about such cases: according to the illusion view, the term fails to express any concept at all, and the subject suffers an illusion of thought; according to the rival descriptive view, the term expresses a descriptive concept of the form the *F*, such as the liquid that actually falls from the skies around here (chap. 1, sec. 4). (Note that it does not follow from the descriptive view that when the term does succeed in naming a natural kind it expresses a descriptive concept.) These different anti-individualist views yield different principles about the case where a subject intends a term to name a natural kind but it fails to do so. The illusion view establishes the following principle:

(B)   If a chemically indifferent subject *S* intends *t* to name a natural kind although it fails to do so, then *S* suffers an illusion of thought.

By contrast, a different principle follows from the descriptive view:

(C)   If a chemically indifferent subject *S* intends a term to name a natural kind although it fails to do so, then *t* expresses a descriptive concept of the form, the *F*.[3]

In what follows I will set aside the reasons that might motivate someone to adopt the illusion or the descriptive view. Instead, I will consider each view in turn and consider whether either could be used to defend (R2): Sally can know a priori that if she thinks that water is wet then her environment contains water.

As a first step in examining this issue, notice that [If ((P and Q) and R) then S] is logically equivalent to [If ((P and Q) and not-S), then not-R]. So principles (B) and (C) above are logically equivalent to:

(B') If a chemically indifferent subject S intends a term t to name a natural kind and it's not the case that S suffers an illusion of thought, then t names a natural kind.

(C') If a chemically indifferent subject S intends a term t to name a natural kind and t does not express a descriptive concept of the form, the F, then t names a natural kind.

The reformulated principles (B') and (C') state entailments from certain psychological conditions to the claim that a certain term names a natural kind. If Sally knows a priori that she meets the conditions mentioned in the antecedent of one of these principles and that the principle is true, then she could use this knowledge to gain a priori knowledge of connections between her thoughts and the world. For instance, suppose that she has a priori knowledge of (B'), that she is chemically indifferent, that she intends 'water' to name a natural kind, and that it's not the case that she suffers an illusion of thought. In that case, perhaps, she could come to know a priori that if she thinks that water is wet, then there is water in her environment. On the assumption that there are philosophical arguments that settle the debate between the illusion and descriptive views, Sally could use knowledge of these arguments to gain a priori knowledge of that anti-individualist view and the corresponding principle. So, the key question is whether she can have a priori knowledge that she meets the conditions in the antecedent.

It seems plausible that Sally could know a priori that she meets two of the conditions mentioned in the antecedent of each principle, namely that she is chemically indifferent and that she intends t to name a natural kind. In particular, it seems that she can know a priori that she has no idea of the chemical composition of what she calls 'water' and that she intends 'water' to name a natural kind. However, the antecedent of each principle contains a further condition: that it is not the case that Sally suffers an illusion of thought (B'); and that it is not the case that 'water' expresses a descriptive concept (C'). So, the success of the reductio turns on whether Sally can have a priori knowledge of these further conditions. However, I will argue that it is implausible that Sally can have such knowledge by using the claim that S's true belief that p is knowledge only if, were p false, she would not believe that p.

Let us start by considering the illusion version of natural kind anti-individualism. Suppose that chemically indifferent Sally is actually on Earth where the lakes and rivers are full of water. Thus, she intends that 'water' name a natural kind, and it does so. Further, suppose that Sally is convinced of the truth of the illusion version of natural kind anti-individualism, and truly believes that she is not suffering an illusion of thought. Nonetheless, her belief is not a case of a priori knowledge, for were she suffering an illusion of thought, she would believe that she is not. Consider a counterfactual situation in which she is suffering an illusion of thought. She would suffer such an illusion if she were on Dry Earth, where there is no liquid in the rivers and lakes although everyone suffers an illusion of there being such a liquid. Alternatively, Sally would suffer an illusion of thought if she were on Motley Earth, where although there is a tasteless, colorless, clear liquid in the rivers and lakes, it is composed of a motley of different natural kinds. In either scenario, it would seem to Sally as if there is a clear, colorless, liquid in the lakes and rivers. She would take it that there is a dominant natural kind in the lakes and rivers to which her term 'water' refers. Thus, if the question were to arise, she would deny that she is suffering an illusion of thought on Dry or Motley Earth, though she would be suffering such an illusion.

Now consider the alternative anti-individualist view, that on Dry and Motley Earth Sally would not suffer an illusion of thought but instead would have a descriptive thought (I use the expression "descriptive thought" as an abbreviation of the more elaborate claim that her thought contains a descriptive component, here one corresponding to the term 'water'). Suppose too that Sally were convinced of the descriptive version of anti-individualism. Even if she were, and the question were to arise, it seems that if she were on Dry or Motley Earth she would deny that she is having a descriptive thought. In either situation, it would seem to her as if there is a liquid present in the rivers and lakes. She would believe that her term 'water' names the dominant natural kind in the rivers and lakes.

In summary, it seems that in the actual situation Sally cannot know a priori that she is not having either an illusion of thought, or a descriptive thought. If she were and the question were to arise, she would believe that she is not. It will be useful to have a shorter way of stating this conclusion. Let the *bad case* cover both the possibility that a subject is having an illusion of thought and the possibility that she is instead having a descriptive thought. Using this terminology, we may say that a subject cannot know a priori that she is not in a bad case, for if she were and the question were to arise, she would believe that she is not in a bad case.

Let us review the results of our discussion so far. We have been considering whether the reductio is successful against natural kind anti-individualism and, in particular, whether Sally can have a priori knowledge that if she thinks that water is wet then her environment contains water. Twin Earth arguments establish only a counterfactual dependence of thought on world; they do not show that having the concept water entails the existence of water. However, I have argued that Sally could use knowledge of the arguments for natural kind anti-individualism to gain a priori knowledge of conditional principles of the form: if a subject is in certain psychological and other conditions, then her environment contains instances of a certain natural kind. Further, I have argued that if Sally can also know a priori that she meets the antecedent of such a principle, then she can gain a priori knowledge of links between her thought and the world, say, that if she thinks that water is wet, then her environment contains water. The antecedent of the first principle we considered, (A), contains the condition that the subject has a concept that names a natural kind. However, Sally cannot know a priori that a concept names a natural kind. We then considered principles whose antecedent states that the subject intends a term to name a natural kind and that she is not in a bad case, where the latter covers either the possibility that she is having an illusion of thought or a descriptive thought. Although a subject can know a priori that she intends a term to name a natural kind, she cannot know a priori that she is not in a bad case, for if she were in a bad case and the question were to arise, she would believe that she is not. So, whether the conditional principles involve the notion of having a concept that names a natural kind, or the notion of having a concept that is merely intended to do so, the reductio is unsuccessful against natural kind anti-individualism.

It is worth pausing to discuss one final issue before moving on to discuss other types of anti-individualism. Recall that the reductio examines what would follow if the assumptions of anti-individualism and privileged access were both true. So, it is legitimate for the proponent of the reductio to appeal to these assumptions and anything that follows from them. It might be claimed that it follows from the assumption of privileged access that a subject can know a priori that she is not in a bad case. If this were correct, then, despite the arguments given above, it would be possible to give a successful reductio of natural kind anti-individualism.

2.1 Privileged Access and the Bad Case

According to the suggestion to be considered, privileged access involves more than merely the claim that a subject can have a priori knowledge of her thought contents, say, that she thinks that water is wet. In addition, it involves the claim that, if a subject is not in a bad case, she can know a priori that she is not in a bad case, that is, depending on the version of anti-individualism at issue, she can know a priori that she is not suffering either an illusion of thought or a descriptive thought.

Before considering the merits of this view, note that this claim about privileged access is employed in Boghossian's version of the reductio. Boghossian (1997) argues that the kind of anti-individualism supported by Putnam's Twin Earth argument about water entails the illusion version of anti-individualism. In his defense of the reductio, he combines this claim with the idea that a subject can know a priori whether or not a term expresses a concept. In more detail, he argues that a subject who knows the philosophical arguments for Putnamian anti-individualism can have a priori knowledge of the following principle: if a chemically indifferent subject intends t to express an atomic concept that names a natural kind, but there is no natural kind for t to name, then t fails to express any concept (pp. 170–174). He argues that a subject can have a priori knowledge that she is chemically indifferent and that she intends 'water' to express an atomic concept that names a natural kind. Thus, so long as a subject can also know a priori that 'water' does express a concept, then she can know a priori that 'water' names a natural kind and that there is water in her environment. Boghossian argues that it is a consequence of privileged access that a subject can know a priori whether or not a term expresses a concept: "privileged access assures him that he will be able to tell a priori whether or not a given term does express a concept" (p. 175). Thus, Boghossian concludes, Putnamian anti-individualism and privileged access have the absurd conclusion that a subject can have a priori knowledge that her environment contains a natural kind, say, water.[4]

Let us consider, then, whether privileged access involves the claim that a subject can know a priori that she is not in a bad case, where the bad case is construed to involve either an illusion of thought or a descriptive thought. As I have defined it, privileged access states that a subject can have a priori knowledge of her thought contents. This seems to amount only to the claim that, for any thought content p that a subject thinks, she can know a priori that she thinks that p. It does not obviously involve the claim that a subject can know a priori whether she is having a thought or, if she is, its type, say, whether it is descriptive. Further, the claim that anti-individualists have argued is consistent with their view is merely the claim that a subject can have a priori knowledge of her thought contents. They have not argued that a subject can know a priori that she is not in a bad case. For instance, defenders of the illusion version of anti-individualism have not argued that a subject can know a priori that she is not suffering an illusion of thought. In general, anti-individualists defend the claim that a subject can know a priori that she is thinking that p even if she does not know much about that thought—the environmental facts which individuate it, whether it is the same or different in content from some other simultaneous thought, or how to properly explicate it (see chap. 2 and 5; and, for the last point, Burge 1988, p. 662). So, it seems unlikely that they would take privileged access to entail that a subject can know a priori whether some thought is descriptive or not.

Last, anti-individualists standardly defend privileged access by pointing out that a subject's second-order judgments of the form "I judge that I think that p" are self-verifying. Consider an Earth subject who thinks that water is wet and self-ascribes this thought. Were the environment so different that she no longer thinks that water is wet, she would no longer self-ascribe this thought. For instance, if she were instead on Twin Earth thinking that twater is wet, then she would believe that she thinks that twater is wet.

Notice that this standard defense cannot be applied to show that a subject can know a priori that she is not in a bad case. A subject's belief that she is not in a bad case is not self-verifying. Indeed, if a subject were in a bad case, she would believe that she is not in a bad case.

It seems, then, that as defined here, and as anti-individualists understand it, privileged access does not directly involve the claim that a subject can know a priori whether she is in a bad case.[5] However, there might be some less direct link between the two. Someone might suggest that if a subject has privileged access to her thought contents, say, that she thinks that water is wet, then she can use this to gain by inference a priori knowledge that she is not suffering an illusion of thought. In the rest of the section I consider this suggestion.

Suppose that Sally thinks that water is wet. Her having this thought entails that she is not instead suffering an illusion of thought. So, there is a possible inference from the premise that she thinks that water is wet to the conclusion that she is not suffering an illusion of thought:

(T1)   I think that water is wet.

(T2)   If I think that water is wet, then I am having a thought rather than an illusion of thought.

(T3)   I am having a thought rather than an illusion of thought.

Given privileged access, Sally can have a priori knowledge of (T1). Further, merely in virtue of understanding the relevant concepts, Sally can have a priori knowledge of (T2). So, if knowledge always transmits across valid arguments, she could use her a priori knowledge of (T1) and (T2) to gain a priori knowledge of (T3), that she is having a thought rather than an illusion of thought.

In the last chapter, we saw that it is a contentious issue whether knowledge always transmits across a valid argument. Davies and Wright try to answer the reductio by arguing that there is a failure of transmission of knowledge across the inference: (W1) I think that water is wet; (W2) If I think that water is wet, then my environment contains water; (W3) My environment contains water. The point currently under consideration focuses on a different claim—that knowledge fails to transmit across the valid argument (T1)–(T3).

We rejected Davies's and Wright's accounts of the failure of transmission of knowledge.[6] Nevertheless, I will argue that there is a failure of transmission of knowledge from (T1) and (T2) to (T3) on a different basis. In doing so, I will use the widely accepted view that S knows that p only if, were p false, she wouldn't believe that p. As Nozick and Dretske point out, this condition entails counterexamples to closure, and thus transmission, of knowledge (chap. 7, sec. 2). It seems that the inference (T1)–(T3) is such a counterexample. In particular, Sally's belief in (T3) fails the relevant condition for knowledge: if she were not having a thought but suffering an illusion of thought, she would falsely believe that she is having a thought rather than an illusion of thought.[7] However, there is no reason to suppose that Sally's belief in (T1) and (T2) fails this condition for knowledge. Consider Sally's belief in (T1): as anti-individualists stress, if conditions were so different that Sally would not think that water is wet, then she would no longer self-ascribe this thought. For instance, if she is instead on Twin Earth thinking that twater is wet, then she would believe that she thinks that twater is wet. If she were not thinking that water is wet, but instead suffering an illusion of thought, she would no longer believe that she thinks that water is wet. Thus, the inference (T1)–(T3) is a counterexample to the transmission of knowledge. Further, it is a counterexample to the closure of knowledge: a subject could have a priori knowledge of (T1) and (T2) and lack knowledge of (T3), whether a priori or empirical, since she lacks empirical evidence that rules it out that she is suffering an illusion of thought.

In conclusion, privileged access neither directly nor indirectly supports the claim that a subject can know a priori that she is not in a bad case, whether this involves her having an illusion of thought or having a descriptive thought. This argument concludes the last part of the discussion of applying the reductio to natural kind anti-individualism. I have argued that the reductio cannot be applied successfully to natural kind anti-individualism, for natural kind anti-individualism does not support (R2): Sally can know a priori that if she thinks that water is wet, then her environment contains water. However, the reductio might be successful against some other version of anti-individualism. In the following two sections, I consider singular anti-individualism and social anti-individualism.

3   Singular Anti-Individualism

According to singular anti-individualism, some singular thoughts are individuated partly by the object(s) they are about. For example, suppose that Sally sees a particular apple and thinks the perceptual demonstrative thought that that apple is red. According to singular anti-individualism, her thought that that apple is red is individuated partly by the apple it is about. Thus, if she had been looking at a different apple or had merely suffered an illusion of seeing an apple, she would have lacked the thought she actually has. Using this example, we might construct a reductio for singular anti-individualism with the original (R1)–(R3) replaced by (P1)–(P3):

(P1)   Sally knows a priori that she thinks that that apple is red. (*From the assumption of privileged access.*)

(P2)   Sally knows a priori that if she thinks that that apple is red, then that apple exists. (*From the assumption of singular anti-individualism.*)

(P3)   Sally knows a priori that that apple exists. (*From P1–P2.*)

As with the case of natural kind anti-individualism, our focus will be on the second step. If Sally knows the arguments for singular anti-individualism, can she know a priori that her thinking that that apple is red entails that that apple exists?

Anti-individualists do not typically claim that whenever a subject thinks about an object, her thought is individuated partly by that object. They accept that a subject may sometimes think of an object by description. Suppose that I don't follow tennis and don't know who the top-ranked players are. Nonetheless, I might surmise that the woman, whoever she is, who is the world's top female tennis player is wealthy. Here, I think about a person via a description. If Venus Williams is in fact the top female tennis player, then I think about Venus. By contrast, if Capriati had been the top player, I would have thought about her instead. In such a case, my thought seems independent of the object it is about. In each situation, I think the same thought, but it is about different players. While accepting the possibility of such descriptive thoughts, anti-individualists argue that subjects may also have nondescriptive thoughts that are individuated partly by the objects they are about. For example, it has been claimed that perceptual demonstrative and recognition-based thoughts are individuated partly by the objects they are about.

It might be suggested that a subject could use singular anti-individualism to gain a priori knowledge of certain conditionals of the form: if S is in condition C, then she is in a certain kind of environment. If she could also know a priori that she meets the antecedent of such a conditional, then perhaps she could gain a priori knowledge of links between her thoughts and the environment. However, I will argue that one cannot know a priori that one meets the antecedent, however condition C is formulated. The argument may be sketched out as follows. One could formulate C so that it involves a real-world relation to the environment, or one could formulate it more weakly so that it does not involve any such relation. When formulated so that it involves a real-world relation, a subject cannot know a priori that she meets condition C. When formulated more weakly, it turns out that condition C is compatible with the absence of a relevant object to refer to. Thus, it is compatible with the bad case, the possibility that the subject either suffers an illusion of thought or has a descriptive thought. But, since a subject cannot know a priori that she is not in a bad case, it turns out that this second weaker formulation cannot support the reductio. Let me illustrate this with the example of anti-individualism about perceptual demonstrative thoughts.

Suppose that we take condition C to be having a perceptual demonstrative thought about an object. Thus, the conditional might state, if a subject has a perceptual demonstrative thought about x, then her environment contains x.

However, so formulated the conditional cannot support the reductio. A subject has a perceptual demonstrative thought about an object only if she is perceiving an object. But a subject cannot know a priori that she is perceiving an object. Alternatively, we could formulate the conditional so that it does not involve any real-world relation. For instance, we could use the notion that a subject seems to see and refer to an object demonstratively. Let's consider, then, what follows from the fact that, say, Sally seems to see a red apple and tries to refer to it demonstratively. If she sees apple *a* and successfully refers to it, then her thought is individuated partly by *a*. However, suppose instead that she suffers an illusion of seeing an apple and thus fails to refer demonstratively to any apple. There are two possible anti-individualist views about this case. According to the illusion view, Sally suffers an illusion of thought. On the rival descriptive view, she has a thought involving a descriptive concept of the apple, for example, she thinks that the apple she seems to see is red. These different versions give us two different conditionals linking thought and the world:

(D)   If a subject *S* seems to see an object and attempts to refer to it in the perceptual demonstrative way but fails to do so, then *S* suffers an illusion of thought.

(E)   If a subject *S* seems to see an object and attempts to refer to it in the perceptual demonstrative way but fails to do so, then *S* has a descriptive thought.

These principles are logically equivalent to:

(D')   If a subject *S* seems to see an object and attempts to refer to it in the perceptual demonstrative way, and does not suffer an illusion of thought, then there is an object *S* sees.

(E') If a subject S seems to see an object and attempts to refer to it in the perceptual demonstrative way and does not have a descriptive thought, then there is an object S sees.

Principles (D') and (E') are analogous to the principles (B') and (C'), considered in the discussion of applying the reductio to natural kind anti-individualism. Each of (D') and (E') states that if a subject is in certain psychological conditions then her environment is some specific way. Like the earlier principles, (B') and (C'), a subject could use (D') or (E') to gain a priori knowledge of links between her thoughts and the environment only if she can know a priori that she meets their antecedents. To use (D') she needs to know a priori that she is not suffering an illusion of thought; to use (E') she needs to know a priori that she is not having a descriptive thought. However, as our earlier discussion of natural kind anti-individualism shows, a subject cannot have such knowledge. Even if a subject is not in a bad case, she cannot know this a priori, where the bad case covers both the possibility that she suffers an illusion of thought and the possibility that she has a descriptive thought. If she were in a bad case and the question were to arise, she would believe she is not in a bad case.

For instance, suppose that Sally actually sees apple *a* and thinks that that apple (*a*) is red. Suppose that Sally also endorses the illusion version of anti-individualism and believes truly that she is not suffering an illusion of thought. This belief does not constitute a priori knowledge. Consider the situation in which Sally suffers an illusion of seeing an apple and thus suffers an illusion of thought. In such a situation, if the question arose, she would believe that she is not suffering an illusion of thought. Now consider the alternative view that when she suffers an illusion of seeing and referring to an apple, she has a descriptive thought. On this alternative view too, were the question to arise, she would deny that she is having a descriptive thought.

It seems, then, that the reductio fails against singular anti-individualism for the same reasons it failed against natural kind anti-individualism. In each case, the relevant type of anti-individualism fails to support the crucial second step of the reductio, according to which a subject can have a priori knowledge of some specific link between her thoughts and the environment. However, these arguments leave it open that the reductio works when applied to social anti-individualism.

4   Social Anti-Individualism

According to social anti-individualism, a subject's thought contents are individuated partly by the practices of her linguistic community. The key question is whether social anti-individualism supports the second step of the reductio, according to which Sally can have a priori knowledge of some specific link between her thoughts and the environment. As we have already seen, Burge's arthritis thought experiment does not directly support the second step for it concerns a subject stipulated to be part of a linguistic community and establishes only a counterfactual dependence of thought on environment (sec. 1). Nevertheless, I will argue that social anti-individualism could be used to gain a priori knowledge of the following conditional principle, which does link thought and the world:

(F)   If a subject S has a concept c and is agnostic about c, then S is part of a linguistic community with the concept c.

(See Brown 1995 and 2001. F's consequent abbreviates the more complex condition that S is now, or used to be, part of a linguistic community with the concept c.)[8] If Sally could have a priori knowledge of (F) and that she meets the antecedent of (F), then she could use this knowledge to gain a priori knowledge that she is part of a linguistic community. But it seems absurd that someone could know that she is part of a linguistic community merely by reflection on her thought contents and some philosophy.

Before examining (F) in more detail, it is important to understand the component notion of agnosticism. Agnosticism is a type of incomplete understanding of a concept distinct from misunderstanding. Misunderstanding amounts to supposing that a concept applies to certain kinds of thing to which it does not apply, or supposing that it fails to apply to certain kinds of thing to which it does apply. For example, one misunderstands the notion of arthritis if one thinks that it applies to problems of the thighs and joints (in fact, it applies only to problems of the joints). By contrast, agnosticism consists in being unsure whether the concept applies to certain kinds of thing where there is a determinate fact about whether or not the concept applies to that kind of thing (see Burge 1979, p. 77). For example, an English speaker who believes that 'arthritis' applies to problems of the joints, but is unsure whether it applies to problems of the thigh, is agnostic.

I will now argue that (F) follows from social anti-individualism. My argument starts from the fact that every kind concept has conditions of correct and incorrect application. Notice that this is so even for concepts that are partly indeterminate or vague. For example, there are certain degrees of hair loss at which it is indeterminate whether one is bald. Despite this, there are some conditions to which the concept determinately applies (e.g., having not a single hair on one's head) and others to which it determinately does not apply (such as having a full head of hair). Thus, every concept has standards of correct and incorrect application, and these application conditions partly individuate the concept. So, for a subject to have some particular kind concept, something must make it the case that she has a concept with the relevant application conditions.

Suppose that Sally applies 'sofa' to sofas, but is unsure whether it also applies to large armchairs. The concept sofa is individuated partly by the fact that it does not apply to large armchairs. Social anti-individualism allows that if Sally is part of a community of English speakers, then she expresses the concept sofa with 'sofa', despite her uncertainty. Thus, Sally fulfils the antecedent of (F)—she has the concept sofa while being agnostic about its application conditions.

Now consider whether Sally could use 'sofa' to express the concept sofa if she had been brought up in an environment in which there are no other speakers. It seems not. A concept Sally possesses can be the concept sofa only if it fails to apply to large armchairs. But, in the counterfactual environment, there is nothing to determine that the concept Sally expresses with 'sofa' has these application conditions. Sally herself is unsure about whether the term 'sofa' applies to large armchairs. She has had no contact with other speakers. And, since the kind sofa is not a natural kind, her natural environment cannot help her to have the concept. (In any case, we are currently considering only social anti-individualism and ignoring natural kind anti-individualism. Thus, even if the relevant concept had been the concept of a natural kind, the natural environment could not have helped the subject to acquire the concept.) Thus, in the counterfactual environment in which Sally is not part of a linguistic community, she cannot have the concept sofa given her uncertainty about whether it applies to large armchairs.

Of course, in this counterfactual environment, Sally may express some concept other than the concept sofa with 'sofa'. Thus, she may express some concept with 'sofa' while being unsure about whether that concept applies to large armchairs. Some critics have taken this to amount to a counterexample to (F), a case in which a subject has a concept and is agnostic about it but is not part of a community (see, e.g., McLaughlin and Tye 1998, p. 317; Falvey 2000, p. 142). However, this objection is based on a misunderstanding of agnosticism. Recall that a subject is agnostic about a concept only if she is unsure whether it applies to things of a certain type, and there is some definite fact of the matter about whether it does so apply. But, in the counterfactual situation in which Sally is the only speaker, there is nothing to determine whether or not the concept she expresses with 'sofa' applies, or fails to apply, to large armchairs. Sally herself is unsure whether it does so, and she has had no contact with no other speakers. So, even if Sally expresses a concept with 'sofa', and is unsure about whether it applies to large armchairs, she is not agnostic about it.[9]

It seems, then, that anyone who holds social anti-individualism should accept (F). Further, it seems that Sally could have a priori knowledge of (F). Admittedly, the argument given for (F) above used a fact of which Sally is ignorant, that the concept sofa does not apply to large armchairs. However, the argument can be formulated independently of this assumption (Brown 2001). If Sally could have a priori knowledge of (F) and of the fact that she meets the conditions mentioned in the antecedent of (F), then she could have a priori knowledge of connections between her thought and the world, say, that if she thinks that sofas are comfy then she is part of a linguistic community. So, the key question for the reductio is whether Sally can know a priori that she meets the antecedent of (F). In particular, can Sally know a priori that she has the concept sofa and that she is agnostic about it?

It seems plausible that Sally may know a priori that she has the concept sofa. However, it is hard to see how she could know a priori that she is agnostic. A subject is agnostic if she is unsure about whether a concept applies to things of a certain kind and there is a determinate fact of the matter whether it does so apply. It seems plausible that Sally can know a priori that she is unsure whether the concept sofa applies to large armchairs. However, Sally may have no idea whether there is a determinate fact about whether the concept sofa applies to large armchairs. For all she knows, it may be indeterminate whether the concept sofa applies to such armchairs. After all, the extensions of some concepts are partly vague or indeterminate. Moreover, even if Sally does believe that there is a determinate fact about whether the concept sofa applies to large armchairs, this belief does not constitute a priori knowledge. Social anti-individualists hold that incomplete understanding of terms and concepts is a ubiquitous phenomenon (see, e.g., Burge 1979). So, it is a relevant alternative that there is no determinate fact whether 'sofa' applies to large armchairs and Sally's belief is incorrect. But, Sally cannot rule out this alternative a priori.

We might put the point more generally as follows. Social anti-individualism undermines the traditional idea that a subject can gain a priori knowledge of how a term or concept applies in virtue of understanding it. On the traditional conception, a subject who understands the relevant concepts can know a priori that the concept of a bachelor applies to unmarried men, and that the concept of a toothbrush is the concept of an artifact. But a social anti-individualist should reject this conception. Consider Burge's arthritis patient who has the concept arthritis while incompletely understanding it, believing that it applies to problems of the joints and thighs. He cannot know a priori that the concept in fact applies only to problems of the joints. However, even if the patient had instead truly believed that arthritis applies only to problems of the joints, this belief would not constitute a priori knowledge. Given the ubiquity of incomplete understanding it is a relevant alternative that he misunderstands the concept. But, he cannot rule out this possibility a priori. (See Brueckner 2002.)

In summary, the reductio fails against social anti-individualism for the same reason it fails against natural kind and singular anti-individualism. In each case, the relevant type of anti-individualism fails to establish the crucial second step, according to which a subject can have a priori knowledge of some specific link between her thoughts and the environment. The classic Twin Earth arguments for anti-individualism establish only a counterfactual dependence of thought on the environment. Nevertheless we have seen that each of the types of anti-individualism supports some conditional claim that states that if a subject is in certain psychological and other conditions, then her environment is some particular way. A subject could use such conditionals to gain a priori knowledge of connections between her thoughts and the environment only if she can have a priori knowledge that she meets the conditions mentioned in the antecedent of the conditional. But she cannot have such a priori knowledge.

5   Combined Views

So far, we have seen that the reductio fails to show that privileged access is incompatible with various forms of anti-individualism when taken singly. At this stage, our discussion of the reductio may seem complete. However, there is one last possibility to be considered, whether the reductio would be successful against some combination of anti-individualist views. Someone might suggest that the objections we have raised to the reductio arise from the fact that we have considered different anti-individualist theses taken singly. So taken, anti-individualist theses establish that if a subject is in a certain condition, then her thought is individuated partly by the environment. Such a condition might be that she is having a perceptual demonstrative thought, or that she intends a term to express an atomic concept of a natural kind and is not suffering an illusion of thought. However, as we have seen, a subject cannot know a priori that she is in such specific conditions. By contrast, a combination of anti-individualist views would apply to a larger range of thoughts and so might not require that a subject can know a priori that she is in such a specific condition.

This line of thought lay behind my suggestion (Brown 1995, 2001) to formulate a reductio of the combination of natural kind and social anti-individualism. I argued that on this combined view, the following principle would be correct:

(G)   If a subject S has the concept c and is agnostic about c, then either c is a concept of a natural kind and S's environment contains instances of that kind, or S is part of a community with the concept c.

Unlike earlier principles, (G) just talks of a subject's having a concept, rather than her having a particular type of concept, such as a natural kind concept. (G) reflects the idea that if both natural kind and social anti-individualism are true, then a subject can have a concept despite being agnostic, either by being in an environment with instances of a suitable natural kind, or by being part of a suitable linguistic community.

However, in fact, once again it is hard to see how (G) could be used in a successful reductio. It could be so used only if a subject could know a priori that she meets the antecedent of (G), in particular, that she is agnostic about a concept. But we have already seen that social anti-individualism undermines the claim that a subject can have such knowledge. This conclusion seems unaffected even if natural kind anti-individualism is also true. It seems, then, that the reductio is no more successful against anti-individualist views when combined than when taken singly.

6 Conclusion

I have argued that the reductio fails to show that anti-individualism is incompatible with privileged access. Anti-individualism fails to support the crucial second step, according to which a subject can have a priori knowledge of some specific link between her thoughts and the environment. The Twin Earth arguments support only the counterfactual dependence of thought on world; they do not show that having a certain concept, say, water, entails that one's environment is some way, say that it contains water.

Someone could use anti-individualism to gain a priori knowledge of certain conditional principles that state that if a subject is in certain psychological and other conditions, then her environment is some particular way. However, such conditional principles could be used to defend a successful reductio only if one can know a priori that one meets the conditions mentioned in the antecedent. But, I have argued that such knowledge is not available.

Appendix to Chapter 8: Comparison with Davies and Wright

I have argued that the reductio fails to show that anti-individualism and privileged access are incompatible since anti-individualism fails to support the second step, according to which a subject can have a priori knowledge of some specific link between her thoughts and the environment. This response to the reductio contrasts with that offered by Davies and Wright, who challenge the transition from the first two premises of the reductio to the third. Despite this difference, I am committed to making one of the claims that they make, namely that there are counterexamples to the transmission of knowledge.

In chapter 8, section 2.1, I denied that a subject could gain a priori knowledge that she is thinking a thought rather than suffering an illusion of thought by inference from her a priori knowledge that she thinks, say, that water is wet, and her a priori knowledge that if she thinks that water is wet, then she is having a thought rather than suffering an illusion of thought. However, my grounds for limiting the transmission of knowledge are different from those endorsed by Wright and Davies. They argue that there is a limitation on the transmission of knowledge since warrant is a necessary condition for knowledge and there is a limitation on the transmission of warrant. Wright argues that warrant fails to transmit across a valid argument when the warrant for one of the premises is conditional on having prior and independent warrant for the conclusion. Davies argues that warrant fails to transmit across a valid argument when warrant for the premises fails to rule out salient or relevant alternatives to the conclusion. I have argued that there is a limitation on the transmission of knowledge on the grounds that S's true belief that p is knowledge only if, were p false, she would not believe that p. So long as warrant is not defined as whatever makes the difference between true belief and knowledge, this does not entail that there are counterexamples to the transmission of warrant.

Given my different reasons for denying the transmission of knowledge, my account does not face the objections raised to Davies's and Wright's accounts in chapter 7. Further, my account has different consequences. First, a limitation on the transmission of knowledge grounded on the above conception of knowledge could not be used to argue for a failure of transmission across the inference (W1) I think that water is wet; (W2) If I think that water is wet, then my environment contains water; (W3) My environment contains water—for (W3) meets the relevant condition for knowledge. Consider a possible situation in which one's environment does not contain water. Given the anti-individualism underlying (W2), in such an environment one would lack the concept water, and thus could not falsely believe that one's environment contains water.

Davies and Wright might object that my solution to the reductio involves denying the closure of knowledge. However, although Davies tries to separate his denial of the transmission of warrant from a denial of the closure of knowledge, in fact his account is committed to denying closure also. To see this, consider Davies's architecturalism argument, which considers the consequences of the view that there are philosophical arguments that provide a priori knowledge that any creature capable of thought has a cognitive architecture that meets the conditions for the language of thought, or LOT (Davies 1998). If this assumption is combined with the assumption of privileged access it might seem to offer an objectionably a priori route to knowledge about the structure of a thinker's brain via reasoning analogous to that central to the reductio:

(A1)   I think that water is wet. (*From the assumption of privileged access.*)

(A2)   If I think that water is wet, then LOT is true of me. (*From the assumption that philosophical arguments enable one to know a priori any thinker meets the conditions for LOT.*)

(A3)   LOT is true of me. (*From (A1) and (A2).*)

However, it seems absurd to suppose that a subject could gain a priori knowledge of the structure of her brain merely by reflection on her thoughts and philosophical arguments.

Since Davies finds it plausible that one has a priori knowledge of the premises of the architecturalism argument (p. 343), he attempts to avoid a priori knowledge of the conclusion by arguing that the argument is a counterexample to the transmission of warrant. Thus, it seems that Davies holds that someone might have an a priori warrant for (A1) by reflection and an a priori warrant for (A2) by philosophical argument without thereby having an a priori warrant for (A3). Given this, Davies can avoid denying closure of warrant only if anyone with such a priori warrant for (A1) and (A2) has some warrant for (A3) independent of the inference. But it is hard to see how this could be the case.

As Davies notes, one could have the relevant a priori warrants for (A1) and (A2) without having any empirical evidence for (A3). But it seems that any justification of (A3) that is independent of the inference from (A1) and (A2) would have to be empirical. Thus, it seems that Davies is committed to holding that the inference (A1)–(A3) is a counterexample to closure of warrant. Given his further view that knowledge requires warrant, he cannot avoid denying closure of knowledge.

By contrast, Wright's conditional analysis is not committed to denying the closure of warrant or knowledge. According to this analysis, warrant fails to transmit across a valid argument if warrant for one of the premises is conditional on prior and independent warrant for the conclusion. Thus, his analysis does not generate the possibility that one could have warrant for the premises of a valid argument yet fail to have warrant for the conclusion. But the very feature that enables the conditional analysis to avoid denying closure is responsible for one of the main objections to it, namely that it has the counterintuitive consequence that a subject can have a priori knowledge of substantive facts about the world (see chap. 7).

Suppose that one has a priori warrant for the premises of an argument across which warrant fails to transmit. To avoid denying the closure of a priori warrant, Wright must say that one has a priori warrant for the premises only if one has prior and independent a priori warrant for the conclusion. The reductio is just such an argument. Wright accepts that Sally has a priori warrant and knowledge that she is thinking that water is wet, and that if she is thinking that water is wet then her environment contains water, but he denies that Sally could thereby come to have a priori warrant and knowledge that her environment contains water. Thus, to avoid denying closure, Wright must accept that Sally has prior and independent a priori warrant and knowledge that her environment contains water.

Thus, as argued in chapter 7, Wright's solution to the reductio is no less problematic than the problem it aims to solve: it is committed to the claim that a subject can have a priori knowledge of substantial facts about the nature of her environment. (This closure argument presents a consideration additional to that presented in chap. 7 for supposing that Wright must accept that Sally has prior and independent a priori warrant for the claim that her environment contains water.)

9   Conclusion

Many have argued that anti-individualism has radical consequences for our knowledge of our own minds, our ability to reason, and our knowledge of the world. After examining these objections in detail, I have argued that anti-individualism does not have these consequences.

The book started with a discussion of whether anti-individualism is compatible with privileged access, the plausible claim that a subject can have a priori knowledge of her thought contents. In the first part of the book, I examined the achievement problem for compatibility, the problem of how a subject can have privileged access to externally individuated thought contents. According to the discrimination argument, anti-individualism threatens privileged access since it undermines a subject's ability to distinguish a priori between the actual situation and alternative situations in which she lacks the thought she has in the actual situation. According to the illusion argument, the illusion version of anti-individualism undermines privileged access by allowing that a subject may suffer an illusion of thought. Compatibilists standardly reply to the discrimination argument by allowing that the alternative situations are relevant and so potentially knowledge undermining, but stressing the reliability of a subject's judgments about her thought contents. By contrast, I have explored and developed the idea that the alternative situations are not relevant. This response finesses two issues facing the standard compatibilist view: the issue of whether knowledge requires discriminative abilities or only reliability, and what the reliabilist requirement for knowledge turns out to involve. As a result, the relevant alternatives strategy may be used by compatibilists with different epistemic views, including those who think that knowledge requires discriminative abilities and those who think that it requires only reliability.

In the second part of the book, I argued that anti-individualism undermines transparency of content, that is, a subject's ability to grasp a priori sameness and difference of content. Anti-individualism thus has the consequence that a subject cannot always grasp a priori the logical properties of her thoughts, so she may make simple logical mistakes. This undermines one idea of rationality, according to which a rational subject can always grasp a priori the simple logical properties of her thoughts and would not make simple logical mistakes. But I argue that anti-individualism does not undermine rationality when properly understood.

In the last part of the book, I examined the consequence problem, the problem of what consequences would follow if anti-individualism and privileged access were both true. It has been argued that the joint assumptions of privileged access and anti-individualism have the consequence that a subject can have a priori knowledge of substantive facts about the world. Some have taken this to be a reductio of the joint assumptions of anti-individualism and privileged access; others have taken it to be an advantage of anti-individualism. However, I have argued that even if anti-individualism and privileged access were both true, they would not enable a subject to gain a priori knowledge of the world.

It seems, then, that anti-individualism does not have the problematic epistemic consequences often suggested. A quite different set of objections to anti-individualism arises from psychological explanation. It has been argued that anti-individualism is incompatible with the idea that a subject's mental states and, in particular, their contents, causally explain her actions. Although this issue has not been my concern here, part of the argument of the book is relevant to anti-individualism's consequences for psychological explanation. In chapter 6, I provided a new reason for thinking that anti-individualism is in tension with the notion of object-dependent sense developed by modern Fregeans. If that is right, then anti-individualists cannot hope to take advantage of the Fregean explanation of psychological phenomena. Thus, the choice between anti-individualism and individualism is also a choice between non-Fregean and Fregean explanations of action. A full defense of anti-individualism would need to address this issue as well as the question of the causal efficacy of content. However, these issues concerning psychological explanation are outside the scope of the present book and must be left for another occasion.

Notes

Chapter 1

1. Functionalism can also be developed as an anti-individualist view.

2. For simplicity, I am ignoring impure intrinsic properties that can be possessed independently of the existence of other objects and events but are not shared by duplicates (Langton and Lewis 1998). To deal with this issue, one could reformulate the definitions of individualism and anti-individualism, replacing the notion of an intrinsic property with the notion of a property shared between duplicates.

3. That a subject's thought contents are individuated partly by her environment does not strictly entail that her thought contents fail to supervene on her intrinsic properties. Jackson and Pettit (1993) argue that a property of an object, x, that is individuated relationally might still supervene on microstructural properties of x, e.g., the property of being water-soluble.

4. These arguments and the resulting nondescriptive model of reference in language and thought can be found, inter alia, in Perry (1979), Kripke (1980), Evans (1982), Peacocke (1983), McDowell (1986), Salmon (1986), Soames (1987), and, Kaplan (1989).

Chapter 2

1. Her thought contents may not change immediately after the switch, for, at that point, the dominant influence on her thoughts is plausibly still the Earth environment. Nevertheless, anti-individualists agree that, after a

suitable period of time, her new relationship with Twin Earth starts to affect her thought contents.

2. This view may be supported by arguing that after the switch, the subject is related mainly to the Twin Earth environment (e.g., Burge 1988; Falvey and Owens 1994; Gibbons 1996; Tye 1998). On an alternative view, after the switch, she is related to both Earth and Twin Earth environments and so either has an "amalgam" concept that applies to both water and twater, or suffers an illusion of thought (see Heal 1998; Sawyer 1999). For further discussion, see chap. 5.

3. For exceptions, see Warfield (1997) and Sawyer (1999). Sawyer suggests that one has a recognition-based thought about an object or kind only if there is no duplicate in the environment. I agree (see Brown 1998 and chaps. 3 and 4 here), but this point does not extend straightforwardly to show that duplicate thoughts are not relevant for other types of externally individuated thoughts, such as perceptual demonstrative or socially individuated thoughts. In addition, in some cases a twin thought is relevant, such as in a slow switch. Sawyer treats slow switch cases as akin to cases in which a subject mistakes a motley collection of natural kinds for a single natural kind. She argues that, after a switch, a subject would not have a twin thought, say, about twater, but rather a thought involving a descriptive concept that applies to both water and twater. But this does not answer the discrimination argument, since, as indicated, it can use any alternative situation in which the subject lacks the thought she has in the actual situation including one in which she instead has a descriptive concept.

4. The self-verifying nature of cogito thoughts cannot be used to explain our knowledge of our past thoughts. A subject's belief that she thinks that p makes it the case that she now thinks that p, but not that she thinks that p at any other time.

5. Compatibilists do not argue that a subject can have a priori knowledge of the contents of her past thoughts. Nevertheless, Sally's mistake supports the claim that she cannot distinguish a priori between the two situations.

6. Whether Sally can correctly report her thought contents depends on the correct account of thought content. Plausibly, after the switch, the meaning of 'water' on Sally's lips is determined by the conventions of the Twin Earth community in which 'water' refers only to twater. But some anti-individualists hold that, after the switch, those of Sally's thoughts that were based on Earth memories involve the concept water. Others argue that, after the switch, with 'water' Sally expresses a concept that applies to both water and twater.

7. Note that this view does not undermine my description of the challenge posed by the discrimination argument: how can a subject know a priori that she thinks that p when there is a relevant alternative situation, in which she lacks the thought that p, that she cannot a priori distinguish from the actual situation? Even if a subject retains her old concept after a slow switch, where p is suitably chosen, she no longer thinks that p after the switch. E.g., let p be the thought S expresses on Earth with 'Water is wet', namely, the thought that water is wet. The content S expresses with 'Water is wet' does not only depend on memory but is caused and sustained by current interactions. Thus, after the switch to Twin Earth, even if S retains the concept of water, she no longer expresses the thought that water is wet with 'Water is wet'. Depending on the anti-individualist view under consideration, she would either have a twin thought, have an amalgam thought, or suffer an illusion of thought.

8. Sally's explication may provide evidence that, before and after the switch, she uses 'water' to express different concepts. E.g., her verbal reports may attribute different contents to her water and twater thoughts, and she might explain 'water' by saying it refers to a natural kind common to lakes and rivers around here. Neither of these points provides evidence that she notices any difference between water and twater thoughts.

9. Here, and throughout this chapter, I concentrate on what Goldman calls a "local reliability" condition for knowledge. This seems appropriate given that compatibilists focus implicitly on this condition; they argue that, even if Sally were in a relevant alternative situation in which she lacks the thought she actually has, she would no longer self-attribute that thought. Goldman holds that knowledge also requires that the belief be produced by a "globally reliable" process, one that tends to produce a high ratio of true beliefs. This distinct reliability condition is relevant to the illusion argument, and I discuss it in chap. 4 (see sec. 3 especially).

10. Burge similarly argues that we (in his view mistakenly) suppose that a subject can know that p only if she can rule out various alternatives because, were one of those alternatives actual, she would be liable to error (1988, p. 659). But he provides no argument for his diagnosis and against the rival hypothesis that we make this supposition because we take it that knowledge that p requires the ability to distinguish the actual state of affairs in which p from relevant alternative states of affairs.

11. McLaughlin and Tye do not aim to show that anti-individualism is compatible with such discriminative abilities, but this issue is crucial to the discrimination argument as I have set it up.

Chapter 3

1. A subject may locate the object egocentrically, rather than allocentrically.

2. Here Evans stresses the idea that the subject would not be disposed to regard an object outside the area of search as the relevant object. Elsewhere, Evans says "any disposition he has to pick out something outside the area of search does not count, and he is disposed to identify just one thing within it" (1982, p. 280). I have concentrated on the first idea, as it seems to go better with Evans's idea of the area of search as the area within which the subject estimates the object to be. On this definition of the area of search, it is not obvious that a disposition to consider an object outside the area of search would not count for the estimated area of search might be incorrect. See sec. 6.

3. In chap. 4, I question whether such alternative situations are usually relevant.

4. I am assuming that a subject may have the same perceptual demonstrative thought at different times. If this were not the case and Sally were to know this, then she would correctly judge that her two perceptual demonstrative thoughts have different contents even if she mistakenly thinks that they concern the same object. However, perceptual demonstrative thoughts are plausibly connected with perceptual tracking of objects over (short) periods of time so that one can have the same perceptual demonstrative thought at different times; this is so even on a Fregean view (Campbell 1987).

5. Sally's inability to pass this test cannot be explained away by saying that there is a period in which it is indeterminate what thought she is thinking. Sometimes indeterminacy may make judgments of change more difficult. E.g., as someone loses weight, there may be a period in which it is indeterminate whether she has become thin, although at a later stage she is determinately thin. However, unlike this thinness example, Sally's problem is not plausibly captured by saying that she has access to the change but is not sure how to classify it. Rather, it seems, she lacks access to the change altogether.

6. Evans's notions of discrimination by perception and by recognitional capacity do not help here. We have already seen that Sally lacks a recognition-based ability to distinguish the actual situation and the relevant alternative situation in which she thinks a twin thought. Perception of an object enables one to distinguish it from all others since it enables one to locate the object and discover its type. It is implausible to suppose that a subject exploits location in distinguishing types of thought.

7. Like the earlier indexical suggestion, this suggestion is compatible with a wide range of anti-individualist views, whether or not they accept Evans's requirement for thought.

8. Notice that this is so whether or not knowledge that p requires the ability to distinguish the actual situation from relevant alternative situations or merely requires that there is no relevant alternative situation in which the subject falsely believes that p.

Chapter 4

1. Introduced in chap. 1, sec. 4.

2. Some prefer to use "reliability" for the statistical or dispositional property I later describe as "global reliability." However, the use of "reliabilist" to characterize Nozick's and Goldman's accounts is widespread and reflects the fact that a belief meeting the relevant conditions could not easily have been false.

3. This conclusion would not be affected if a local reliabilist accepted two further conditions Goldman places on knowledge—(1) his nonundermining condition: that the subject neither believe that the process is unreliable nor be in a mental state from which reliable processes would lead her so to conclude; and (2) that the belief be produced by a reliable process that was itself acquired by a reliable method for acquiring belief-forming processes (Goldman 1986, pp. 52–54). In particular, Sally may be ignorant of the fact that she is liable to suffer illusions of hearing wasps; and this fact does not undermine the reliability of the belief-forming process if we take reliability to be local reliability.

4. By contrast, the distinction between local and global reliability makes no difference to whether Sally's a priori knowledge of her actual thoughts is undermined by the possible situation in which she is hearing, and thinking about, a different wasp w^*. If Sally were hearing w^*, then she would neither self-ascribe the thought that that wasp (w) is near nor suffer an illusion of thought.

5. Someone might suggest that illusions of thought are normally so infrequent that even if global reliability is required for knowledge, illusions of thought present no problem for this condition. I ultimately agree with this line of thought (sec. 11), but it is interesting to see whether a defense of privileged access needs to rely on this point about frequency. If it does, the fact that some subjects—like Sally—frequently suffer illusions of thought may threaten their privileged access to their thoughts. In secs.

4–5, I examine whether a compatibilist could respond to the illusion argument in a different way, by arguing either that knowledge does not require global reliability or that illusions of thought are not relevant to global reliability.

6. Nozick's alternative formulation (if p weren't true, then S would not believe that p) does not help since we have no satisfactory theory of the truth value of conditionals with impossible antecedents.

7. The case cannot obviously be dealt with by using Goldman's nonundermining condition and his condition that the belief result from a process that was itself acquired by a reliable method for acquiring belief-forming processes. I may have no evidence that forming beliefs on the basis of my informant's testimony is unreliable; and this process may have been produced by a reliable method for acquiring belief-forming processes.

8. The barn example is not likely to be solved by Goldman's other conditions for knowledge. E.g., Laura may have no evidence that she is disposed to mistake fakes for barns. In addition, the process that produced Laura's belief may itself have been produced by a reliable process for acquiring belief-forming processes.

9. Someone may argue that Laura's case instead motivates a modification of local reliabilism. Consider the two perceptual demonstrative propositions that that object (b) is a barn, and that that object (f) is a barn. Calling such pairs of object-dependent propositions *counterparts*, the objector may suggest the following modified view: the true belief that p is knowledge iff it is produced by a method that is reliable with respect to p and its counterparts. However, this response ignores the argument for global reliabilism from knowledge of necessary truths, and it is inadequate if the illusion version of anti-individualism is correct. Consider S who regularly hallucinates barns but is in an environment in which there are only real barns. At t, she sees the barn, b, and thinks that that object (b) is a barn. This belief is not knowledge given her frequent hallucinations. But the modified local reliabilist account cannot agree; all it requires for knowledge is reliability with respect to the believed proposition and its counterparts. On the illusion version of anti-individualism, when S hallucinates a barn she does not believe a relevant counterpart proposition but rather suffers an illusion of thought. It is hard to see how the objector could deal with the barn-hallucinator without thereby conceding that the illusion version of anti-individualism may threaten privileged access. For example, she could say that S knows that that object (b) is a barn only if there is no nearby situation in which S would suffer an illusion of thought. But, if that is right, then the illusion version of anti-individualism may threaten privileged access,

for subjects can suffer illusions of thought at both first- and second-order levels.

10. Not always: the two typings considered in the last paragraph do not obviously affect the range of propositions relevant to global reliability, but rather affect the range of circumstances relevant to reliability.

11. Most compatibilists accept the relevance of alternative situations. However, Sawyer (1999) argues that if a subject is thinking a recognition-based thought about an object or kind, then the possibility of thinking a twin thought is not relevant. However, this claim does not easily extend to other types of externally individuated thoughts. In addition, the discrimination argument can exploit not only twin situations but also no-reference situations. Warfield (1997) suggests that real-world slow switches are infrequent.

12. It is logically possible that a subject could apply a term only to instances of a natural kind for which she lacks a recognitional capacity, e.g., if by accident she never comes across instances of a duplicate that she would mistake for the relevant kind. However, the more usual explanation is that she can recognize the relevant natural kind. Further, where she lacks such a capacity and applies a term to instances of one kind only by accident, this undermines the idea that she has a concept of that kind.

13. For Campbell (1987), the ability to perceptually track is crucial to our making the seems/is distinction.

14. Although the discussion considers the paradigm examples of externally individuated thoughts, it does not cover all possible examples, e.g., memory-based demonstrative thoughts.

Chapter 5

1. It should be clear from this example, and throughout the discussion, that I am focusing on validity as a property of thoughts, rather than as a property of sentences.

2. Is transparency further undermined by the illusion version of anti-individualism, according to which someone who takes herself to have two thoughts with the same content may in fact be suffering one or more illusions of thought? Such cases are not direct counterexamples to either transparency of sameness or transparency of difference of content, for they do not involve a subject having two thoughts with the same (or different) content and being unable to realize this a priori. Further, if such cases are

rare, they do not prevent a subject from grasping a priori that she has two thoughts with the same content when she does. Compare: if perceptual illusion is rare, it does not prevent one from knowing that one is perceiving when one is.

3. Chapter 6 considers a different argument due to Frances for the incompatibility of anti-individualism and transparency of difference of content. Since this argument does not show that a subject may make an invalid inference it is less relevant to the discussion of reasoning in this chapter.

4. Many of Owens's other arguments depend on the truth of anti-individualism, including his arguments from belief ascription (1989) and his Pierre and Bugsy Wabbit arguments (1990). Owens's (1992) Rudolf case aims to show that regardless of the truth of anti-individualism, without empirical information a subject cannot tell whether or not two of his earlier thoughts involve the same concept. However, this example does not threaten transparency since that concerns a subject's epistemic access only to her current thoughts, not her past thoughts.

5. Could a Fregean individualist challenge the claim that all of Burge et al. express the same thoughts by (i) and (ii) on the basis that although Kripke and Church assent to (i) and (ii), Burge and Mates assent to (i) but dissent to (ii)? Recall that Fregeans hold that content is partly individuated by difference of attitude. So, it might be suggested that although Church and Kripke express the same attitude by (i) and (ii), Burge and Mates do not. However, this argument rests on a mistake about the Fregean test for difference of content. The Fregean test for difference of content applies only to extensional contexts, not intensional ones.

6. In fact this claim does not follow logically from the failure of transparency. Even if a subject cannot always grasp a priori that two of her thoughts are contradictory, it does not follow that she can never grasp a priori that two of her thoughts are contradictory.

7. By contrast, Millikan (1993) argues that the processing of empty and equivocal thoughts, and failures of transparency, are so frequent that the standard principles are not true even considered as generalizations.

Chapter 6

1. Even on the descriptive understanding, the claim is compatible with her thought being individuated by some environmental factor other than x. So anti-individualists, whether Fregean or not, can accept that subjects sometimes think of objects via a description (see chap. 1, sec. 1). The point is

only that if a subject thinks of a particular object, x, by description, then her thought is not individuated by x.

2. Salmon, Owens, and Millikan reject transparency of sameness of content and argue that a subject may have contradictory beliefs without anything being wrong with her faculty of reasoning (Salmon 1986, appendix A; Owens 1989, 1990; Millikan 1993, p. 289). Millikan further concludes that a rational subject may fail to make simple valid inferences (ibid.).

3. Dummett (1973) makes a related claim about the Fregean argument for sense formulated at the level of language: "[t]he underlying assumption [of the Fregean argument from informative identity statements to the notion of sense] is the compelling principle that, if someone knows the senses of two words, and the two words have the same sense, he must know that they have the same sense: hence, if the sense of a name consists merely in its reference, anyone who understands two names having the same reference must know that they have the same referent" (p. 95).

4. The case may undermine the different principle that if a subject has two thoughts or thought constituents with the same content at the same time, then she can know (cf. realize) a priori that they have the same content. Suppose that S correctly thinks that two perceptual demonstrative thoughts involve the same sense. It might be argued that her belief is not a priori knowledge since she cannot rule out a priori the possibility that she is mistaken because, say, between her thinking these two thoughts, there has been an unnoticed switch in the object perceived. Whether this argument succeeds depends on which error possibilities one needs to rule out to have knowledge. However, the classic Fregean argument for sense does not require the stronger principle concerning knowledge. That argument involves the idea that, in simple cases, a rational subject would not have contradictory beliefs or fail to make valid inferences. But this requires only the weaker transparency principle in the text.

5. If, instead, Eve believes that she has lost track of the original apple, she might think of it as the apple that caused certain memories. Thinking of apple a by this description enables Eve to meet Evans's discrimination requirement. However, this thought is conceptually more complex than Evans takes perceptual demonstrative thoughts to be. Further, if Eve thinks she has lost track, she would not be inclined to put the two thoughts together in inference.

6. Both social and natural kind anti-individualism accept that a subject can have the concept of a natural kind while being ignorant of its chemical composition. Further, both views accept that a subject can have the concepts expressed by two terms even if she is ignorant that they have different

extensions. E.g., in Burge's arthritis thought experiment, a subject has the concepts expressed by 'arthritis' and 'rheumatoid ailment of the joints and thighs' although thinking mistakenly that they have the same extension. And a subject may have such causal relations that a natural kind anti-individualist would accept that she has the concepts of two distinct natural kinds even though she is unsure if the relevant terms name the same natural kind. E.g., she may think that she may have encountered two different forms of the same underlying natural kind just as, say, diamond and graphite are instances of the element carbon.

7. Even if someone disputed this conclusion, the Fregean response establishes that Clara can realize the difference in content only either by gaining empirical information or by acquiring Fregean theory via philosophical argument. In neither case is the difference of content readily available a priori. But, even this minimal conclusion establishes tension between Fregean sense and anti-individualism. The classic arguments for sense assume that a rational subject would not have simple contradictory beliefs and would not fail to make simple valid inferences. That requires that sameness of content is readily available a priori. But why hold that sameness of content is so available if difference is not?

8. Given that Clara is uncertain about whether the terms name the same element, she does not actually make an invalid inference.

9. This might not be so if the relevant principles were formulated using the notion of knowledge instead of realization. See note 4.

10. The Fregean cannot motivate transparency of sameness of content or the accompanying conception of rationality by appeal to the notion of sense, for this would be circular: transparency of sameness of content and the accompanying conception of rationality are key assumptions of the classic Fregean arguments for sense.

Chapter 7

1. Many anti-individualists hold that if one had always been envatted then one would lack any contentful thoughts and/or experiences.

2. I have formulated transmission and closure slightly differently from Wright, who says "[c]losure [of warrant], unrestricted, says that whenever there is warrant for the premises of a valid argument, there is warrant for the conclusion too. Transmission, unrestricted, says more: roughly, that to acquire a warrant for the premises of a valid argument and to recognise its validity is to acquire—perhaps for the first time—a warrant to accept the

conclusion" (Wright 2000, p. 141). My formulation is designed to apply with minimal change to both warrant and knowledge. It is implausible to claim that if a subject has warrant for, or knowledge of, the premises of a valid argument, then she has warrant for, or knowledge of, the conclusion. She might not believe the conclusion of the argument or realize that the argument is valid, and, even if she does, she might believe the conclusion on completely different grounds. Some of the same problems affect the standard definition of closure for knowledge: if S knows that p and S knows that if p then q, then she knows that q.

3. Davies and Wright concentrate on a failure of transmission of warrant. But to solve the reductio they need to deny that knowledge transmits across the reductio.

4. Wright expresses this by saying that the arguments are "question-begging." I am following Jackson's different usage in which an argument is question-begging iff someone who doubts the conclusion would have background beliefs relative to which the evidence for the premises is no evidence.

5. Wright (2002) revises condition (ii) to read: "that C depicts a situation of a general kind incompatible with the reliable operation of the cognitive capacities involved in generating the warrant for A." This revision does not affect my discussion.

6. Pritchard (2002) makes the different objection to Wright's analysis, that the water argument is not analogous to Moore's argument since the presuppositions for having warrant for the first premises of these two arguments are different, and it is only in the case of Moore's argument that there is no possible evidence for the relevant presupposition. However, neither Wright nor Davies claims that the arguments are analogous in these respects. McLaughlin (2003) poses a more serious challenge to Wright, claiming that Wright's template for a failure of transmission has the result that warrant fails to transmit across any valid argument from A and if A then B, to B, where A has a noninferential nonlogically conclusive warrant.

7. This is so even if the relevant warrant is taken to be nonevidential. Merely lacking evidence against a possibility, q, does not entail that one has nonevidential warrant for not-q.

8. In this passage, by "reliability," I mean what I earlier called "global reliability" (chap. 4).

9. Wright's conditional analysis would also be rejected by some internalists. Pryor (2000) argues that, for some propositions, having an experience

as of *p* provides a justification for *p* that does not presuppose or rest on one's justification for anything else. On this basis, Pryor (forthcoming) rejects Wright's conditional analysis of the BIV argument, although he accepts this view of the zebra argument.

10. "Externalism about [a natural kind] concept may involve all or only some of a variety of claims: for instance that the concept is *rigidly associated* with its actual extension, that it is *identified* by its extension, that it *cannot so much as exist* without a (non-empty) extension. The last is what is germane to the second premise of the McKinsey paradox" (Wright 2000, p. 145). Wright argues that the reductio argument meets his template, taking A = "I believe that water is wet"; B = "I, or my speech community, have had such and such encounters with water"; and C = "the seeming thought which I attempt to token by 'I believe that water is wet' is content-defective owing to the reference failure of the purported natural kind term, 'water', in my language" (p. 156).

11. See also Wright (2000), p. 157. Wright claims that, on his view of the reductio, one's warrant for the premise (W1) I think that water is wet depends on antecedent entitlement to discount the possibility (C) that one is instead suffering an illusion of thought. This entitlement in turn depends on one's having "antecedent reason to think that [one's] tokenings of 'water' comply with appropriate externalist constraints," namely that oneself or one's community has had such-and-such encounters with water. But, Wright says, "if such an antecedent reason for discounting C had to be empirically acquired, this line of thought would after all involve dismissal of the groundlessness of self-knowledge in the relevant kind of case." In other words, if one could have only empirical warrant for supposing that oneself or one's community has had contact with water, then one could not have a priori knowledge of one's thought contents. He goes on to defend the idea that there is an a priori entitlement against the possibility of illusions of thought.

12. For any valid argument, doubt about the conclusion may lead someone to doubt the premises, but such a doubt does not necessarily involve having background beliefs relative to which the evidence for the premises is no evidence. Thus, Davies's account does not threaten transmission across all valid arguments.

13. By contrast, the experience of seeing a striped horselike animal combined with one's warrant for thinking that if the animal is a zebra then it is not an elephant does rule out the relevant alternatives to the claim that the animal is not an elephant. Thus, Davies's account does not threaten a failure of transmission across all valid arguments.

14. By contrast, McLaughlin (2003) challenges Davies's analysis by objecting to the limitation principles.

15. Since Davies provides no independent account of the notion of a
relevant alternative, it is reasonable to assume that he is using the extant
epistemological notion. If he is not, then it is not clear how to interpret the
notion.

16. Davies might try to avoid this objection by restricting his account of
warrant to true beliefs. So restricted, the account of warrant is radically
incomplete and has the counterintuitive consequence that different
accounts of warrant apply to true and false beliefs. In any case, even with
this restriction, Davies's account would still have counterintuitive consequences in Gettier cases.

17. On Goldman's more recent account, "S's believing p at t is justified iff
a) S's believing p at t is permitted by a right system of J-rules; and b) this
permission is not undermined by S's cognitive state at t" (Goldman 1986,
p. 63). Condition (a) is explained in reliabilist terms. Note that (McE1) and
(McE3) meet Goldman's nonundermining condition, (b).

18. Some accounts of warrant might accept these consequences. Plantinga
(1993) elucidates justification as a deontological notion associated with the
concept of duty. By contrast, he defines warrant as that which makes the
difference between true belief and knowledge. Thus, a belief cannot be both
warranted and true and yet fail to be knowledge. So, Gettier cases cannot
involve true warranted beliefs that fail to be knowledge. Merricks (1995)
argues that, on Plantinga's conception, warrant entails truth. However,
Plantinga's conception of warrant is highly controversial. So, if Davies were
to support his account with Plantinga's views, it would not provide a compatibilist response to the reductio acceptable to a wide range of theorists
with different approaches to warrant.

Chapter 8

1. Boghossian (1997) distinguishes atomic and compositional concepts
(p. 165).

2. See Nozick (1981) and, for similar conditions, Dretske (1970, 1981) and
Goldman (1976, 1986). In chapter 4, following McGinn and Goldman, I
called such conditions "local reliability" conditions for knowledge.

3. Each view also endorses the different principle that if a chemically indifferent subject S intends t to name a natural kind and it does so, then it

expresses a nondescriptive concept of that kind. But this principle is of no use in defending (R2).

4. McLaughlin and Tye (1998) and Stoneham (1999) deny that Putnamian anti-individualism about natural kinds entails the illusion view. Even if this is correct, Boghossian's argument might still apply to the illusion view. Brown (1998) objects to Boghossian's argument that if natural kind and social anti-individualism are both true, then a subject cannot know a priori that she intends *t* to express an atomic concept of a natural kind. However, this objection is not relevant at this point when we are considering only natural kind anti-individualism.

5. Nor is this merely the result of an overly restrictive definition. E.g., it seems no part of folk psychology to suppose that a subject can know a priori the type of her thought and, in particular, whether it is descriptive or not.

6. Interestingly, Davies's and Wright's accounts have the consequence that warrant, and thus knowledge, fails to transmit from (T1) and (T2) to (T3).

7. Someone might argue that Sally's belief in (T3) meets the Nozickean condition when relativized to methods: *S* knows *p* via *M* only if *S* truly believes *p* via *M* and, if *p* were false and *S* were to use *M* to arrive at a belief whether *p*, *S* wouldn't believe that *p* via *M* (Nozick 1981, p. 179). If the relevant method were inferring whether one is suffering an illusion of thought from having an actual thought, then the method seems inapplicable when one is suffering an illusion. So, formed via this method, one's belief that one is not suffering an illusion of thought meets the Nozickean condition. However, it is not clear what justifies the selection of this method rather than the method of inferring whether one is suffering an illusion of thought on the basis of having an apparent thought. Nozick's understanding of the notion of method favors the latter specification, for he says "any method experientially the same, the same 'from the inside' will count as the same method" (p. 185). Notice that if Nozick's principle for the individuation of methods is rejected then one does have a method for producing the belief that one is not a BIV that meets the relevant condition, namely inference from visual perception (as opposed to inference from visual experience).

8. Social anti-individualists are also committed to the following entailment: if *S* has a concept *c* and misunderstands that concept, then *S* is, or used to be, part of a community with the concept *c*. However, since a subject cannot have a priori knowledge that she misunderstands a concept, knowledge of this entailment is of no use in the reductio.

9. A similar objection applies to McLaughlin and Tye's example involving the concept of the a priori (1998, p. 317).

References

Anderson, Anthony, and Owens, Joseph (eds.). 1990. *Propositional Attitudes: The Role of Content in Logic, Language and Mind*. CSLI Press: Palo Alto.

Armstrong, David. 1973. *Belief, Truth, and Knowledge*. Cambridge University Press: London.

Barber, Alex (ed.). 2003. *Epistemology of Language*. Oxford University Press: Oxford.

Beebee, Helen. 2001. "Transfer of Warrant, Begging the Question, and Semantic Externalism." *Philosophical Quarterly* 51: 356–374.

Boghossian, Paul. 1989. "Content and Self-Knowledge." *Philosophical Topics* 17: 5–26.

———. 1992. "Externalism and Inference." *Philosophical Issues* 2: 1–28.

———. 1994. "The Opaqueness of Mental Content." *Philosophical Perspectives* 8: 33–50.

———. 1997. "What the Externalist Can Know A Priori." *Proceedings of the Aristotelian Society* 97: 161–175.

Boghossian, Paul, and Peacocke, Christopher (eds.). 2000. *New Essays on the A Priori*. Oxford University Press: Oxford.

Brewer, Bill. 1999. *Perception and Reason*. Oxford University Press: Oxford.

———. 2000. "Externalism and A Priori Knowledge of Empirical Facts." In Boghossian and Peacocke (2000), 415–432.

Brown, Jessica. 1995. "The Incompatibility of Anti-Individualism and Privileged Access." *Analysis* 53: 149–156.

———. 1998. "Recognitional Capacities and Natural Kind Terms." *Mind* 107: 275–303.

———. 1999. "Boghossian and Privileged Access." *Analysis* 59: 52–58.

———. 2000a. "Against Temporal Externalism." *Analysis* 60: 178–188.

———. 2000b. "Critical Reasoning, Understanding, and Self-Knowledge." *Philosophy and Phenomenological Research* 61: 659–677.

———. 2000c. "Reliabilism, Knowledge, and Mental Content." *Proceedings of the Aristotelian Society* 100: 115–135.

———. 2001. "Anti-Individualism and Agnosticism." *Analysis* 61: 213–224.

———. 2003. "Externalism and the Fregean Tradition." In Barber (2003).

Brueckner, Anthony. 1992a. "Semantic Answers to Scepticism." *Pacific Philosophical Quarterly* 73: 200–219.

———. 1992b. "What an Individualist Knows *A Priori*." *Analysis* 52: 111–118.

———. 2002. "Anti-Individualism and Analyticity." *Analysis* 62: 87–91.

Burge, Tyler. 1976. "Belief and Synonymy." *Journal of Philosophy* 75: 119–138.

———. 1979. "Individualism and the Mental." *Midwest Studies in Philosophy* 4: 73–121.

———. 1982. "Other Bodies." In *Thought and Object: Essays on Intentionality*, ed. A. Woodfield, 97–120. Oxford University Press: Oxford.

———. 1986a. "Individualism and Psychology." *Philosophical Review* 95: 3–45.

———. 1986b. "Intellectual Norms and the Foundations of Normativity." *Journal of Philosophy* 83: 697–720.

———. 1988. "Individualism and Self-Knowledge." *Journal of Philosophy* 85: 649–663.

———. 1993. "Content Preservation." *Philosophical Review* 102: 457–488.

———. 1996. "Our Entitlement to Self-Knowledge." *Proceedings of the Aristotelian Society* 96: 91–116.

———. 1998. "Memory and Self-Knowledge." In Martin and Ludlow (1998), 351–371.

Campbell, John. 1987. "Is Sense Transparent?" *Proceedings of the Aristotelian Society* 61: 273–292.

———. 1994. *Past, Space, and Self*. MIT Press: Cambridge, Mass.

Carnap, Rudolf. 1946. *Meaning and Necessity*. University of Chicago Press: Chicago.

Church, Alonzo. 1954. "Intensional Isomorphism and Identity of Belief." *Philosophical Studies* 5: 65–73.

Churchland, Paul. 1970. "The Logical Character of Action Explanations." *Philosophical Review* 79: 214–236.

Crimmins, Mark, and Perry, John. 1989. "The Prince and the Phonebooth." *Journal of Philosophy* 86: 685–711.

Dancy, Jonathan. 1985. *Introduction to Contemporary Epistemology*. Blackwell: Oxford.

Davidson, Donald. 1969. "On Saying That." In Davidson, *Essays on Truth and Interpretation*, 93–108. Oxford University Press: Oxford.

———. 1987. "Knowing One's Own Mind." *Proceedings of the American Philosophical Association*, 441–458.

Davies, Martin. 1998. "Externalism, Architecturalism, and Epistemic Warrant." In Wright, Smith, and Macdonald (1998), 321–361.

———. 2000. "Externalism and A Priori Knowledge." In Boghossian and Peacocke (2000), 384–432.

Davies, Martin, and Humberstone, Lloyd. 1980. "Two Notions of Necessity." *Philosophical Studies* 38: 1–30.

DeRose, Keith. 1995. "Solving the Sceptical Problem." *Philosophical Review* 104: 1–52.

———. 2000. "How Do We Know We're Not Brains in a Vat?" *Spindel Supplement to the Southern Journal of Philosophy* 37: 121–138.

DeRose, Keith and Warfield, Ted (eds.). 1999. *Scepticism*. Oxford University Press: Oxford.

Devitt, Michael. 1980. *Designation*. Columbia University Press: New York.

Dretske, Fred. 1970. "Epistemic Operators." *Journal of Philosophy* 67: 1007–1023. Reprinted in his *Perception, Knowledge, and Belief*, 30–47. Cambridge University Press: Cambridge.

———. 1981. *Knowledge and the Flow of Information*. MIT Press: Cambridge, Mass.

Dummett, Michael. 1973. *Frege*. Duckworth: London.

Dupré, John. 1981. "Natural Kinds and Biological Taxa." *Philosophical Review* 90: 66–90.

Evans, Gareth. 1982. *The Varieties of Reference*. Oxford University Press: Oxford.

Falvey, Kevin. 2000. "The Compatibility of Anti-Individualism and Privileged Access." *Analysis* 60: 137–142.

Falvey, Kevin, and Owens, Joseph. 1994. "Externalism, Self-Knowledge, and Scepticism." *Philosophical Review* 103: 107–137.

Fodor, Jerry. 1987. *Psychosemantics*. MIT Press: Cambridge, Mass.

———. 1992. *A Theory of Content*. MIT Press: Cambridge, Mass.

Frances, Bryan. 1999. "Contradictory Belief and Epistemic Closure." *Mind and Language* 14: 203–226.

Frege, Gottlob. 1892. "On Sense and Reference." In *Philosophical Writings: Translations*, eds. P. Geach and M. Black. Blackwell: Oxford.

———. 1980. *Philosophical and Mathematical Correspondence*, ed. by Gabriel et al., abridged for the English edition by McGuiness, and trans. by Kaal. Blackwell: Oxford.

Gallois, Andre, and O'Leary-Hawthorne, John. 1996. "Externalism and Scepticism." *Philosophical Studies* 81: 1–26.

Gibbons, John. 1996. "Externalism and Knowledge of Content." *Philosophical Review* 105: 287–310.

Goldberg, Sandford. 1999. "The Relevance of Discriminatory Knowledge of Content." *Pacific Philosophical Quarterly* 80: 136–156.

Goldman, Alvin. 1967. "A Causal Theory of Knowing." *Journal of Philosophy* 64: 355–372.

———. 1976. "Discrimination and Perceptual Knowledge." *Journal of Philosophy* 73: 771–791.

———. 1979. "What Is Justified Belief?" In *Justification and Knowledge*, ed. George Pappas. Reidel: Dordrecht.

————. 1986. *Epistemology and Cognition*. Harvard University Press: Cambridge, Mass.

Heal, Jane. 1998. "Externalism and Memory." *Proceedings of the Aristotelian Society* 72: 95–110.

Heil, John. 1988. "Privileged Access." *Mind* 386: 238–251.

Jackson, Frank. 1987. *Conditionals*. Blackwell: Oxford.

Jackson, Frank, and Pettit, Philip. 1993. "Some Content Is Narrow." In J. Heil and A. Mele, *Mental Causation*, 259–282. Oxford University Press: Oxford.

Kahneman, Daniel. 1982. *Judgement under Uncertainty*. Cambridge University Press: Cambridge.

Kaplan, David. 1989. "Demonstratives." In *Themes from Kaplan*, eds. J. Almog, J. Perry, and H. Wettstein. Oxford University Press: Oxford.

Kimbrough, Scott. 1998. "Anti-Individualism and Fregeanism." *Philosophical Quarterly* 48: 470–482.

Kripke, Saul. 1980. *Naming and Necessity*. Blackwell: Oxford.

————. 1979. "A Puzzle about Belief." In Margalit, ed., *Meaning and Use*, 239–283. Reidel: Dordrecht.

Langton, Rae, and Lewis, David. 1998. "Defining 'Intrinsic.' " *Philosophy and Phenomenological Research* 58: 333–346.

Lewis, David. 1996. "Elusive Knowledge." *Australasian Journal of Philosophy* 74: 549–567.

Ludlow, Peter. 1995a. "Externalism, Self-Knowledge, and the Prevalence of Slow Switching." *Analysis* 55: 45–49.

————. 1995b. "Social Externalism, Self-Knowledge, and Memory." *Analysis* 55: 157–159.

————. 1996. "Externalism and Memory: A Problem." *Acta Analytica* 14. Reprinted in Ludlow and Martin (1998), 311–318.

Ludlow, Peter, and Martin, Norah (eds.). 1998. *Externalism and Self-Knowledge*. CSLI Publications: Stanford.

Mates, Benson. 1952. "Synonymity." In Linsky, ed., *Semantics and the Philosophy of Language*, 111–138. University of Illinois Press: Urbana.

McDowell, John. 1977. "On the Sense and Reference of a Proper Name." *Mind* 86: 159–185.

———. 1986. "Singular Thought and the Extent of Inner Space." In *Subject, Thought, and Context*, eds. J. McDowell and P. Pettit, 137–168. Oxford University Press: Oxford.

McGinn, Colin. 1984. "The Concept of Knowledge." *Midwest Studies in Philosophy* 9. Page references from *Knowledge and Reality*, C. McGinn, 7–35. Oxford University Press: Oxford.

McKinsey, Michael. 1991. "Anti-Individualism and Privileged Access." *Analysis* 51: 9–16.

———. 1997. "Accepting the Consequences of Anti-Individualism." *Analysis* 54: 124–128.

McLaughlin, Brian. 2000. "Self-Knowledge, Externalism, and Scepticism." *Proceedings of the Aristotelian Society* 74: 93–117.

———. 2003. "McKinsey's Challenge, Warrant Transmission and Skepticism." In S. Nuccetelli (ed.), *New Essays on Semantic Externalism and Self-Knowledge*. MIT Press: Cambridge, Mass.

McLaughlin, Brian, and Tye, Michael. 1998. "Content Externalism and Privileged Access." *Philosophical Review* 107: 349–380.

Merricks, Trenton. 1995. "Warrant Entails Truth." *Philosophy and Phenomenological Research* 55: 841–855.

Millikan, Ruth. 1993. *White Queen Psychology and Other Essays for Alice*. MIT Press: Cambridge, Mass.

Nozick, Robert. 1981. *Philosophical Explanations*. Oxford University Press: Oxford.

Owens, Joseph. 1989. "Contradictory Belief and Cognitive Access." In *Midwest Studies: vol. 14, Contemporary Perspectives in the Philosophy of Language II*, eds. P. French, T. Uehling, and H. Wettstein. University of Notre Dame Press: Notre Dame.

———. 1990. "Cognitive Access and Semantic Puzzles." In Anderson and Owens (1990), 147–174.

———. 1992. "Psychophysical Supervenience: Its Epistemological Foundation." *Synthese* 90: 89–117.

Peacocke, Christopher. 1983. *Sense and Content*. Oxford University Press: Oxford.

————. 1996. "Entitlement, Self-Knowledge, and Conceptual Redeployment." *Proceedings of the Aristotelian Society* 96: 117–158.

————. 1998. *Being Known*. Oxford University Press: Oxford.

Perry, John. 1979. "The Essential Indexical." *Noûs* 13: 3–21.

Plantinga, Alvin. 1993. *Warrant: The Current Debate*. Oxford University Press: Oxford.

Platts, Mark. 1983. "Explanatory Kinds." *British Journal for the Philosophy of Science* 34: 133–148.

Pritchard, Duncan. 2002. "McKinsey Paradoxes, Radical Scepticism, and Transmission of Knowledge across Known Entailments." *Synthese* 130: 279–302.

Pryor, James. 2000. "The Sceptic and the Dogmatist." *Noûs* 34: 517–549.

————. Forthcoming. "Is Moore's Argument an Example of Transmission Failure?"

Putnam, Hilary. 1975a. "The Meaning of 'Meaning'." In *Language, Mind, and Knowledge*, vol. 2 of *Minnesota Studies in the Philosophy of Science*, ed. K. Gunderson, University of Minnesota Press: Minneapolis. Reprinted in Putnam (1975d), 215–271.

————. 1975b. "Explanation and Reference." Reprinted in Putnam (1975d), 196–214.

————. 1975c. "Is Semantics Possible?" Reprinted in Putnam (1975d), 139–152.

————. 1975d. *Mind, Language, and Reality*. Cambridge University Press: Cambridge.

Salmon, Nathan. 1986. *Frege's Puzzle*. MIT Press/Bradford Books: Cambridge, Mass.

Sawyer, Sarah. 1998. "Privileged Access to the World." *Australasian Journal of Philosophy* 76: 523–533.

————. 1999. "An Externalist Account of Introspective Knowledge." *Pacific Philosophical Quarterly* 80: 358–378.

Segal, Gabriel. 2000. *A Slim Book about Narrow Content*. MIT Press: Cambridge, Mass.

————. 2003. "Ignorance of Meaning." In Barber (2003).

Soames, Scott. 1987. "Direct Reference, Propositional Attitudes, and Semantic Content." *Philosophical Topics* 15: 47–87.

Stoneham, Tom. 1999. "Boghossian on Empty Natural Kind Concepts." *Proceedings of the Aristotelian Society* 99: 119–122.

Stroud, Barry. 1984. *The Significance of Philosophical Scepticism.* Oxford University Press: New York.

Tversky, Amos, and Kahneman, Daniel. 1983. "Extensional versus Intuitive Reasoning: The Conjunction Fallacy in Probability Judgement." *Psychological Review* 90: 293–315.

Tye, Michael. 1998. "Externalism and Memory." *Proceedings of the Aristotelian Society* 72: 77–94.

Warfield, Ted. 1994. "Knowing the World and Knowing Our Minds." *Philosophy and Phenomenological Research* 55: 525–545.

———. 1997. "Externalism, Self-Knowledge, and the Irrelevance of Slow Switching." *Analysis* 57: 282–284.

———. 1998. "A Priori Knowledge of the World: Knowing the World by Knowing Our Minds." *Philosophical Studies* 92: 127–147.

Wason, Peter, and Johnson-Laird, Philip. 1972. *The Psychology of Reasoning.* Harvard University Press: Cambidge, Mass.

Wright, Crispin. 2000. "Cogency and Question-Begging: Some Reflections on McKinsey's Paradox, and Putnam's Proof." *Philosophical Issues* 10: 140–163.

———. 2002. "Anti-Sceptics Simple and Subtle: Moore and McDowell." *Philosophy and Phenomenological Research* 65: 330–348.

———. 2003. "Some Reflections on the Acquisition of Warrant by Inference." In Nuccetelli (2003), 57–78.

Wright, Crispin, Smith, Barry C., and Macdonald, Cynthia. 1998. *Knowing Our Own Minds.* Oxford University Press: Oxford.

Zemach, Eddy. 1976. "Putnam's Theory on the Reference of Substance Terms." *Journal of Philosophy* 73: 116–127.

Index